CREATE WEALTH
WITH QUICKEN®

CHRISTOPHER E. VOGT, CFP

PRIMA PUBLISHING

Project Editor: Jeff Ennis

Selected figures and material are reprinted with permission of Vogt Financial Concepts & Strategies, Inc.
Certified Financial Planner is a trademark of the International Board of Standards and Practices for Certified Financial Planners, Inc.
Quicken is a registered trademark of Intuit Inc.

If you have problems installing or running Quicken please contact Intuit at (800) 624-8742 or (520) 295-3220. Appendix B contains additional information on contacting Intuit technical support. Neither Prima Publishing nor the author can provide software support.

Prima Publishing and the author have attempted throughout this book to distinguish proprietary trademarks from descriptive terms by following the capitalization style used by the manufacturer.

A great deal of care has been taken to provide accurate and current information; however, the ideas, suggestions, general principles, and conclusions presented in this book are subject to local, state, and federal regulations, court cases, and any revisions of the same. We urge readers to consult their legal counsel regarding any points of law, their tax advisor regarding tax issues, and their other advisors as appropriate. This publication is not intended as a substitute for competent legal, tax, or other professional advice.

Information contained in this book has been obtained by Prima Publishing and the author from sources believed to be reliable. However, because of the possibility of human or mechanical error by our sources, Prima Publishing, and the Author do not guarantee the accuracy, adequacy, or completeness of any information and are not responsible for any errors or omissions or the results obtained from use of such information.

ISBN: 0-7615-0338-2
Library of Congress Catalog Card Number: 95-70828
Printed in the United States of America
95 96 97 98 AA 10 9 8 7 6 5 4 3 2 1

CONTENTS

FOREWORD

People are never more cautious than when handling their own money. This probably contributed to the fifteen years it took both credit cards and automatic teller machines (ATMs) to become accepted. For much the same reason, personal financial software has been slow to be embraced by the non-technical marketplace. *Quicken* combined with electronic bill paying and the new online banking services, represents revolutionary changes and should be considered for inclusion in your personal financial planning strategy.

Like many people, I am constantly searching for ideas and tools to simplify and improve the quality of life. *Quicken* has been a tremendous asset in this regard and actually transformed the way my wife and I manage our personal finances.

For every financial management software user I find out there, I meet four potential users who have been thinking about it for a few years. Many even have a dated copy of *Quicken* along with many years of good intentions to start using it. While over a dozen *Quicken* books are available at your local bookstore, most merely serve as replacements for the program's manual. They will tell you how to set up accounts and record transactions but don't really have any meat on the bone when it comes to showing how to apply *Quicken* to everyday life.

I believe the time to start is now and *Create Wealth with Quicken* can show you the way. *Create Wealth with Quicken* stands apart from the crowd of "me too" *Quicken* books. This book will show you step-by-step how to use many of the program's commands and features, but it doesn't stop there. Christopher E. Vogt draws heavily on his experience as a Certified Financial Planner. Whether you are struggling to manage your debt, make investment decisions, inventory your assets or determine if you should refinance your mortgage *Create Wealth With Quicken* will provide valuable guidance. Chris weds the science of financial planning to the technology of *Quicken* to produce an exciting new level of *Quicken* book.

Applying Chris' principles with *Quicken* is more important to you and your family's future than ever before. Don't procrastinate. Start now. If you are hesitating about upgrading, do it today. Don't just read this book, study and practice it.

Brian J. Morse, CPA
Senior Technology Partner
Coopers & Lybrand

PREFACE

Your computer and each piece of software on your system should contribute to improving your lifestyle. Financial software, in particular, should contribute to your financial situation. Quicken is a product that is capable of making a significant contribution to improving your bottom line. The purpose of this book is to provide you with practical, usable knowledge to make Quicken a strategic tool to put, or keep, more money in your pocket. You will learn to maximize your income and minimize your taxes. My goal is to help you help yourself use Quicken to optimize your personal financial situation.

A number of my friends, associates, and clients have Quicken. Few of them know how to use it to optimize their financial situation. Personally educating each person would be a frustrating exercise, nor cost-effective. This book is for each of you who desire to achieve financial excellence.

It was a struggle to determine what to include and what not to include in the chapters that follow. After more than a decade of assisting employees and executives, small businesses and corporations, and the less fortunate and the affluent with their financial concerns, I have accumulated a wealth of knowledge to share. I have chosen to concentrate our efforts on the ideas most likely to have long-term impact.

This book is for those who are not content with the status quo. The concepts and strategies that follow will empower you to create wealth beyond your highest realistic expectations. Most of the ideas will apply to the majority of you. Some of them will only apply to a limited number. I trust that you will benefit from the ideas we include.

Your comments and suggestions are important to me. I would appreciate any feedback you have to offer. Your input is an important factor as I continue to perfect *Create Wealth with Quicken.*

Many readers and friends have asked for ongoing information about Quicken and financial matters. We are constructing a home page on the World Wide Web and setting up a special section for *Create Wealth with Quicken,* where we plan to regularly publish items of interest about Quicken and financial topics. We are also searching for other valuable resources on the Internet to provide links to them. Check us out at `http://www.c3rn.com`.

Thank you for purchasing *Create Wealth with Quicken.* I am looking forward to hearing how your life improves as you apply the time-tested principles for creating wealth that fill this book to your personal finances.

ACKNOWLEDGMENTS

> WITHOUT A RICH HEART, WEALTH IS AN UGLY BEGGAR.
>
> —RALPH WALDO EMERSON

Books are projects that require the efforts of many people. This book certainly was not an exception to the rule. Without the assistance of more individuals than we can identify here, you would not be reading this.

The most important member of the team is my lovely, gracious, and intelligent wife, Wendy. She spent hours reviewing the text in-house for technical accuracy. You can thank her for entering the sample data into Quicken over and over again as beta versions of Quicken ate the numbers for lunch.

My children, Christopher II, Joshua, and Victoria, are the real reason I wrote this book. I want their future to be as bright as possible. My kids are too young to really understand what Daddy and Mommy did all those hours in front of their computers. Now that the work is complete, I can once again spend quantity, not just quality, time with them!

Dr. Winona Wellsfry and her husband, Ward, are also important players on the team. Winona spent countless hours scrutinizing the original text for grammatical errors and readability issues. Ward is responsible for the clever comics. I am also thankful for them taking care of their grandchildren for several days while Wendy and I slaved over hot computers on the manuscript.

The next group of players are at Prima Publishing. I am most appreciative of Jeff Ennis who played the key role of Project Editor. I also appreciate the diligent efforts of Maryanne Brown who has faithfully served as our Technical Reviewer since the first edition. Our copyeditor, Kelley Mitchell, considered every phrase with an eye for perfection.

There are many other fine folks at Prima who aided in many aspects of producing and marketing this book. I tip my hat to each of you, even though you remain anonymous.

This book would never have been possible without Intuit's development of the Quicken family of products. The Quicken for Windows Beta Support Team had the most contact with Wendy and me on this edition. We logged many hours together on the Beta Hotline. Thanks to each of you, especially those who answered our questions. The members of the Window Beta Team were (in alphabetical order): Ravi Bellur (Beta Coordinator), Tom Bernota, Terri Brubaker (Team Lead), Marie Caracci, Anthony Coca, Tammy Gallegos, Russ Gardener, Joseph Herrera, Dina Hennsey, John James, CJ (Charles Jones), Andrew Lee (Beta Supervisor), Teale Magierek, Greg Mewhinney, Stefani Odom, Jennifer Pollard, and David Shelander.

Finally, my heartfelt thanks go to each reader of this book. You will make the vision contained in the pages of *Create Wealth with Quicken* a reality.

INTRODUCTION

> HE DOES NOT POSSESS WEALTH THAT ALLOWS IT
> TO POSSESS HIM.
>
> —BENJAMIN FRANKLIN

The inspiration to create this book arose from seeing so many Quicken users take so little advantage of the program's power to better their financial situation. People buy software to make their lives better, easier, and more productive. Most computer books show you the mechanics of using a piece of software. This book will show you how to make money and even create wealth using the tools Quicken provides.

WHO SHOULD READ THIS BOOK

You are reading this because you have the desire to increase your wealth or you know someone with that desire. This book is not for people happy with the status quo. Anyone who wants to make their current income stretch further and work harder will appreciate this book. We have received letters from pleased readers throughout the United States and Canada. We even received a thank-you note from someone creating wealth with Quicken in Moscow, Russia.

We won't teach you to create wealth by working harder or longer; we will teach you to achieve financial success by working smarter. True prosperity does not occur overnight. Some people gain a large sum of money in a short time, e.g., winning the lottery or receiving an inheritance. But according to U.S. Treasury Department studies, such people will find themselves, on average, in the same financial condition as before the windfall within two years of receiving the large sum of money. In other words, they blew their opportunity to create a lasting legacy for themselves and future generations.

Is it wealth if it is fleeting? Get-rich-quick schemes don't create wealth; steady plodding toward prosperity does. When the money controls the individual, it will soon disappear. Lasting wealth is only possible when you control your money. *Create Wealth with Quicken* gives you the lifestyle and mental secrets necessary to develop the attitudes and habits to acquire and retain wealth. Anyone interested in attaining a sound financial position should read this book.

How This Book Is Organized

No other Quicken book is like *Create Wealth with Quicken*. This book will logically lead you through the steps required to achieve lasting financial success. Each chapter includes Practical Applications to help propel you along the path to prosperity. We also include exercises in most chapters. We tested each exercise with an inexperienced Quicken user. The longest chapter required about 1½ hours to read and complete the exercises. The text includes complete instructions for using Quicken to complete the assigned tasks. We also include plenty of graphics to keep visually oriented readers on track!

As you progress through these pages you will learn the secrets of financial success. Part I explains the principles necessary to lay a firm foundation for your financial future. After you learn the basics, you are ready to plot a path to success in Part II, where you will start to tackle one of money's most difficult issues—cash flow. Then you will learn to control cash flow, as well as learn about opportunities for creating wealth. The next step is to learn and apply the financial concepts and strategies that will help you maximize those opportunities.

Finally, in Part III, we will wrap up the package by discussing home ownership and synthesizing the secrets of creating wealth. Homes play an important role in many people's planning. We will destroy some of the myths of home ownership and show you how to increase the value of home ownership in your financial future. We tie the package together in the final chapter, where we briefly review some of the key concepts covered throughout the text. Don't read the last chapter first. It won't make sense if you have not read the rest of the book!

The appendixes are important components of this book. Appendix A has a list of short-cut keys (called "Quick Keys" in Quicken) for DOS and Windows Quicken users. Appendix B is a guide to resources including contact information for people and companies discussed in the book. We suggest that you obtain the recommended materials and read them as you progress through this book. You will also find a list of authors and titles that we recommend.

The glossary can contribute to your knowledge as well. You will find a significant number of financial terms explained in simple English. Please refer to it whenever you come to a term you do not understand. The index is also a powerful aid for using this book effectively. We have tried to make it as comprehensive as possible.

If you read the entire book quickly, you will not fully benefit from the experience. We recommend that you take each chapter in turn. Complete the exercises in it before moving on for the maximum benefit. By the time you complete the text, you should have a solid plan and have made significant progress to creating wealth with Quicken!

AIDS INCLUDED IN THE TEXT

The DOS and Windows versions of Quicken have much in common. The Windows version of Quicken operates identically and is visually identical under both Windows 3.1 and Windows 95. There are subtle and substantial differences in the DOS and Windows program designs. We wrote the book using the Windows version and added any instructions necessary for DOS users so they could benefit from the exercises equally. When appropriate or necessary, you will find additional instructions following the general instructions described for the Windows version. These instructions are clearly defined by the DOS Instructions icon. We also provide a number of Q-Tips, Quicken tips, that give helpful hints to using Quicken more efficiently.

This is not simply an instruction book on using Quicken. Although we provide complete instructions on the parts of Quicken used, we don't provide any instructions for the parts of the software that do not apply to the financial concepts and strategies presented. If you want another book covering additional features, buy one from your local bookseller. Windows users will especially appreciate *Quicken 5 for Windows: The Visual Learning Guide* also available from Prima Publishing.

This book is also an excellent financial planning tool. We have strategically placed numerous financial concepts, tips, and strategies throughout the text. Four types are specifically identified: Financial Alerts, Key Concepts, Money Matters, and Tax Tips.

Financial Alerts caution or warn of potential dangers you may face.

 Key Concepts are philosophical statements or nuggets of wisdom meant to stimulate your thinking.

 Money Matters are financial tips.

 Tax Tips provide short tax-saving ideas and strategies.

CONVENTIONS USED IN THE TEXT

Our desire is to make this book an enjoyable experience. To make the book as easy to use and understand as possible, we try to present information consistently throughout the text.

Type on your keyboard any **bold** words or characters that are part of instructions.

To avoid confusion between your bank account and the Account that Quicken sets up to track your bank account, we capitalize the words *Account* and *Register* when they refer to Quicken Accounts or Registers. We also capitalize command and window names as we use them in the text.

Keys on your computer keyboard are set in a special key-cap font when used in instructions, e.g., E and T. When you need to press multiple keys sequentially, we connect the keys with a hyphen, as in Ctrl-A.

In addition to providing practical Quicken and financial advice, concepts, and strategies in this book, we provide additional FREE resources of particular interest for *Create Wealth with Quicken* readers on the World Wide Web site of *The Computer Connection*, America's friendliest computer talk show. Visit us at http://www.c3rn.com.

Thank you again for contributing to the continuing success of *Create Wealth with Quicken*!

To my grandparents with love and gratitude:

Ed J. and Opal Vogt

&

David E. and Edna Riemer

I am thankful to my grandparents for instilling sound financial principles

and a strong work ethic in my parents, who in turn passed those

characteristics on to my brother and myself.

PART I

FOUNDATION CONCEPTS

CHAPTER 1

BASIC PRINCIPLES

> MONEY IS PLENTIFUL FOR THOSE WHO UNDERSTAND THE SIMPLE LAWS WHICH GOVERN ITS ACQUISITION.
>
> —GEORGE S. CLASON

Have you ever wondered why some people have money and others don't? Have you ever noticed that two people with very similar backgrounds and earnings can have very different financial situations? I think it is very curious that America's educational system spends 12 to 20 years training us to earn a living but only a few hours teaching us how to make wise use of the money we earn. Most of us learn about money by trial and error—probably more by error.

Almost anyone can aspire to and achieve financial success. Even if you are wallowing in a swamp of debt, you can overcome the obstacles that stand between you and financial security. You *can* become wealthy. Throughout this book, we'll examine some financial successes and failures to learn from others' experiences. Here are two examples of actual people who are well on their way to achieving financial success.

Richard and Laura[1] were floundering in debt just two and a half years ago. They never planned to live on the brink of financial collapse. They simply failed to use their earnings appropriately. Eventually, they determined that they needed help. With the assistance of a financial expert, they learned how to manage their cash flow strategically. Richard and Laura are now free from the bondage of consumer debt. The level of stress in their home has diminished. They now have a plan to create wealth and achieve financial freedom.

Several years ago, Dan and Anne, another couple, were off to a good start. Their only debt was their home mortgage. They were DINKs—Double Income, No Kids—with good-paying jobs. They had begun to save a little money each month but hadn't yet developed a plan for financial success. With the advice of a Certified Financial Planner®, they devised a plan.

Seven short years later, Anne only works part-time. She enjoys staying home with the kids. Dan and Anne are also well on their way to financial freedom. They live in a larger home with a smaller mortgage. At the same time, they have accumulated over $70,000 in investments and built up more than adequate cash reserves.

The path to financial freedom is strewn with stumbling blocks. You need the proper tools and a strategy to reach your goals. You already have two useful tools that will be invaluable to you on your journey—Quicken and *Create Wealth with Quicken*. Whether you are using the DOS or Windows version of Quicken, in this book you will find the concepts and strategies you need to create wealth.

---

1. Many of the individuals described in this book are living, breathing people. The situations presented are based on actual situations and experiences. Names of actual people have been changed to protect the innocent—and the guilty!

WELCOME TO QUICKEN

Intuit's Quicken is the market leader for personal financial management software. If you have not yet installed Quicken on your computer, please do so. After installing Quicken on your computer, you will be ready to proceed.

The primary focus of this book is to enable you to take full advantage of the financial "Swiss Army Knife" we call Quicken. Categorizing expenses is crucial to using Quicken properly to create wealth. In Chapter 3, we provide an organized list of categories and additional information on harnessing their power. You may want to compare Intuit's list of categories to our list before entering your financial information into Quicken. You will need to delete any unnecessary categories and type in your individual categories. You will use the categories we provide in Chapter 3 throughout this book.

Intuit designed Quicken for average computer users. It is friendly and easy to use. As we proceed, we will try to show you the most intuitive or easiest method when Quicken allows multiple approaches. The most straightforward method usually employs your mouse. For example, Quicken's HomeBase window, shown in Figure 1-1, allows quick access to the program's major features and functions. Later, after you are familiar with the program, you will want to use shortcut keys to execute tasks quickly. You might find the listing of Quicken quick keys in Appendix A useful. The ultimate goal of *Create Wealth with Quicken* is to teach you how to employ Quicken to put more money into your pocket or purse. We will explore how you can use America's most popular personal finance software to build your assets and create wealth! You may find the listing of Quicken quick keys and other short-cuts in Appendix A useful.

Intuit designed Quicken 5 for Windows with an intuitive interface that allows you to perform routine tasks with minimal effort. Your initial view of HomeBase may vary from ours depending which version of Quicken

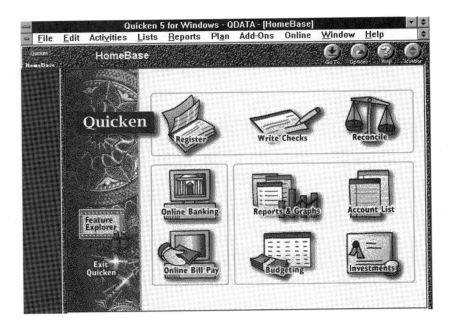

Figure 1-1.   Intuit designed Quicken 5 for Windows with an intuitive interface that allows you to perform routine tasks with minimal effort.

for Windows you purchase and which options you install. If your iconbar is not visible, click the round iconbar button.

LAYING A MENTAL FOUNDATION

To create wealth you must make a commitment to the process. You also need a positive mental attitude and outlook. Just as it is true that houses need strong foundations to stand the test of time, you need a strong foundation to build your financial future. The most important foundation required to build wealth is a proper mental attitude, not a lot of money in the bank or a stock portfolio. Throughout this book, you will learn many helpful financial concepts that you can use for the rest of your life—whether you are young or old.

Figure 1-2. Planning your finances is like planting a money tree. Plant it today, so that its fruit will be ready when you need it.

One of the most important concepts to understand is the effect of time on money. Procrastination is the biggest temptation most people must conquer on the road to riches. Creating wealth will take some time. Time is your friend—if you start now. It will be your enemy if you wait "just a little longer" before you begin your journey to financial success. As Figure 1-2 suggests, the sooner you plant your personal "money tree," the sooner your harvest will be ready. As a picture may be worth a thousand words, the following exercise illustrates this key concept.

EXPLORING THE EFFECT OF TIME ON MONEY

Time makes a big difference to your pocketbook, whether you realize it or not. Let's begin our exploration with an exercise that will visually demonstrate time's effect on your ability to accumulate wealth. You will also learn to use one of the financial planning tools included in Quicken.

Consider John and Jane, two young people who graduated from high school together. They are both the same age. Just before graduation, John found a job as a salesperson at the local electronics superstore. He was soon earning a respectable income. After a few months, John had purchased all of the electronic equipment he wanted. So on his 18th birthday, he decided to start "investing for his future." He began to invest $100.00 on the first day of each month.

Jane went to college after graduating from high school. Four years later, she had earned a business degree with a management emphasis and landed a good job. She decided to start investing $100.00 on the first day of each month, exactly four years after John began.

If John continues investing $100.00 per month until he is 65 years old, he will have invested for 47 years. Assume that John and Jane both find investments that pay 12 percent per year until they are 65. Do you think their investments will be worth a million dollars? How much more money do you think John will have than Jane?

To keep things simple, we'll assume that John and Jane are each putting their money into an investment account that pays a 12 percent return and is not subject to current income taxation. Don't laugh. There are a few places left in America that produce high rates of return and are not subject to current taxation.

Quicken includes financial tools to help you solve challenges like this. Now let's walk through the problem together using Quicken's Financial Planners. We will launch the planners from the main menu bar.

1. Chose Plan from the menu bar.
2. Click on Financial Planners from the drop-down menu.
3. Select Savings on the submenu shown in Figure 1-3 to open the Investment Saving Planner. We are now ready to calculate the Ending Savings Balance. The Investment Saving Planner window has three sections: Savings Information, Calculate, and Inflation.

Figure 1-3. The most direct route to reach the Financial Planners in Quicken 5 for Windows is via the main menu bar.

 Financial Planners are available only when you have a Register on the screen.

1. From the Main menu, select the Use Register command to access a Register.
2. Choose Activities, [Alt]-[A] or [F6], from the menu.
3. Select Financial Planning.
4. Finally, choose Investment to open the Investment Planning window. The DOS version does not have separate Savings Information, Calculate, and Inflation sections.

We will begin by answering the questions in the Calculate and Inflation sections. The Calculate section should already have the Ending Savings Balance—Future Value in DOS—marked as the default setting, which is correct. We won't be considering the effects of inflation in these examples. Change the Predicted Inflation rate to **0.000**. After you make this change, the other selections in the inflation section will not affect our calculations.

Now we are ready to complete the Savings Information section. John and Jane start without any savings, so their Opening Savings Balance—Present Value in DOS—is **$0.00**.

1. Type the number **12** in the Annual Yield box. The annual yield is the percentage return per year.
2. John and Jane are investing every month, so select **Months** from the Number Of drop-down list box. (DOS users press F7 repeatedly to change the Additions each to Months.)
3. When you pick Months, the Contribution Each list box on the next line automatically changes to Months, also.
4. John is planning to invest for 47 years times 12 months per year, for a total of 564 months. Place the number **564** in the box to the right of the Number of Months.
5. John is investing $100.00 per month, so enter **100** (note that Quicken automatically adds the dollar sign and decimal point for whole dollars) in the Contribution Each Month box (Additions each in DOS).
6. You have entered all of the required information. Press Tab once, and the Ending Savings Balance (Future Value in DOS) is calculated automatically.

It seems pretty incredible, but John is able to accumulate $2,726,874.06 in our scenario!

Your Investment Savings Planner should look like the one shown in Figure 1-4.

Now let's see how much of a difference waiting a mere 48 months makes. Since Jane is saving four years, or 48 months, less, change the Number of Months to **516** and press Tab once. Jane's Ending Savings Balance is only $1,687,574.61. If you calculate the difference, you will see that the four years Jane waited cost her over a million dollars! The old saying that "time is money" certainly seems accurate. Figure 1-5 shows the result of this seemingly minor change.

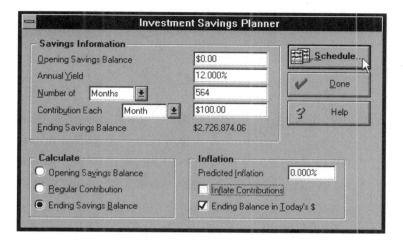

Figure 1-4. This is the Investment Savings Planner properly completed to calculate John's Ending Savings Balance after 47 years of investing $100.00 per month at a 12 percent rate of return. Confirm that the Predicted Inflation rate is 0.000%.

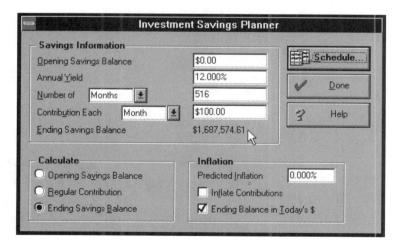

Figure 1-5. Jane's Ending Savings Balance is over $1,000,000 less than John's, although Jane invested only 48 fewer months than John.

The Investment Savings Planner is fairly sophisticated compared to software tools available to financial professionals only a few years ago. Let's have the Investment Savings Planner compute how much Jane would need to invest each month to end up with the same ending balance as John—$2,726,874.06.

To calculate the amount Jane must invest each month, you need to change the setting in the Calculate section (the lower left part of the window) from Ending Savings Balance to Regular Contribution. DOS users move the ✓ from Future Value to Additions Each Month by pressing F8 until the latter item is checked.

Now confirm the figures in the Savings Information section. The Number of Months should be 516. Change the Ending Savings Balance— Future Value in DOS—to **$2,726,874.06**. After making any necessary adjustments, press Tab once. The result shows that Jane must invest $161.59 per month to have as much money as John when she turns 65! Figure 1-6 shows the proper settings to reach this result.

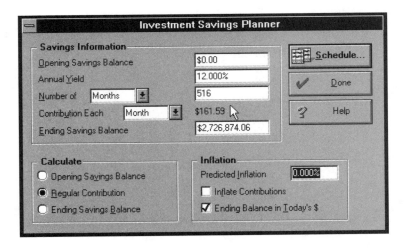

Figure 1-6. The Investment Savings Planner determines that Jane would need to invest $161.59 each month to accumulate as much money as John has by only investing $100.00 per month.

Another way to measure the effect of time on these computations is to total the amount of John's investment and compare it to how much Jane needs to invest to achieve the same result. If John puts $100.00 in his account each month for 564 months, his total investment is $56,400.00. Jane must add $161.59 for 516 months, which totals $83,380.44. Matching John's balance will cost Jane $26,980.44, or 48 percent, more than John.

You have just observed the power of time on money. Take a few minutes to personalize the numbers. Enter the number of months until you intend to retire, how much money you can invest each month, and how much you can earn on the types of investments you are making today. In Chapters 5 and 6, we will discuss some investment options you may not have considered and what results they have produced in the past.

Congratulations! You have just learned a very important lesson. Time is very important to your wealth creation process. You've just seen how much difference a short period of time can make if you procrastinate before initiating your investment program.

This concept is known as "compound interest" or "the time value of money." Compound interest refers to the fact that the interest remains in the account to accumulate even more interest on itself. The time value of money refers to the fact that, over time, the value of money changes. Students of wealth creation sometimes call compound interest the "eighth wonder of the world."

Anyone can accumulate a fortune over a lifetime. Just plan to pay yourself first each month—put some money into an investment before spending any—and allow the money and its interest to accumulate. The trick is to set something aside each month and then not touch it!

MONEY MATTERS

The key to long-term financial success is to spend less than you make over a long period of time and invest the excess wisely.

THE DANGERS OF COMPOUND INTEREST

Compound interest can work wonders for creating wealth. The problem is that most people have compound interest working against them. Instead of earning interest, most of us are paying more interest than we earn. Madison Avenue and America's money lenders have hoodwinked us into believing that debt is good. Although debt is useful in certain limited situations, debt causes most people more financial problems than successes. Of course, our own government has been a less-than-stellar model in the practice of wise debt management.

For years, political candidates have exhorted against the dangers of our nation's debt. Unfortunately, the numbers are so large that most of us can't fathom the magnitude of the problem. As this book is being written, we are enjoying (unless you are holding a Certificate of Deposit) some of the lowest interest rates in twenty years. These low rates will not last forever. Interest rates are cyclical and will eventually increase. When they do, I predict our government will experience severe financial difficulties. My goal for the next few pages is to help you understand the real dangers of debt.

FINANCIAL ALERT

Our federal government's debt load is increasing rapidly. Some economists and other financial experts predict that the government will not be able to pay even the interest on the massive debt that is accumulating. Watch out—if interest rates begin to rise, the national debt will escalate even faster. In 1993, just paying the interest on that debt required more than 60 percent of the personal income tax revenue collected. Experts estimated that the national debt exceeded $16,000 for each person, including children, living in America!

As we entered the '90s, an increasing number of financial gurus began to recommend the elimination or reduction of personal debt. I agree. In fact, paying off your personal debt, including your home mortgage, may be one of the best investments you'll ever make. We'll revisit this subject in Chapter 5.

Let's explore the principles of debt by considering the way home mortgages work.

DEBT'S DESTRUCTIVE FORCES

Owning your home is an important part of the American Dream for most of us. Unfortunately, home ownership can be an expensive proposition. Minimizing these costs is an important factor in creating wealth.

Mortgage interest is the largest expense of home ownership for most new home owners today. Quicken provides a nice tool to help you calculate the impact of debt on your finances. We will use the Financial Planners again to demonstrate this tool. Go back to the menu bar and choose Plan. This time select Loan from the submenu (see Figure 1-7) to see how much a home mortgage costs over the life of a typical mortgage.

Figure 1-7.   Select Loan from the Financial Planners submenu to determine how much your home mortgage is really costing you.

To return to the Financial Planners you must have an open Register on the screen.

1. From the Main Menu, select the Use Register command to access a Register.
2. Choose Activities, Alt-A or F6, from the menu.
3. Select Financial Planning.
4. Finally, choose Loan to open the Loan Calculator.
5. Use F8 to check Regular Payment.

The Loan Planner is a very easy tool to use (see Figure 1-8). Just enter your loan's current balance, how many years remain, and how many times per year your payments are due. For example, assume you are going to purchase a new home. You want to borrow $100,000 using a 30-year, fixed-rate loan with a nine percent interest rate. How much will your monthly payment be? How much will the loan cost you over the next 30 years? How much of each payment is interest, and how much is principal?

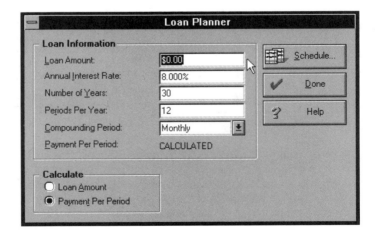

Figure 1-8. Notice that the Loan Planner default settings are appropriate to calculate standard fixed-rate home mortgages. Plug in your loan amount and adjust the interest rate to match your loan's rate.

1. Enter **$100,000** for your Loan Amount (called Principal in the DOS version).
2. Enter **9** for your Annual Interest Rate.
3. Use **30** for the Number of Years and **12** Periods Per Year.
4. Confirm that the Compounding Period is **Monthly**. This is a new feature in Quicken for Windows version 5 and is not available in the DOS version.
5. The Calculation area should have Payment Per Period selected.
6. Press Tab once, and the Loan Planner will calculate your monthly payment to equal $804.62.

If you have a different answer, confirm that your settings match those shown in Figure 1-9.

Now we want to see the loan details. Click on the Schedule button (press F9 in DOS), and Quicken will display a schedule showing each monthly payment, like the one in Figure 1-10. A breakdown shows the principal, interest, and remaining loan balance for each payment during

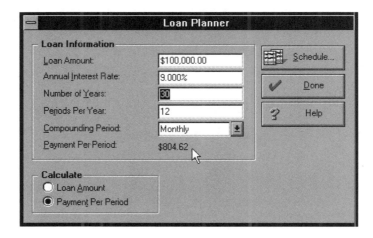

Figure 1-9.   The Loan Planner quickly calculates the monthly payment for our hypothetical home mortgage.

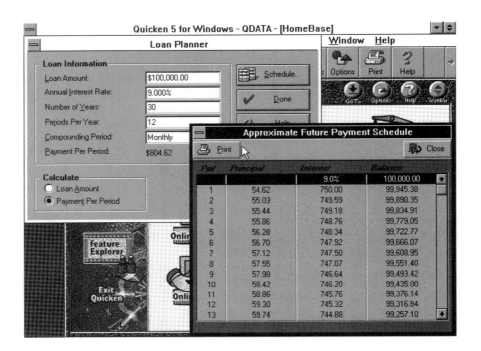

Figure 1-10. The Schedule button on the Loan Planner creates an Approximate Future Payment Schedule for the life of the loan. You can print out the schedule for future reference.

the life of the loan. In Quicken, this is called an Approximate Future Payment Schedule, but it is commonly referred to as a loan amortization schedule.

If you haven't looked over the Approximate Future Payment Schedule yet, take a minute to see how much of each payment that goes toward principal versus the amount of interest the mortgage company collects. Most people don't realize how much their interest costs add up over the life of their loan.

Multiply the monthly payment of $804.62 by the length of the loan. In our example, we are considering a 30-year loan, so there are a total of 360 monthly payments. The total of those payments is $289,663.20 for a $100,000 loan. You will pay $189,663.20 in interest over the life of your $100,000 loan. That's almost twice as much as your original loan amount!

However, home mortgages are really a good deal compared to credit cards. Most people I know who owe on their credit cards have outstanding balances that are earning their friendly banker or department store 18 to 21.9 percent interest—compounded daily!

COMPOUND VERSUS SIMPLE INTEREST

There are two basic types of interest—compound and simple. Simple interest is calculated only one time per payment period. Lenders for most consumer loans calculate your interest daily, even though they bill you monthly, which is compound interest. The difference between simple and compound interest is significant. If you happened to own a bank, you would consider this difference crucial to your profitability.

Assume for a minute that you really do own a small bank. Your little bank likes to issue credit cards. Who wouldn't? Credit cards have much higher interest rates than auto loans or home mortgages. Suppose you issue a thousand "Premier" credit cards to your best customers, each of whom has a $1,000.00 balance on their existing card. You want to earn as much interest as possible on these credit cards, so you make your Premier customers a special offer. You allow them to stop making payments for a year but continue to charge them interest. After that year, they will resume making regular payments.

Your Premier cards charge only 16.9 percent interest, while your competitors charge 18 percent or more. If you compute the interest you earn only once a year, a $1,000 balance will grow to only $1,169 during the first year. If you recompute interest charges each day, that same $1,000 balance will grow to $1,184.07 in a year. That is a difference of only $15.07 per account. You have a thousand customers with $1,000 balances. Now you're talking $15,070. You also know that many of your cardholders will accumulate larger balances because they will continue to use your cards to buy even more great things they can't live without.

I would venture to guess that you don't own a bank. Rather, you probably are a valued customer of a bank that has invested $1,000 or more with you and is earning 16.9, 18.9, or even 21.9 percent on your account.

Let's have Quicken compute how much a typical credit card will cost you over time. It is not unusual for an average American to have a $1,000 average balance on a 20 percent credit card for his or her entire working life. Assume that you decide to pay off that card. You have a two-part plan: 1) You will cut the card in two, and 2) you will pay the current minimum payment due and continue paying that amount each month until the balance is zero. The typical card requires a minimum payment of two percent of the current balance. On a $1,000 balance, that will be $20.00 per month. Even though the card will require a smaller payment each month, you will continue to pay the full twenty bucks every month until you have paid the card in full.

Most lenders compute and accrue the interest you owe them compounded daily. Fortunately, the Loan Planner will compute interest that is compounded daily—Quicken for Windows version 5 is the first version of Quicken with this important feature. Now, if the Loan Planner could calculate how long it takes to pay off a loan when you enter all of the other parameters, the program would be almost perfect.

Enter the following numbers into the Loan Planner: Loan Amount = **$1,000.00**, Annual Interest Rate = **20**, Number of Years = **9**, Payments Per Period = **12**, and Compounding Period = **Daily**. The Planner calculates your actual payment to be $20.13—the extra thirteen cents are because Quicken only calculates the number of entire years until your loan is paid in full. See Figure 1-11 if you come up with a different payment. Click on the Schedule button to see a monthly schedule of the amount of principal and interest paid each month. Click on the Schedule button to create a

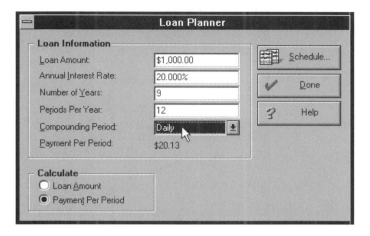

Figure 1-11. Use the Loan Planner to compute payments to pay off a credit card with a 20 percent interest rate in nine years by paying $20.13 each month. If you pay exactly $20.00 each month, it will take slightly longer than nine years to pay off the card.

hard copy for future reference. DOS users please notice that Quicken automatically tracks the total interest paid to date on your loan schedule.

As you work through *Create Wealth with Quicken*, you will continue learning the significance of compound interest on long-term financial success. You can see that how often interest is compounded affects an account by changing the Compounding Period from Daily to Monthly. Notice the slight difference in the monthly payment. Now change the Compounding Period to Semi-Annual. The change is even more significant.

Have you noticed that advertisements often don't bother telling you how much expensive things, like cars, cost? Madison Avenue knows that most people don't think about total cost anymore. Typically, people think in terms of monthly payments rather than total cost. Most people don't ask themselves, "Can I afford to spend $1,000 on a new (stereo system, couch, etc.) today?" Instead they think, "All right! I can afford twenty bucks a month!"

The problem is that a "twenty-spot" a month for 108 months is actually $2,160 over the life of the loan. Would you really pay $2,160 for that wonderful $1,000 gismo? Consider saving $20.00 a month for awhile and earning interest on that savings. Use your accumulated savings and interest to purchase your dream gismo for cash! If you are saving for a new computer, you can probably buy a better system for less money in a few months.

Plug a few numbers from your credit cards, personal loans, business debts, and home mortgage into the loan planner. How much interest are you paying for the privilege of having debt?

DONALD THE TRUMPED

The halls of history are littered with the crumpled carcasses of financial empires crushed by paying compound interest to their lenders. Donald Trump is a national figure. In the '80s, we watched in awe as he built an empire based on an ever-increasing load of debt. By the end of the '80s, the load was too heavy for his empire to bear, and he crashed into bankruptcy. Trump is now slowly recovering from his trials. His recovery is due, at least in part, to refinancing much of the debt at lower interest rates. Will Trump triumph? Only time will tell. I would be willing to bet a large lunch at a drive-up window that he has learned a lot about the perils of too much debt.

Compound interest is a foundational concept. Learn how compounding can work for you. Understand the devastating danger posed by debt's despicable effects!

PRACTICAL APPLICATIONS

Knowledge is power. Knowledge without action is useless. Now is the time to begin applying what you are learning. Each of these practical applications will be useful to you as you work through the exercises in future chapters. Consider them to be building blocks. This first block is the cornerstone that will serve as a base on which to build your financial future.

You have read about and demonstrated for yourself the power—positive and negative—of compound interest. Understanding this concept is the key to creating wealth. Spend some time projecting the effects of compounding on your own financial situation.

How old do you want to be when you can wake up in the morning and know you are financially secure? When do you want to wake up in the morning and have the freedom to decide whether you are going to work or spend the day occupied with your favorite pastime? That is the age we will call your retirement age.

Use the Investment Savings Planner to project how much your investment assets will be worth at retirement. You may want to refer to the instructions associated with Figure 1-4. Consider each asset or savings program separately. Project the value of your IRA or pension plan based on its current rate of return. Don't use a 12 percent rate of return if it is now earning three percent in a Certificate of Deposit. If you invest in a stock or mutual fund, use the last five-year average performance for your projections.

If you know your income tax bracket, reduce your rate of return by your combined state and federal tax rate. If you don't know your tax rate, use 20 percent if you make $20,000 or less per year, use 30 percent if you make $50,000 or less, and use 40 percent if you make over $50,000 a year. These percentages are only rough approximations. Your actual tax rate will vary over time, and it will probably be higher if you live in a high-tax area like New York City or California. Your rate may be lower if you live in a state that doesn't impose income taxes, such as Nevada. There are a number of other factors that influence your actual yield, but we are only trying to get a rough idea of our future now. We can refine our projections as we learn about these other factors throughout the book.

Let's work through an example together. We will use the Investment Savings Planner for this exercise. Assume that you own a mutual fund whose shares are currently worth **$1,257.00** (the Opening Savings Balance). This particular fund has averaged 14.5 percent per year, compounded annually, for the last five years, even though you have only recently become an investor. It is important to use a meaningful time frame when examining investments with fluctuating values and returns. This particular fund is not sheltered in an IRA, so we need to reduce your rate of return by your tax bracket. Assume your combined state and federal tax rate is 25 percent. That means you get to keep 75 percent of the profits. Multiply 14.5 percent by 75 percent to get **10.875** percent Annual Yield. Assume you have **19** years (Number of Years) until your projected retirement date. You want to see how much your investment might be worth if you do not add any more to it (Contribution Each Year—not Month—it makes a big difference). Don't forget to set the Predicted Inflation rate to zero percent. The Investment Savings Planner predicts your mutual fund to be worth $8,936.64 when you retire. Your window should look like Figure 1-12.

Examine the Schedule the Investment Savings Planner produces, shown in Figure 1-13. Notice how the investment grows each year. The amount of each increase is larger than the prior year's as the net profits (gross profits less taxes) are left in the account to accumulate. It is important to realize that many investments, like mutual funds, don't grow at an even rate. The actual investment results will vary from year to year. Depending on the type of investment, the value can vary considerably each year.

Many people have an investment program in place that includes making additional investments each month. Let's assume that you are investing

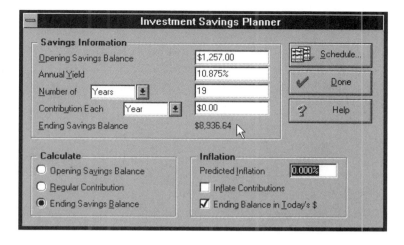

Figure 1-12. The Investment Savings Planner is useful for predicting the future value of investments. This example shows the value of a mutual fund investment given in the Practical Applications.

Deposit Schedule

The effect of 0.0% annual inflation over the period of 19 years will make $8,936.64 worth $8,936.64 in terms of today's purchasing power.

Number	Deposit	Total
0	0.00	1,257.00
1	0.00	1,393.70
2	0.00	1,545.26
3	0.00	1,713.31
4	0.00	1,899.63
5	0.00	2,106.22
6	0.00	2,335.27
7	0.00	2,589.23
8	0.00	2,870.81
9	0.00	3,183.01
10	0.00	3,529.16

Figure 1-13. Examine the Schedule available from the Investment Savings Planner. It shows the investment's growth on an annual basis without any additional money being added. The statement at the top of the window tells us that we are not considering the effects of inflation.

only $50.00 a month into your mutual fund. You need to make a couple of changes in the Investment Savings Planner. Change the time frame from Years to Months. (Press F7 repeatedly to make the change in DOS.) The number of months is **228** (19 years times 12 months per year). Your Contribution Each Month is **$50.00**. Quicken calculates your investment value at $47,471.04. See Figure 1-14 if you get a different result.

After you run projections on all of your savings and investment accounts, you will want to print out repayment schedules for each of your debts. Compute repayment schedules for all of your loans, including auto loans, intra-family loans, mortgages, personal loans, loans from your pension plans, student loans, and any other loans you may have. Use the Loan Planner to make your calculations. You may want to review the steps given earlier in the chapter for using the Loan Planner.

Credit cards and some other loans do not usually have specific loan lengths. You can find out how long the loan will take to pay off by trying

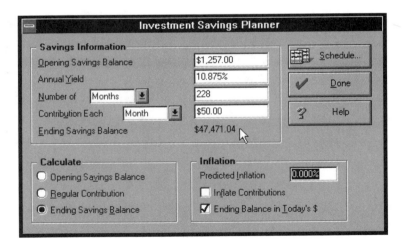

Figure 1-14. Many people invest in mutual funds on a monthly basis. This example shows how to set up the Investment Savings Planner to project the fund's value in 19 years (228 months) with monthly contributions of $50.00.

different numbers of years until the payment is close to your current monthly payment. When calculating the loan in Figure 1-11, I had to try a couple of different figures for the loan length before finding that nine years produced a payment of approximately $20.00 per month.

After you complete the printouts for your loan amortization schedules and project the future values for your investments, you are ready to start Chapter 2.

To learn more about acquiring wealth, I recommend that you also read *The Richest Man in Babylon* by George S. Clason. This is an excellent book that presents the key concepts to acquiring wealth in terms that even children find enjoyable. There are two editions available; the only differences are the page and type sizes making it easier to read, and price. Signet publishes the less expensive edition, and Plume produces the larger-type edition. Your local bookseller probably carries one or the other.

CHAPTER 2

LET'S GET STARTED

EIGHTY PERCENT OF AMERICA'S MILLIONAIRES ARE
FIRST-GENERATION RICH.
—THOMAS J. STANLEY

It's time for us to begin using Quicken for what it is actually designed to do—keep track of your money! Over the last few years, I've done an informal survey of Quicken users. Most people use Quicken simply to maintain their checkbooks. They record all of their checks and deposits. Some people actually use Quicken to print out their checks every month. The average user is not taking full advantage of the real power of the program. In this chapter, we'll show you how to begin to really harness that power to help you create wealth.

THE BIG PICTURE

Your checking account is only one small piece of the big picture. As we work through this chapter, we will organize your assets and determine your debts.

As we begin, I would like to introduce you to the Richies—a fictitious family we'll be watching throughout this book. Sam and Sally Richie are fairly typical Americans. They're middle-class, with two cars in the garage, two children—Tina and Tom—a cat, a dog, and three guppies (there were more guppies until the kids fed some to Sparky, their cat). Throughout this book, you will be able to practice setting up Accounts and using various Quicken features. Take a minute to set up a Quicken file for the Richies and, if you have not yet started using the software for your own finances, create a file for yourself, too.

In Quicken for Windows (DOS instructions follow), use the File command on the Main menu:

1. Choose File from the menu bar. Then choose New, and press ⌈Enter⌋.
2. A window appears asking you if you are creating a new file or new Account, as in Figure 2-1. The default is to create a New File: Click

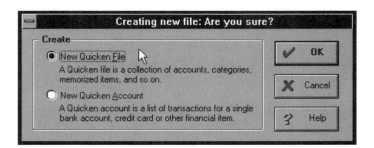

Figure 2-1. Most Quicken 5 users will see this window only when they create a new file or Account. If you have not previously loaded an existing file or created a new file in Quicken 5, you will go directly to the Quicken New User Setup window.

Figure 2-2. Create a data file for the Richies using the settings described in the text.

on OK or press Enter. If you are creating the file for the first time the Create Quicken File window will appear as in Figure 2-2.

Note: Any time you load Quicken for Windows version 5 without any data files in the default directory, the Quicken New User Setup automatically steps you through the process of creating Quicken data files. This is a valuable process, especially for those who have never used Quicken before. Unfortunately, the process does not allow you to set up the data files properly for our exercises. You can either run through the set up process once for experience's sake and then set up your permanent data file or click Cancel, then choose New from the file menu.

3. The Create Quicken File window appears, as shown in Figure 2-2. Type **Richie** for the File Name. You don't need to type ".qdb" (".qdt" in Quicken for DOS and earlier versions of Quicken for Windows) after Richie; the software will automatically add your file extension for you. Please note the Q-Tip on Quicken files that follows.

4. We will be using our own categories instead of Quicken's predefined categories throughout this book for Home and Business Predefined Categories. Check boxes to make these selections are located in the lower right corner of the window, as pictured in Figure 2-2. Uncheck the checkmark in the Home Predefined Category checkbox by clicking the checkbox. If you are using the Quicken New User Setup, you must select either Home or Home and Business categories. Please review the note in Step 2.

5. Click OK or press ⌷Enter⌷. The Create New Account window appears. We will set up Accounts later, so click Cancel to close this window for now. We will return to Quicken in a few minutes.

To set up the Richies' file in Quicken for DOS, follow these steps:

1. **From the Main menu, choose File Activities.**
2. **The File Activities menu appears. Choose Select/Set Up File.**
3. **Double-click <Set Up New File> (or press ⌷Home⌷, then ⌷Enter⌷) in the Select/Set Up New File window.**
4. **Type Richie in as your File Name and press ⌷Enter⌷.**
5. **The Standard Categories window appears. Type 4 for Neither (Home nor Business) categories. Press ⌷Enter⌷.**
6. **The Select/Set Up New File window appears with RICHIE highlighted. Press ⌷Enter⌷, and the Set Up New Account window appears. Please continue reading. We will return to Quicken in a few minutes.**

Q-TIP

Quicken creates a data file for you when you install and set up the software. In Quicken 5 for Windows you must name the file yourself, the file will have the .QDB extension. In previous versions of Quicken for windows and DOS, it names your data file QDATA.QDB. This is your personal data file unless you give it another name. Quicken automatically places new files in the

current directory that Quicken is using to store data. The default directory is where the Quicken software is. If you want to store your data in the default location, press [Enter], or type in a new directory name.

Wealth creation doesn't occur overnight. It is a long-term process. The first step in this process is to get a firm grasp on where you are and where you want to go. If you haven't already done so, it is a good idea to set some goals so that you know where you're going. Couples should take time together to set mutual and individual goals. Set financial and non-financial goals for the coming year, the next five years, the next ten years, and the distant future. These goals may be to send your children to college or to retire early. Do you want to take a long vacation in a few years or travel around the world?

Whatever your goals are, make sure you write them down. Try to be as specific as possible when you set your goals. If you want to buy a new home, determine where you want to live, how many bedrooms you want, and how many square feet you'd like to have. Do you want a pool or not? Do you want to live in the mountains or near the beach? Make your written goals as detailed as possible. Goals set in writing are much more apt to happen than goals that are just nebulous ideas in your mind.

Once you've written down your goals, post them someplace conspicuous. The mirror where you brush your teeth and comb your hair in the morning, is appropriate. You'll see your goals every day as you get started in the morning. You'll think about them throughout the day and make better financial decisions.

ORGANIZE YOUR ASSETS

Your first stop on the path to prosperity is to organize your assets. Properly organizing your assets is necessary to get a good look at the big picture. Quicken is an excellent tool for organizing assets and keeping

them organized. You will be very happy you have all of your assets organized the next time you apply for a loan. For example, home mortgage
applications require you to list all of your assets and liabilities. After we
organize your assets, then we'll deal with your liabilities.

You will find that you have several types of assets. We will set up
Accounts for each of your assets or groups of assets. We will set up all of
the Accounts using the Account List that we will access from HomeBase.
DOS instructions follow.

1. Open HomeBase by clicking the HomeBase icon or clicking any
   portion of HomeBase that is exposed on your screen.
2. Click the Account List graphic. The Account List window opens, as
   shown in Figure 2-3. Since this is the first time you have accessed
   the Account List since creating a new data file, your Account List is
   empty. Please note for future reference that you can also open the
   Account List by using the Accts icon on Quicken's icon bar.
3. Click the New button on the Account List window's button bar to
   open the Create New Account window, shown in Figure 2-4. We
   will set up our first Quicken Account in a few minutes.

**When you create a new Quicken data file, no Accounts are set up.
The first time you use the new file, Quicken will automatically
take you to the Set Up New Account window.**

The first, and probably most obvious, type of assets are bank and other
deposit accounts—checking, money market, and savings accounts. A
deposit account is simply an account where you place money for temporary storage, usually in a bank or another financial institution. Next are
other assets—your house, cars, computer system, and personal property.
Hopefully, you also have investments. Investments are another type of
asset you want to keep in separate Accounts. Finally, we will discuss Cash
Accounts and why it is important to keep track of your cash expenditures.

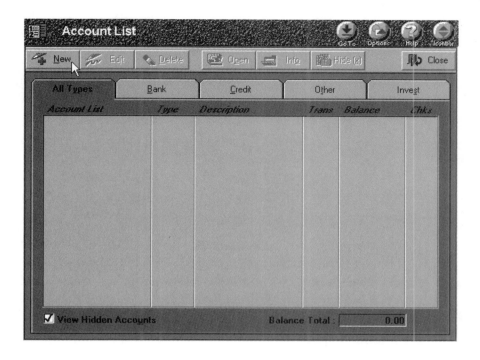

Figure 2-3.   We will start setting up new Accounts from the Account List window.

Quicken keeps track of each of these items in various types of Asset Accounts.

When you create a new Account, Quicken gives you several choices for the type of Accounts to create, as shown in Figure 2-4. The Create New Account window has buttons for Asset, Cash, Checking, Credit Card, Investment, Liability, Money Market, and Savings Accounts. Although Quicken for Windows includes buttons to create Checking, Money Market, and Savings Accounts, these are all listed as Bank Accounts in your Account List. Your Account choices in the DOS version are Asset, Bank, Cash, Credit Card, Investment, and Liability.

Figure 2-4. The Create New Account window helps you select which type of Quicken Account to set up.

You need to choose a particular point in time to value your assets (and liabilities). Each day your financial picture probably changes slightly. You can choose the first day of this month, last Friday, or even today. If you have time, value your assets today, even if you do not enter the data into Quicken until tomorrow or next weekend.

You may not be able to determine exact values for each of your assets today, but that's okay. Estimate any values that you can't determine exactly. Update the estimates when you get a chance. Don't let the inability to place exact values on each item deter you from getting started! Some items, such as stocks and mutual funds, have their closing market values published in the newspaper after each business day. Some mutual funds list two prices in the paper: Bid and NAV, which refers to net asset value. If your mutual fund quotes two prices, use the lower one for valuing your holdings. It is perfectly acceptable to use the last published value for any assets, such as limited partnership interests, for which you don't have current values.

Just use the date the assets were valued as your opening date. Each Asset Account may have different opening dates.

Eventually, you will want to update your check Register with any transactions from the beginning of the year that relate to your income taxes. You will also want to enter historical records for other assets that have tax implications. We will explore investment-related issues in Chapters 6 through 8.

At this point, we only want to determine account balances or asset values as of a particular date. Sam and Sally Richie chose the December 31, the last day of the year. They felt that they should start the year on the right foot. On January 2, after the holiday guests left, they sat down to organize their assets. Sam and Sally decided to start by setting up their bank and other deposit accounts.

Q-TIP

As we follow the Richies' finances, you need to adjust your computer's internal date to the point in time where the Richies are: January 2, 1996. If you are running Quicken from the DOS prompt, exit the program and type date **at the DOS prompt. Then type** 1-2-96 **and press** Enter**. In Windows, press** Alt**-**Esc **as many times as necessary to bring up My Computer, in Windows 95, or the Program Manager, in Windows 3.1. Double-click on the Control Panel icon (usually in the Main group in Windows 3.1) to open it. Now, double-click on the Date/Time icon to open it and change your system date to 1/2/96.**

Date/Time

WARNING: Please be certain to change your system date back to the current date when you leave Quicken. Some programs are date-sensitive.

BANK AND DEPOSIT ACCOUNTS

Almost everyone has a checking account, so it's an obvious place to start. Last December, Sam and Sally began to consider how to better manage their finances with the advent of a new year. They decided to open up a new personal checking account at MegaBank. Their old account had become a hopeless mess. They never could get it to balance. They initially purchased Quicken just to keep track of their check register. They opened the new MegaBank personal checking account with $1,000. We will enter their outstanding checks in Chapter 3. Let's create a checking Account in Quicken for the Richies. DOS instructions follow the Windows instructions.

If you are having problems balancing one of your checking accounts (maybe you've lost track of an old checking account's balance), open a new checking account at your bank and in Quicken. Close out the old one at the bank after all your checks clear, but don't delete the Quicken Account. Use Quicken to keep track of the new account. You will never lose track of your account balances if you use all of the program features, including Account Reconciliation.

1. We will start from the Create New Account window, where we stopped a couple of minutes ago. Click the Checking button. Quicken will immediately open the Checking Account Setup window. Quicken's EasyStep will walk you through the process of setting up a new checking Account. Press (Enter) to continue.

2. By default, Quicken fills "Checking" in the Account Name box, as shown in Figure 2-5. If you accidentally erase it, type **Checking** in that field. Press (Tab) to move from the Account Name field to the Description field. Note: pressing (Shift)-(Tab) moves you backwards.

3. Type **MegaBank Checking** in the Description field and then click Next or press (Enter).

4. The Checking Account Setup window now asks if you have your last account statement. The default is Yes. We do, so click Next or press (Enter).

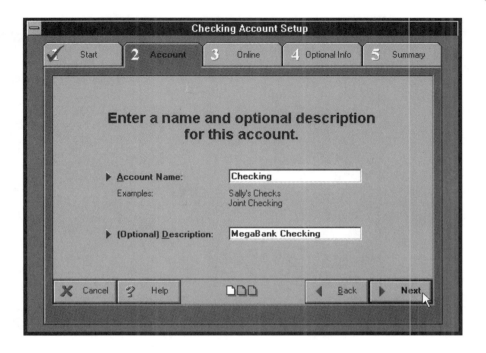

Figure 2-5. The Checking Account Setup window initially requests your Account name and description.

5. The next Checking Account Setup window, Figure 2-6, asks for your Statement Date and Ending Balance. You can use the date on your bank statement or any other date for which you know the exact amount of money in your account for the Statement Date. Quicken automatically defaults to your computer's system date. If you adjusted your computer clock as we suggested earlier, the default Statement Date is 1/2/96. Therefore you need to click the miniature calendar icon to the right of the Statement Date field to pop up an interactive calendar. Then click on December 31, 1995, on the calendar or type **12/31/95** in the field. Press Tab.

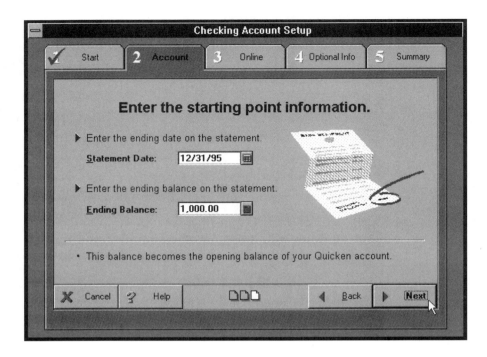

Figure 2-6. The Checking Account Setup window now requires your last statement date and your statement's ending balance. Quicken often provides handy pop-up calendars and calculators, as it does in this window to make your life easier.

6. Sam and Sally are beginning the new year with exactly $1,000.00 in their checking account, so type 1000 (it is not necessary to use the dollar sign or commas when entering numbers in Quicken) for the Ending Balance. Please note the small calculator icon to the right of the Ending Balance field. Click the calculator and try it out, then click Next or press Enter to continue.

7. The Richies are not planning to use the Online Banking services. So leave the default settings at No. Click Next or press Enter to continue.

8. The next screen gives you an opportunity to record information about your account. Check Yes and press ⟨Enter⟩ to continue to the information entry screen. Take a couple of minutes to gather and enter as much of the information as you have available when you create your own Accounts. You should be able to find most of the data on your account statement, but you may need to look elsewhere for your contact's name and phone number. Take the time now; you may need quick access in the future. Meanwhile, use the information in Figure 2-7 for this Account. Click Next or press ⟨Enter⟩ to continue.

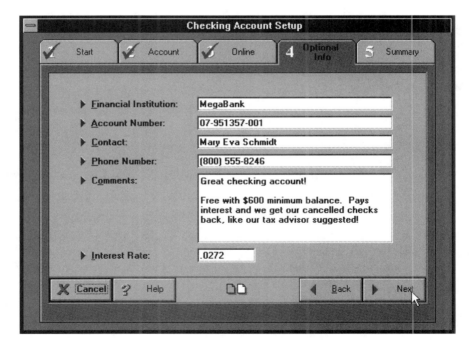

Figure 2-7. You can enter additional Account data in the Optional Information window, where you can record useful information about your Accounts for quick reference when you are using Quicken.

9. The final EasyStep window gives you a summary of your Account. Review it for accuracy. Please read the following Q-Tip before selecting Done.

Q-TIP **Quicken's EasyStep process is helpful the first time or two you create an Account. You must use EasyStep the first time you create a new Account for each type of Quicken Account—Asset, Cash, Checking, Credit Card, Investment, Liability, Money Market, and Savings Accounts. The lower-left corner of the last step of the series has a checkbox that allows you to Start with Summary when you setup future Accounts. Check this box to go directly to the summary screen where all of the data may be entered in one place. You can click the Previous button to view EasyStep's detail screens.**

After you enter the information necessary for Quicken to create your new Account, the Account List automatically opens, showing the Checking Account's Opening Balance, as shown in Figure 2-8. The Opening Balance is the amount you entered as your last bank statement's Ending Balance.

Please note the file folder-style tabs across the top of the list. These tabs allow you to select groups of Accounts to display based the Account type. We will use these tabs later in this chapter. Another helpful feature in the Account List window is the iconbar. If you don't have all of the optional information available when you create an Account, or if the information changes, simply click the Info icon when you want to edit it.

Highlight the Checking Account on the Account List and press [Enter] to Open the Account Register, shown in Figure 2-9. You will see how Quicken creates the Opening Balance for the Account using the Ending Balance you provided when you created an Account.

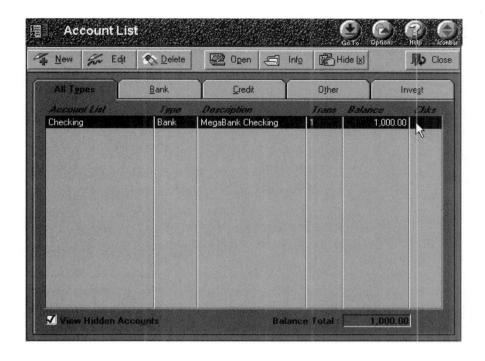

Figure 2-8. Your Account List window should look like this after you finish creating the Richies' Checking Account.

Setting up Accounts in the DOS version of Quicken is stream-lined in comparison to the method we used above in the Windows version. Since this is a new file, we left off with the Set Up New Account window open.

1. Since the Richies' checking account is a bank account, type 1 for Account Type. Press Enter or Tab to go to the Name for this account field and type Checking. Press Enter to go to the next window when you are satisfied with your answers.

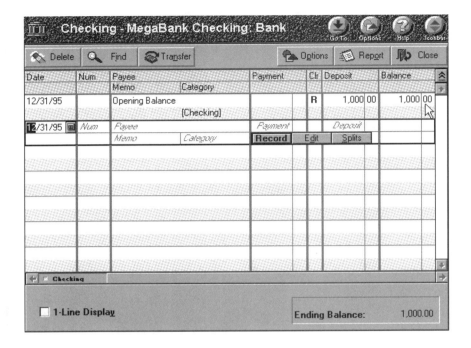

Figure 2-9. Open the Checking Account Register to see how Quicken sets up Opening Balances.

2. The Starting Balance and Description window is now open. Enter 1000 (it is not necessary to use the dollar sign or commas when entering numbers in Quicken) for the Balance as of: 12/31/95. Press ⌷Enter⌷ or ⌷Tab⌷ again to go to the Description field. Type MegaBank Checking.

3. Press ⌷F8⌷ to go to the Additional Information window. This is where Quicken stores useful information about your Accounts, so it is handy when you are working with Quicken. Press ⌷Enter⌷ when you finish viewing this screen to return to the previous window.

4. Press ⌈Enter⌉ again to close the Starting Balance and Description window. Quicken creates the Checking Account and returns to the Account List.

5. Highlight Checking and press ⌈Enter⌉ to open the Checking Register, where you will see that the Account has an Opening Balance of $1,000.00.

Q-TIP

Quicken is loaded with more program features and functions than we will be able to explore fully in this text. If you ever need more help than we provide, try to find the information you need in the on-line help system. Use the Help command or press ⌈F1⌉ to access Help.

New users may find Quicken's Qcards, small windows with instructions for the task you are performing, to be of tremendous assistance. After a while, you may find that they interfere with your ability to use Quicken efficiently. You can easily change the Qcard settings through the Help menu by checking or unchecking the Show Qcards line.

DOS users choose Set Preferences from the Main menu and then Qcard Settings from the submenu. In the Qcard Settings window, press ⌈F9⌉ to turn the Qcards off and on.

Please set up all of the Richies' Accounts, assets, and liabilities in Quicken. A complete list of the Richies' banking and deposit Accounts and Account descriptions appear in the Account List shown in Figure 2-10. We will describe these Accounts in the following paragraphs. A complete list of all of the Richies' Accounts and balances, as set up in this chapter, is available in Figure 2-27 and 2-28. If you are keeping track of the Richies' assets and liabilities, you can refer to them as needed. You should use the Account names and descriptions in that list, because we will be referring to them as we work through the next several chapters.

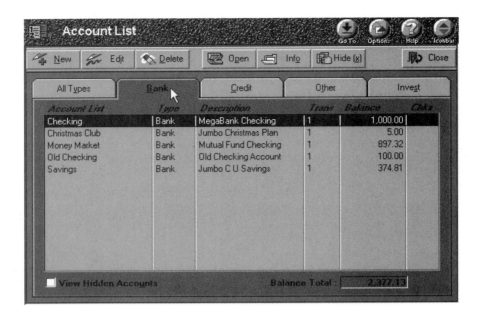

Figure 2-10. Use the Account List shown here to set up the Richies' deposit Accounts. Enter these names and descriptions if you plan to follow the Richies throughout this book. You can use December 31 1995, as the statement date for all of these accounts. Notice that file folder-style tabs allow you to select groups of Accounts, like the Bank Accounts in this figure. The Account List window conveniently provides a subtotal of balances of all the Accounts selected.

Sam and Sally also have an old checking account. They made their last mortgage payment and paid all of their other bills from that account before the end of last year. They think they will probably have about $100 left in that account after the outstanding checks clear. Set up the **Old Checking** Account with a **$100** Opening Balance. They also have a **Mutual Fund Checking** Account—a money market account through a mutual fund that has checking privileges—that had an **$897.32** balance as of December 31.

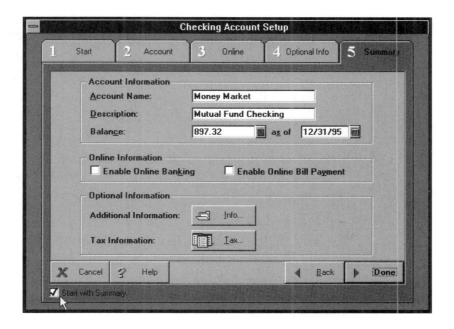

Figure 2-11. By checking Start with Summary (selectable at the bottom of the Summary screen in the New Account Setup windows), you can create new Accounts by entering Account data into one window instead of a series of windows.

 Follow these steps to set up additional Accounts in the DOS version of Quicken:

1. We want to start from the Account List. You can get to the Account List from any Register by pressing Ctrl - A . Access a Register from Quicken's Main menu.

2. Select the first item on the list, <New Account>, and press Enter to open the Set Up New Account window. You can use the Ctrl - Insert Quick Key to pop up the Set Up New Account window from anywhere in the Account List window.

3. Finish setting up the Account the same way we set up the Richies' Checking Account.

Q-TIP

The ability to link transfers in and out of an Account to a federal income tax form can be helpful in some situations. This capacity is most useful when you are making a series of tax-deductible contributions to an IRA or other pension plan or receiving a series of taxable withdrawals from a pension plan or IRA. In most cases, you will not need to link an Account to a tax form, because your transfers will not have tax consequences.

To use this function, click the Tax button in the Checking Account Setup Summary window to open the Tax Schedule Information window, shown in Figure 2-12. The checkbox at the top of the window allows you to quickly identify tax-qualified accounts, like IRAs and 401(k)s. Use the drop-down lists to find the tax form or schedule you want to link your transfers to and click OK when you finish.

Should you determine that an Account should be linked or should have a different link, you can change the link. Highlight the Account in the Account List. Click on the Edit button on the buttonbar. Click the Tax button in the Edit Account window.

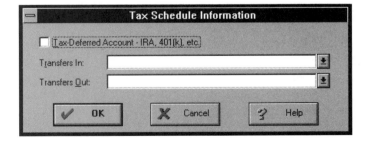

Figure 2-12. The Tax Schedule Information window allows Quicken to automatically keep track of transfers in and out of Accounts that have an impact on your federal income taxes.

In addition to their checking accounts, the Richies have a Christmas Club account at their credit union. It has a balance of only $5—they used most of the money for Christmas. They also have a savings account at their credit union, with a year-end balance of $374.81.

Tina and Tom, the Richie children, also have savings accounts of their own. We will not include these accounts in Sam and Sally's assets since they belong to the kids.

MONEY MATTERS

Parents often want to begin savings and investment accounts in their children's names using their children's Taxpayer Identification Numbers (TIN), better known as Social Security Numbers (SSN). This certainly has numerous advantages, but there are disadvantages, too.

Using this method, high-income taxpayers will save some money on their annual income tax returns. Unfortunately, Congress changed the tax laws in the 1980s to severely limit parents' ability to shift income from their own high tax bracket to their children's tax brackets, which are usually lower. This is commonly referred to as the "kiddie tax." Under current law, children age 14 and younger may earned up to $1,300 in investment and other unearned income at their own tax rate. Assuming that the child has no wage income, the first $650 of the investment earnings are tax-free because the child has a $650 standard deduction. Any unearned income in excess of $1,300 is taxable at the parent's highest tax bracket. Few middle-class children have this problem.

The other major disadvantage of investing in your children's names relates to college aid. The current college aid system discourages children's investment and savings accounts by requiring children to use most of their funds to pay for their education. In 1995, federal and college aid guidelines expect the student to spend 35 percent of their savings each year on college

tuition and other qualified expenses[1]. If the funds are in the parents' names, the aid formulas only require the parents to spend 5.65 percent of their savings[2], allowing parents greater latitude to earmark funds for retirement planning and other pursuits besides paying for their children's education.

Don't let the disadvantages of children having their own savings and investments discourage you from encouraging your children to set aside a portion of everything they earn. Training your children to save and invest their hard-earned cash will build character, encourage responsibility, and strengthen our national economy.

Now that you have established Quicken Accounts for Sam and Sally's deposit accounts, your Account List should match the Richies' shown in Figure 2-10.

It is time for you to set up your own bank, credit union, and other deposit accounts. Remember to open your data file if you have the Richies' data on screen (remembering to change your system date from Richie Standard Time, of course). Take as much time as necessary to set up all of your banking and deposit accounts. Set up separate Accounts for each CD, checking, Christmas Club, mutual fund checking, and savings account that you have. Do not set up Accounts for any Individual Retirement Accounts (IRA) or other pension accounts at this time. We'll be dealing with pensions and IRAs later in the chapter, when we deal with investments. After you set up Accounts for all of your deposit and banking accounts, you're ready to move on to the next section, which covers setting up Accounts for all other non-investment assets you own.

---

1. College-Education Savings Require A Decree of Investing Know-How, *The Wall Street Journal*, Jonathan Clemets, p. C1, September 26, 1995.
2. *ibid.*

ASSET ACCOUNTS

Asset Accounts include your home, automobiles, collections, antiques, jewelry, and anything else that is an asset but is not a bank deposit, investment, or cash. As you enter these assets into your system, you need to determine realistic values for them. It doesn't do any good to inflate or deflate the values from their actual amounts. As you value items, you should use their current market value. Determine an amount that would be reasonable if you were selling them at a garage sale or in a second-hand or thrift store. If you have a refrigerator that cost $995 two years ago, it is probably worth less than half as much now.

Most people own a number of different assets. Let's start with the largest asset most people will ever purchase—a home. Our friends the Richies own a home. Actually, the mortgage company owns most of it.

Open the Richies' Quicken file, if you are in a different file. (As we move back and forth between the Richies' and your data files, you do not need to adjust your computer's system date to 1/2/95. Simply enter 12/31/95 in EasyStep, the Account Setup windows, or the Registers.) You have probably already found that there are multiple ways to set up an Account. You can use the menu commands to create a new Account or use the buttons on the top of the Account List to open, edit, delete, or create new Accounts. Use the New button on the top of your Account List or press Ctrl-N to create a new Account. Quicken 5 for Windows also allows you to click the right mouse button anywhere inside the Account List window to open a pop-up list, then click New. DOS users can use the Ctrl-Insert key combination. Select Asset Account.

Fill in the following information in the Asset Account Setup screens, as shown in Figure 2-13. Type **Residence** for Account Name. Under the description, you can put **Family Home**, Residence, etc. In the next field, enter **December 31, 1995**, for the Richies. The Richies' home is now worth about **$105,000** you can put **Family Home**, Residence, etc. At this point, you will not need to enter any more information (you don't need to use

Figure 2-13. Your home, if you have one, is one of your most important assets. It is essential to maintain detailed records on your home. Chapter 8 has all of the details, but you should set up an Asset Account for your home now. Remember to check the Start with Summary box to avoid the EasyStep process in the future.

the Tax Schedule Information fields). Your Asset Account Setup summary screen should look like Figure 2-13.

Open your data file and set up an Account for your home. Your local newspaper can be a good reference for your home's value, but your friendly neighborhood Realtor® is probably the best free source of information. Look for homes for sale in your area that are similar to yours. Find out from the Realtor the listing price or how much the homes have sold for in the last couple of months. Since this figure is for your own use, you don't need to be very accurate. Try to come within three or four thousand dollars of what your house could actually sell for now. After creating an Asset Account for your home, open the Richies' data file again.

The next largest asset that most Americans own is a car or other vehicle. Very few American families have only one car; most have multiple vehicles. Check the local newspaper to see how much your vehicles are worth, based on their condition. If you belong to a credit union, call and ask about your vehicles' *Blue Book* values. Local automobile dealers also have Blue Book values, but they are less likely to help you determine the values of your vehicles.

The Blue Book lists high, average, and low values. High-value cars are in excellent condition, like the ones dealers put at the front of their auto lot. Average autos are in okay condition. Poor-quality vehicles need some cosmetic or mechanical work. Again, it doesn't do you any good to come up with a higher or lower value than your cars are actually worth. In addition to cars, you will probably want to include pickups, trucks, recreational vehicles, motorcycles, airplanes, and other such items in this Asset Account.

The Richies have three vehicles. Sally has a car that she uses for getting around, Sam has an old pickup truck, and they also have a moped that the kids like to ride around on their property since they're not old enough to get their driver's licenses. The total value of their **vehicles** is currently **$14,000**, as of the first of the year, as shown in Figure 2-14.

Regardless of whether you own a home and a car or two, you have some personal possessions. You probably have some furniture, a computer or two, and some other items of value. You can lump all these things together in one Account and call it Personal Property or Personal Assets. Set up separate Accounts for any items you feel deserve special attention.

Our friends the Richies set up separate Accounts for some of their more important assets and then lump everything else into an Account called Personal Property. They feel that their computer system, hardware and software, being such an important part of their life, should have an

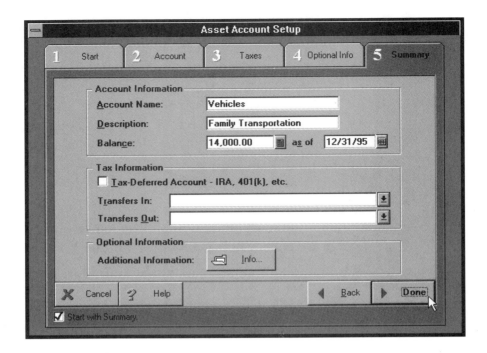

Figure 2-14. Few Americans are able to survive without one or more cars. Include your cars, pickups, recreational vehicles, motorcycles, airplanes, and other modes of transportation in this Account.

Account of its own, too. They figure their hardware and software are currently worth about $2,500. They also collect jewelry and antiques, worth about $2,500, which they put in another Account. All of their other personal property is worth about $15,000, including clothing, books, furniture, the barbecue set in the backyard, lawn furniture, and the doughboy pool. Set up Accounts for these assets using Figure 2-15. The Richies are valuing these assets as of December 31, 1995. They decided to use the last day of the year since these assets have approximate values that don't fluctuate on a daily basis.

Take a few minutes now to make a list of all of your personal possessions. Load your data file and set up Accounts for each of your personal

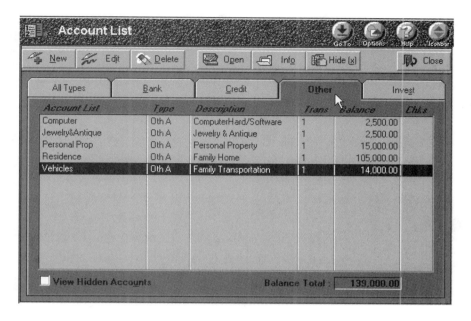

Figure 2-15. Add the above Asset Accounts into Quicken for the Richies. Notice that the Asset Accounts group together under the Other tab for quick reference. Use December 31, 1995, for the valuation date for each of these Accounts.

assets or groups of assets. You can either make a very rough guess and just enter one number as an opening balance in a personal property Account or list each item individually and increase the Account value with each entry. I recommend that you make a rough guess initially and return later to list the individual items.

It is a good idea to keep a list of all the items you own for your insurance policy. If your house burns down, your insurance typically will cover the replacement cost of your belongings. You need to have a good estimate and descriptions of all the items you own. Quicken is not the best place to keep your list, but it's better than not having any itemization. If you don't have a record of all your assets, at least keep a list in Quicken. Of course, it would be a good idea to keep a backup copy of your data files someplace besides in your own home, in case of a catastrophe. As you purchase more assets, remember to add them to the appropriate Asset Account. You will be able to keep a running balance of all of your assets. The Deluxe version of Quicken has an additional module to help you keep track of your household inventory. Contact Intuit for additional information at (800) 624-6930.

Your investments are among the items that you won't want to include with your other assets. Let's talk about those now.

MONEY MATTERS

Is your computer equipment insured under your homeowners or renters' insurance policy? Many policies only provide minimal coverage in the base policy. Some companies have reasonably priced riders that will cover up to $5,000 of additional computer equipment and software. Read your policy or call your insurance agent today to determine the amount of risk you have in the case of theft, fire, or other covered calamity.

Q-TIP

When you purchase additional assets in the future, choose the appropriate Asset Account's name in the Category field of your Register, and the value of that Account will increase automatically. Account names appear at the end of the list of categories in the drop-down window in the Category field. You will learn more about Categories and Transfers as we progress.

INVESTMENT ACCOUNTS

Successfully traveling the road to riches requires that you invest in a number of different items. For each of those items, you should create an Investment Account. Generally, each Investment Account should contain only one investment or type of investment. It is not advisable to mix your investments in Accounts with investments that belong to your children, other family members, or friends. We will discuss investments at length in Chapters 5 and 6.

All your investments can be broken down into two basic types: personal and pension.

PERSONAL INVESTMENTS

Many people "invest" in "savings"-type accounts. Certificates of Deposit are a good example. Many people consider CDs to be an investment. I consider them to be simply "bank deposits." Bank deposits pay such low rates that, after you subtract taxes and inflation, you probably will have little, if any, profit. If you are in an upper tax bracket, you probably lose money on your CDs. Thus, I recommend that you classify your CDs as Bank Accounts. The only CDs we want to set up in Investment Accounts are those in an IRA or other pension plan. In this case, go ahead and call them an investment—even though you will probably lose money after counting the effects of inflation and paying taxes on your distributions.

If you own U.S. Savings Bonds, all of them belong in a single Account of their own. Mutual funds are a different animal. You should have a different Investment Account for each mutual fund, unless your funds are owned by your IRA or another pension plan. Some people like to lump all of their mutual funds from one family of related funds into one Account. It is much easier for you to keep track of the information for tax purposes if each individual fund has its own Account. Some people like to buy stocks and bonds. If you have individual stocks and bonds, then each stock or bond should have a separate Account, unless you own them in your pension plan or IRA. What I mean by each stock or bond is, for example, if you buy ACME and you buy many different shares of ACME multiple times throughout the years, all of those shares of ACME go into one Account, unless you own different types of shares in ACME. If ACME has common and preferred shares, keep them in separate Accounts.

MONEY MATTERS

As investors change brokers and grow more sophisticated in their investment selections, they often open multiple accounts with banks, brokerage houses, mutual funds, and retirement

accounts, like IRAs. Many of these accounts charge maintenance fees for the privilege of keeping them open. Over time,
average people tend to lose track of individual investments as
their portfolio grows. The flurry of paperwork is frequently over-
whelming, especially at tax time. Make life simpler for yourself
and your tax advisor by consolidating the number of open
accounts you maintain. Add the fees you save to your
investment fund!

PENSION INVESTMENTS

Most people start "investing" by opening an Individual Retirement
Account. Again, I'd venture to say that the majority of individual pension
money is "invested" in annuities, CDs, and savings—all of which are
bank-style deposit accounts.

You may have an IRA, a Tax Sheltered Annuity (TSA), a 401(k) plan, or
another type of pension plan. When you set up an Investment Account
for a pension plan, mark the Tax-Deferred Account check box in the New
Account Information window. Each of your pension plans should have a
separate Account. Set up a single Account for each plan, even if it contains multiple investments. Some plans have multiple mutual funds,
limited partnerships, and CDs along with a cash balance in the same
Account. It's okay and even preferable to lump all of those items into one
Quicken Account. Be certain to keep your IRA, your spouse's, and other
family members' IRAs in separate Accounts. You should also keep each of
your IRAs in separate Accounts. For example, if you have an IRA at your
local bank and another IRA with a brokerage house, you should keep
track of them in separate Accounts.

THE RICHIES' INVESTMENTS

Our friends the Richies own a few investments. In a minute, we will set up
Accounts for them in their data file. The first thing they thought of when

they set up their Investment Accounts was their U.S. Savings Bonds. Grandma Richie gave "Sammy" three U.S. Savings Bonds for his birthday a couple of years ago. They don't know how much the bonds are worth, but they do know that each bond has a face value of $50.

Set up an Investment Account for their Savings Bonds (DOS instructions follow):

1. Create a new Account by clicking the New button at the top of the Account List.

2. Click the Investment button in the Create New Account window. (Please note that these instructions assume that you have not already practiced setting up an Investment Account for Sam and Sally and have not already checked Start with Summary on the Summary screen in the Investment Account Setup window.)

3. You are now looking at the Investment Account Setup window. We want to fill in only two pieces of information to create our Accounts: the name of the new Account, **US Savings Bond**, and the description, **U.S. Savings Bonds**, as shown in Figure 2-16. The other requested information is optional and does not apply to our situation. Click OK when you are ready to continue. Quicken will now add your new Account to the Account List.

The main icon bar has a Portfolio View icon, which allows you to quickly view your investments. We will discuss this interesting topic in greater detail in chapters 6 and 7.

1. **Choose Select Account from the Main menu.**

2. **From the Select Account to Use window choose <New Account>.**

3. **Type 6 to set up an Investment Account and then press** Tab**.**

4. **Name the Account US Savings Bond. Press** Enter **to accept.**

Figure 2-16. Create the US Savings Bond Account for Sam using the Investment Account Setup window. The only fields we want to enter data in are Account Name, Description, and Date.

5. In the Investment Type & Description window, accept N, since U.S. Savings Bonds are not mutual funds. Press Tab and type U.S. Savings Bonds for the Account Description. Tab to the next field and accept N for not Tax-Deferred. Press Enter four times to step through the tax information fields and accept the entries on the screen.

6. Quicken creates the Investment Account and enters its name in the Account List.

TAX TIP

Whenever you receive an item as a gift or an inheritance, it is always a good idea to make a note to yourself with the date you received the gift. If you receive an inheritance, ask the executor to provide you with a letter or distribution receipt. It must show the date you receive the inheritance and the value given to the Internal Revenue Service or Probate Court. You will find this information to be very important when you sell the item. Your income tax liability depends on these figures.

Investment Registers are different from other asset Registers (as shown in Figure 2-17). Quicken provides two lines for each transaction. The first

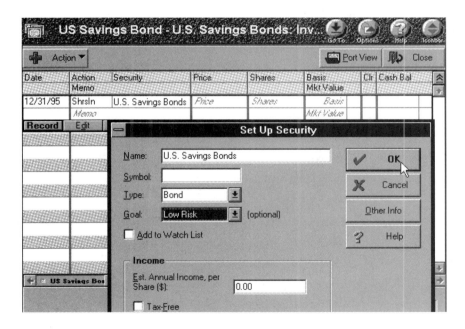

Figure 2-17. Each security you set up has its own Name, Symbol, Type, and investment Goal. When you attempt to enter a security that is not in the Security List in an Investment Register, the Set Up Security window appears. Qcards walk you through the set-up process while you are learning.

line has fields for Date, Action, Security, Price, Shares, Basis, Cleared, and Cash Balance. The second line has a Memo field and Market Value field. The Action field tells Quicken what you're doing—whether you're buying or selling, transferring shares in or out. The easiest way to set up an Account with an existing balance is to transfer shares in. Then you won't affect any other Quicken Accounts. Follow these steps (DOS instructions follow):

1. Double-click on US Savings Bond in the Account List to access the Register.
2. Check the date. Is your Register set to 12/31/95?
3. Press [Tab] to the Action field. Choose ShrsIn from the drop-down list and press [Tab].
4. Type **U.S. Savings Bonds** for the Security name.
5. Press [Tab] and the Setup Security window opens. U.S. Savings Bonds are not on the Securities List. Quicken will automatically take you to the Set Up Security window and place U.S. Savings Bonds in the Name field as you can see in Figure 2-17. The Symbol field is optional and is available for entering stock symbols.
6. A drop-down menu presents you with a few choices. Choose Bond. (If you want an unlisted description for other securities, exit this window. Select the Lists command from the main menu bar, then choose Security Type to open the Security Type list window where you can add to or edit the Security Type list.)
7. The final field to complete is your investment Goal, an optional item. Another drop-down menu appears. Choose Low Risk or you will need to modify the list of available goals. To modify the list, close this window then choose Lists from the main menu bar. Select investment goal to open the Investment Goal List widow where you can customize the list.

8. Don't check the Tax-Free Security check box. Since U.S. Savings Bonds do not pay an annual income, leave Est. Annual Income equal to **0.00**. Figure 2-17 shows the Set Up Security window and how to set up the Richies' U.S. Savings Bonds. When you finish, press Enter to continue.

9. Enter **50** in the Price field and then tab to the (number of) Shares field.

10. Type **3**. Press Tab again and you will notice that the Basis field shows that the total value of the bonds is $150.00 (see the following Tax Tip for more information).

TAX TIP

Basis is a very important concept in determining how much or little tax you owe when you sell an investment. Basis refers to the cost of an item for tax purposes. This figure may be the same, greater than, or even less than what you paid for the item. Quicken calculates the basis for an investment to equal the price of the shares multiplied by the number of shares. It is important to keep any physical documentation of the initial value of any investments you make. In most cases the initial value of the investment will equal the basis. Items you receive as gifts or an inheritance may require additional data to determine their actual basis, but the computation and consideration of these is beyond the scope of this section.

11. In the Memo field, type a note that the bonds were **Birthday gifts from Grandma**. Press Enter to record the information in the Register. After Quicken records the transaction, the total Market Value of the investments in the portfolio appears at the lower-right corner of the Register. Figure 2-18 shows how your Register should appear when you finish.

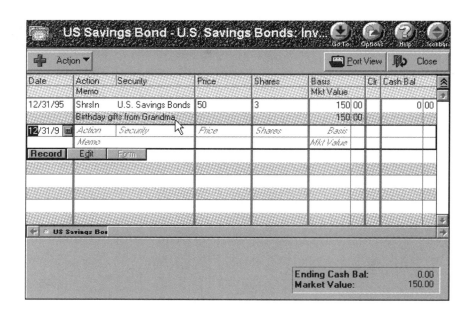

Figure 2-18. Keep each investment, such as these U.S. Savings Bonds, in a separate Account. Similarly, place individual stocks in separate Accounts for each company and type of stock, and, for easier tax computations, place each mutual fund in its own Account. For example, ACME Common and ACME Preferred would have separate Accounts. Some people like to keep their mutual funds in a common Account—one Account for each family of funds. You will probably find it easier to keep each fund in a separate Account, especially at tax time!

1. Press Enter to open the US Savings Bond Register.
2. The First-time Setup window appears. Press Enter to continue.
3. You will be in the Account's Portfolio view. There are two portfolio views: Portfolio Details and Portfolio Summary. Press Ctrl-R to switch between the portfolio view and the Register. To change between portfolio views, press F8.

Check the As Of date near the top right of the portfolio screen. If your computer system is set to a date before 12/31/95, our entry date, your portfolio Market Value will equal $0.00. If you are running Quicken for DOS under Windows, you must exit Quicken before changing the system date, or Quicken will not recognize that the date is different.

4. Press Ctrl-R to go to the US Savings Bond Register.

5. Check your date. Is it 12/31/95?

6. Press Tab to the Action field and then use Ctrl-L to bring up the Action List.

7. Select Add/Remove shares from the Action List and then choose ShrsIn— (Shares In).

8. Type U.S. Savings Bonds in the Name field and press Tab.

9. The Security Not Found window pops up and asks you to either: 1. Add to Security List or 2. Select from Security List. Choose 1.

10. Quicken opens the Set Up Security window. Use the following data to complete this window: Name = U.S. Savings Bonds, Type: choose Bond from the pick list, Goal: choose Low Risk from the pick list, Estimated annual income = $0.00, and Display Mode = Open. Press Enter when you are ready to continue.

11. Type $50.00 in the Price field.

12. Press Tab to the (number of) Shares field and type 3. Press Tab again, and you will notice that the Amount field shows that the total value of the bonds is $150.00. After Quicken records the transaction, the total value of the investments in the portfolio appears at the lower-right corner of the Register.

13. In the Memo field, type a note that the bonds were Birthday gifts from Grandma. Press [Enter], and the Leaving Transaction window appears. Read the instructions, confirm that your entries are correct, and press [Enter] to record your entry in the Register. Confirm your work with Figure 2-18.

Since Sam and Sally do not actually know how much the U.S. Savings Bonds are worth in cash, they entered the price as $50 —each bond's face amount. They can determine the current value for the bonds by calling their bank. Then they can update the values in the Account.

TAX TIP

If you own United States Savings Bonds and decide to redeem them, take them to a bank to convert them to cash. The interest on U.S. Savings Bonds accrues and is all paid upon redemption. Your bank will issue you a Form 1099 for your tax records when you redeem your bonds. Do not misplace the 1099. You will not receive another one at the end of the year. If you forget to declare the interest on your tax return, the Internal Revenue Service will send you a reminder and a bill for penalties and interest for underpaying your taxes.

MONEY MATTERS

What is the difference between savings and an investment? Savings is simply money that is put away to be spent later— deferred spending. An investment is money set aside to grow for an extended period of time. Eventually, your investment can provide an income for your "golden years" or be liquidated to meet a long-term goal.

After setting up their savings bonds, Sam and Sally want to set up Sally's IRA. Her IRA is currently "invested" at the local bank in a CD that matures on 4/12/96. It is currently paying 6.09 percent interest.

We will set up Sally's IRA as an Investment Account, as shown in Figure 2-19. We hope that Sally will soon understand that a Certificate of Deposit isn't really an investment. We expect that when the CD matures in April, she will want to transfer the money in a real investment. Sally—and the rest of us—will understand investments better after reading Chapters 6 and 7.

Sam and Sally set up this Account with the **12/31/95** year-end balance. We are using the year-end balance since pension plans, including IRAs, always report December 31 values. The last day of the year is also a logical and convenient date. Please note that an IRA is a Tax-Deferred account, so you will want to mark that option when you create the Account.

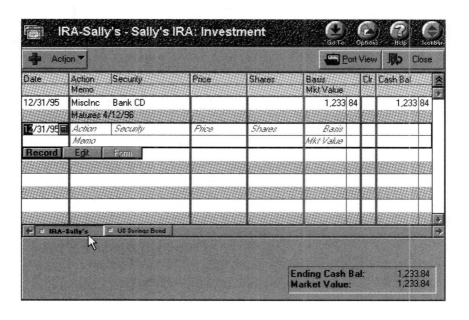

Figure 2-19. We hope that Sally will soon understand that a Certificate of Deposit isn't really an investment. We expect that when the CD matures in April, she will want to transfer the money in a real investment. Sally—and the rest of us—will understand investments better after reading Chapters 6 and 7.

One problem with setting up an Opening Balance in an Investment Account is that the money has to come from someplace. Quicken expects the money to come from an existing Account, which affects the value of the originating Account. When we set up the Savings Bonds, that feature did not present a problem because we used ShrsIn as the Action. The difference is that the bonds are not cash;— CDs are. We want to have a Cash Balance in the Investment Account, not a Share Balance. We can work around this by specifying MiscInc, miscellaneous income, as the source of the funds in the Action field. (DOS users press Ctrl-L to pop up the Action List, and choose Other transactions to find MiscInc, miscellaneous income.) This is not the proper use of miscellaneous income, but it does accomplish our goal of establishing a Cash Balance in an Investment Account without affecting another Account's balance.

The Security is a Bank CD, which isn't really a security. You will need to set up **Bank CD** on the Securities List. The Type is CD. There's no Price because CDs are not based on a price per share. There are no Shares, either. The Basis for the Account is **$1,233.84**. That amount automatically transfers to the Cash Balance column when Quicken records the transaction, shown in Figure 2-19. Use the Memo field to note that the CD **Matures 4/12/96 - 6.09%**. Quicken will ask you to provide a Category when you attempt to Record this transaction. Answer **No** to the request.

One good reason to use the Memo field is so you don't have to dig through all of your papers to find this information in a couple of months, when the CD is nearing maturity. The information you need will all be there in Quicken, ready for you to review. You can also record the interest rate and maturity date in the Account Information window. The disadvantage is that the interest rate and maturity date are not visible when you open the Register. The information on Sally's IRA will be very handy as our couple starts shopping for a better place to reinvest the money. Do they want to reinvest it in another CD at the bank? Is the bank paying a competitive rate? Perhaps Sally will want to reinvest her money in a mutual fund or another place that may provide a greater rate of return.

Sam recently began participating in his company's 401(k) plan. So far, he has had $300 deducted from his paychecks. Set up an Investment Account for his 401(k) called **401(k)-Sam's**, and use **Sam's 401(k)** as the Description.

When the Account is created, we can open it from the Account List. Open the Account list. Click the Invest tab to only display Investment Accounts. Double-click 401(k)-Sam's to open the Register. Complete the first registry entry using Figure 2-20 and the following directions. Use MiscInc (Other Transactions then MiscInc in the DOS version) as the Action. He is currently investing his contributions in the plan's **Guaranteed Account**, so use **Guaranteed Account** for the Security name. We should use Guaranteed Account as the Security Type but will use **CD** as the Security Type in the Set Up Security Window because it is the most

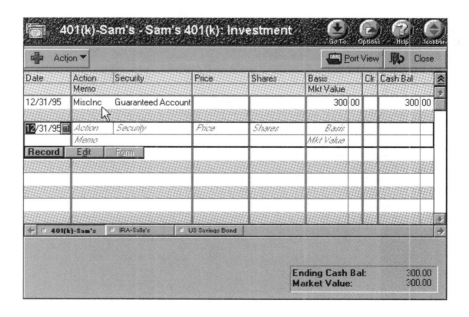

Figure 2-20. Use this Register to set up Sam's 401(k) Opening Balance.

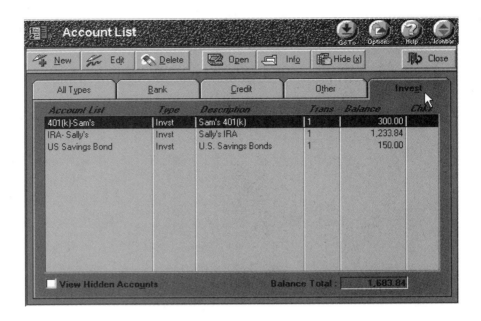

Figure 2-21. Use this Account List to set up the Richies' Investment Accounts and set up the Opening Balances. The Richies are valuing the Accounts as of December 31, 1995. Please note that the IRA and 401(k) are Tax-Deferred investments and no Tax Information is necessary. Windows users will use MiscInc for the Action, while DOS users will choose Other transactions and then Miscellaneous Income.

similar type on Quicken's default list. We will learn to set up and edit new Security Types in Chapter 5.

When you finish, your Account List should look similar to the one in Figure 2-21.

Reset your computer's date to today, if it is on Richie Standard Time, and take time now to set up Accounts for each of your investments in your data file. When you finish, we will set up a Cash Account.

FINANCIAL ALERT Guaranteed Accounts and Guaranteed Investment Contracts are often choices in company pension programs. These "investments" are no more than interest-bearing accounts, also known as annuities, offered by insurance companies. The "guarantee" is no better than the strength of the insurance company offering the contracts. In the past decade, some very large insurance companies suffered financial hardship and were taken over by government regulators. Some people, including a number who "invested" their life savings, suffered losses of at least a portion of the funds they invested or were unable to have their money returned to them for long periods of time. If you are invested in a fixed annuity, your money is in a small "Guaranteed Investment Contract."

CASH ACCOUNTS

Cash Accounts may not seem very important when you first think about them. As you use a Cash Account over time, however, you will see that it can have a very significant place in your plan to create wealth.

Set up a Cash Account for the Richies with an **$89.00** balance. Sam and Sally have a few bucks in their possession and loose change stashed around the house where the kids haven't found it yet. The $89.00 is only a good "guesstimate." Figure 2-22 shows the Cash Account being set up.

In dealing with clients over the past decade, I have found that most of them struggle financially for two reasons: Automatic Teller Machines and Credit Cards. They have an ATM card and use it frequently. Somehow they overlook recording many of those ATM transactions in their check registers. The checkbook never seems to be around when they pull out the cash. Once the funds in the bank's computer are converted to the convenience of currency, the money runs through their fingers like water.

Water is a good analogy for cash. The water company sent out a notice during our recent drought in California. The notice warned that a faucet with a slow drip could easily waste 20 gallons of water a day. The significance of a little irritating drip is astounding. The significance of a

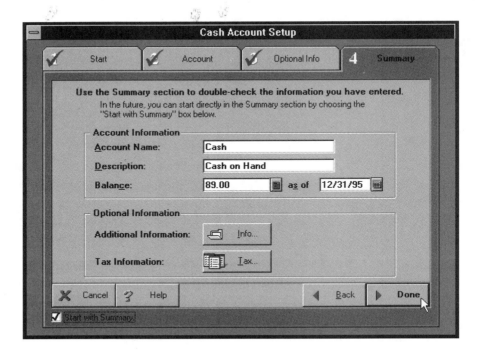

Figure 2-22. You will want to set up a Cash Account at this time. You will find this Account very helpful as you work your way along the path to prosperity. You do not need to enter any Additional Information or Tax Information for the Richies' Cash Account.

sawbuck here, a twenty-spot there, and a few ones sprinkled through the day is simply amazing.

Credit cards are a lot like cash because it is so easy to lose track of how much money you owe. As with cash, most people don't track use of their cards through the month. We'll come back to the subject of credit cards soon.

Setting up a Cash Account will help you with the first problem— spending money with hardly a clue to where it all went. Many people, who begin without the benefits of wealth and who create their own wealth during their lifetime, have found that keeping track of their cash transactions is extremely useful. We will discuss Cash Accounts in more detail in Chapter 3.

Take a minute to estimate how much cash you have and set up a Cash Account with that amount as the opening Balance. Often, it's a good idea for couples to have separate Cash Accounts. There tend to be fewer disagreements when you have separate Accounts. If you choose not to use your Cash Accounts for all cash transactions, at least keep track of those transactions that have tax implications—telephone calls for business use, charitable cash contributions, etc.

You should now have Quicken Accounts for all of your assets. It's time to take a look at your liabilities. Let's determine your debts.

DETERMINE YOUR DEBTS

Very few people now are debt-free. Once, most Americans were free from debt's shackles. Let's consider a few statistics. Almost all American home owners have mortgages. In 1946, 98 percent of American homeowners had mortgages, and that is probably still a fairly accurate figure today. In 1928, only two percent of Americans had a mortgage. That means 98 percent of Americans had no mortgage and were probably debt-free or close to it.

Auto loans first appeared in 1948. The first auto loan was only two years long. In 1952, auto loans had finally made it to three years in length. Now we're seeing auto loans with five- to seven-year terms.

One surprising fact is that credit cards were first introduced by department stores. Then service stations began issuing gas cards. Finally, banks began issuing cards—VISA (first known as Bank AmeriCard) and MasterCard.

Quicken has two types of debt Accounts—Credit Card Accounts and Liability Accounts. Let's look at Credit Card Accounts first.

CREDIT CARDS

Credit cards are almost as American as baseball and apple pie. It seems as if everyone has a pocket or purse full of them. The problem is, most people lose track of how much they charge on their credit cards. At least when people write checks, most people enter the amount of the check and who it is payable to in their checkbook register. With credit cards, it's very easy to whip that little piece of plastic out of your pocket, plop it down on the counter, and say "Charge it!" Very few people keep track of what they're charging. Unfortunately, that can cause a lot of grief at the end of the month when the statement arrives—especially the first statement after Christmas.

Consequently, most people owe something on one or more of their credit cards. Set up a separate Credit Card Account for each card you have and use on a regular basis or each card with a balance due. You may not use all of your credit cards regularly throughout the year. Some are used only occasionally—during the holidays, on vacations, or for major purchases. If you use your card only during the holidays and don't have a current balance, you don't need to set up an Account for that card yet. You can set its Account up when you begin to use the card again. Although some sources disagree, I strongly advise that you set up a separate Account for any credit card you use, even if you use it only occasionally.

The Richies, like most true-blue Americans, have balances on several of the numerous cards they carry. They owe $481.66 on their Mega-Stores department store card. The Gas & Go gas card, which is paid in full each month, has a balance of $38.91. The MasterBank MasterCard has the largest balance—$3,847.94. Their SpendPlus VISA card is last, but not least, with a $1,953.77 balance.

Set up the MasterBank MasterCard first, since it has the largest balance. When you create a new Account, choose Credit Card Account for the Account type. You will find that this New Account Information window is very similar to the ones we have previously seen. In addition to the usual information, it adds a field for your credit limit. Figure 2-23 shows you the Summary screen from the Credit Card Account Setup window for the Richies' MasterBank Card Account. When you finish, use the information in Figure 2-24 to set up Accounts for the Richies' other credit cards.

Take a few minutes to set up each of your credit cards. You may need to call your credit card issuers' toll-free numbers to get current balances. While you're on the line, find out how much your current interest rate is. After you set up all of your Credit Card Accounts, you're ready to move on to other types of loans.

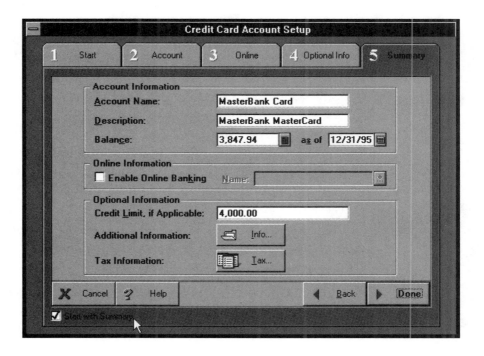

Figure 2-23. Each credit card that you use should have a separate Account. Set up Accounts for any cards that have unpaid balances or that you use on an ongoing basis. Note that the Start with Summary box is checked, saving time with each card entry.

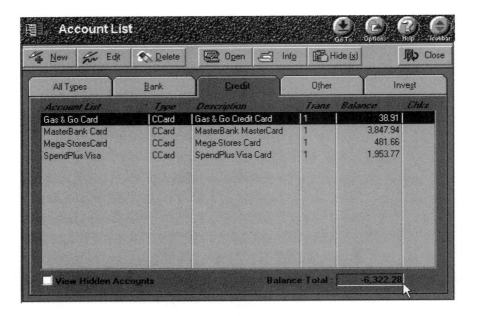

Figure 2-24. Use the above Account List of the Richies' Liability Accounts to set up the Richies' Credit Card Accounts. The Account balances are all as of December 31, 1995. None of these Accounts need Additional Information or Tax Information. Have fun setting the Richies' credit limits!

It is now possible to lose your home if you get behind on your credit card payments. A financial institution in Wyomissing, Pennsylvania, offers first "Tax Deductible Card" we have heard about[3]. The interest on this gold MasterCard is tax deductible because it is secured by a lien against the cardholder's home. Although the interest on the card is tax deductible under most circumstances, because the amount you borrow on the card uses your home as collateral, the lender could foreclose on your property if you get behind on your payments!

---

3. Bloomberg News Service, reported in the September 21, 1995, *Sacramento Bee,* Business Section, page 2.

LOANS

Most people have several loans. Home mortgages are common, but auto loans are even more popular. It may be my imagination, but many people who cannot "afford" a house can "afford" one or more trendy imports. They usually finance these vehicles.

Since vehicle loans are the most common loans, let's start by setting up a Liability Account for an auto loan. The Richies have an auto loan through the Jumbo Credit Union. They found that credit unions often have the most competitive loan rates. Sam telephoned the credit union and learned that their auto loan had a balance of $9,834.62 on 12/31/95. Figure 2-25 shows you how they set up their auto loan. When you are done, set up other types of loans the same way: student loans, mortgages, personal loans from relatives or friends, investment loans, etc.

Leases are a popular form of financing. A lease is simply a loan by another name. Although businesses are the main users of leases, individuals occasionally use leases to finance an auto or other vehicle. Consider a lease to be a liability as you determine your debts. To calculate the total amount you owe, multiply the number of payments remaining by your monthly payment. Set up a separate Liability Account for each lease.

Sam and Sally have two liabilities in addition to their credit union auto loan and their credit cards. They have a first mortgage on their house with a current balance of $74,909.47 and owe $3,579.55 on a home equity loan. Use Figure 2-26 to set up these Accounts.

In addition to liabilities for which you are directly responsible, you may have agreed to cosign or act as a surety for someone else's liability. Many times, parents will cosign a loan for their children. They may cosign the application for their child's first credit card, first auto loan, or first mortgage. One of the aspects of planning your financial future is determining whether you will end up being liable for any of those loans. If you

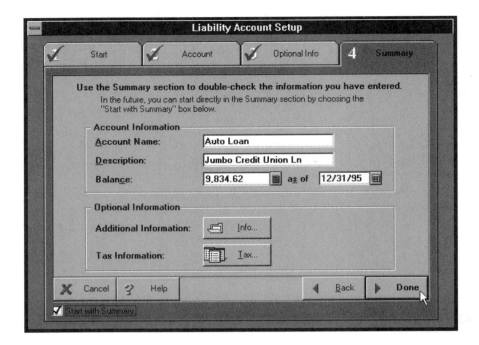

Figure 2-25. Establish a separate Quicken Liability Account for each loan you have. This window shows how to set up the Richies' auto loan from their friendly credit union. After you Click on OK, a window asking if you want to set up an amortized loan with this Account appears. Click No; this feature does not interest us at this time.

believe that there is a good possibility of becoming liable for any of those obligations, you should include those loans and their current balances. You should also attempt to have your name removed from those liabilities. By including liabilities to which you are a cosigner, you will increase your liabilities and decrease your net worth.

It is surprising how many parents end up being liable for one or more of their children's debts. Recently, I have noticed an increase in the number of parents with marred credit records due to their children's irresponsibility. These parents are now paying their children's obligations.

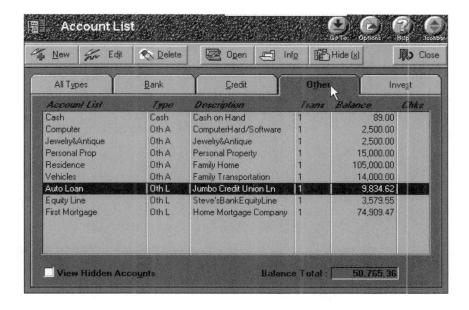

Figure 2-26. Use the Richies' Account List to set up the Richies' other Liability Accounts. The loan balances are as of December 31, 1995. None of these accounts requires Additional Information or Tax Information.

You may have "cosigned" a loan for a complete stranger without even realizing it! Some people enable total strangers to purchase their home and assume their Veterans Administration or FHA mortgage without qualifying for the loan. When this occurs, you will be held personally liable if the person who purchases your home defaults on the mortgage. Protect yourself by requiring any potential purchasers to fully qualify to assume your loan. Require your lender to provide you with a release of liability.

Take time to set up Accounts for each of your outstanding loans and leases. Include all non-interest bearing and low-interest rate loans, even loans from family members, friends, and relatives. After you finish setting up all of your loans, it's time to look at your net worth.

ESTABLISH YOUR NET WORTH

Your net worth is simply all of your assets, less all of your liabilities. If you enter all of your assets and liabilities in Quicken and keep your Accounts current, you can see your net worth by looking at the lower right corner of the Account List. Figures 2-27 and 2-28 show all of the Richies' Accounts and their net worth. (Since our Account List is too long to fit on one screen, we simply snapped two screen captures.) It's a good idea for you

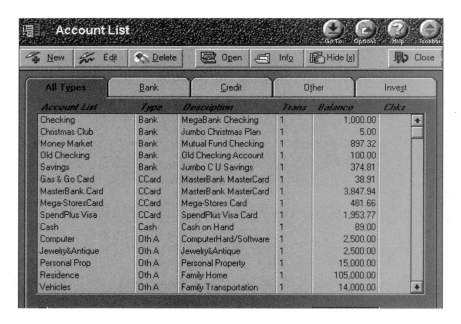

Figure 2-27. The Richies' Account List is complete, unless they forgot about some of their assets or liabilities. Since they list all of their assets and liabilities, the Balance Total at the bottom of the window equals their net worth. Since this window may not be resized in Quicken 5 for Windows, we divided the list of the Richies accounts in two parts. The remainder of the list is in Figure 2-28.

All Types	Bank	Credit	Other	Invest

Account List	Type	Description	Trans	Balance	Chks
Auto Loan	Oth L	Jumbo Credit Union ...	1	9,834.62	
Equity Line	Oth L	Steve'sBankEquityL...	1	3,579.55	
First Mortgage	Oth L	Home Mortgage Co...	1	74,909.47	
401(k)-Sam's	Invst	Sam's 401(k)	1	300.00	
IRA-Sally's	Invst	Sally's IRA	1	1,233.84	
US Savings Bond	Invst	U.S. Savings Bonds	1	150.00	

Figure 2-28. This list shows the balance of the Richies' Accounts.

to track your net worth on an ongoing basis. If your net worth is increasing, you're on the right track.

One nice Quicken feature is the ability to graph your net worth on an ongoing basis (DOS instructions follow).

1. Load the Richies' data file, if it is not active, and go to HomeBase by clicking the HomeBase icon.
2. Click the word Graphs on the Reports & Graphs graphic.
3. This opens the Create Graph window, shown in Figure 2-29, which contains the necessary settings to create the Richies' Net Worth Graph, shown in Figure 2-30.
4. Click Create after entering the settings shown in Figure 2-29.

1. **From a Register, select Graph from the menu bar.**
2. **Choose Net Worth from the drop-down list.**
3. **Select Monthly Assets and Liabilities. Press Enter to accept the default settings, and Quicken will draw your graph.**

Net Worth Graphs have three components. They have a baseline at zero. The bar below the baseline represents the total liabilities. The bar

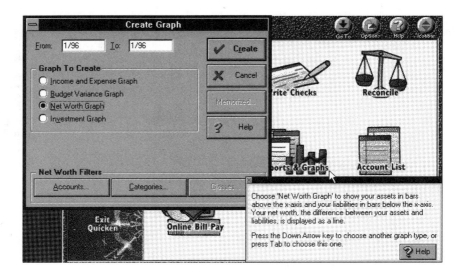

Figure 2-29. To create your Net Worth Graph, go to HomeBase and then choose Create to open the Create Graph window.

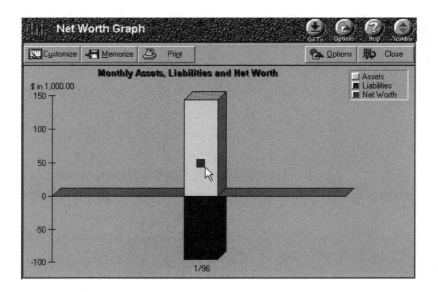

Figure 2-30. Use your Net Worth Graph to get a quick look at your total assets and liabilities.

above shows the total assets. A box in the middle of the bar shows your current net worth—assets less liabilities, as shown in Figure 2-30.

Although graphs have pizzazz, they don't provide the detailed information you need to analyze your situation properly. You need to create a Net Worth Report. DOS users simply Click the Report button. Windows users:

1. Return to HomeBase by clicking the HomeBase icon.
2. Click on the word Reports on the Reports & Graphs graphic to open the Create Report window.
3. Choose the "What am I Worth as of Today" button shown in Figure 2-31. Note: this only works if you have set your computer's internal clock to Richie Standard Time.
4. Quick rapidly creates the Richies' Net Worth Report, shown in part in Figure 2-32.

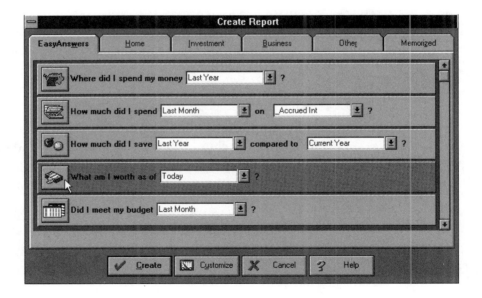

Figure 2-31. The Create Report window allows you to quickly produce many different reports including the Net Worth Report.

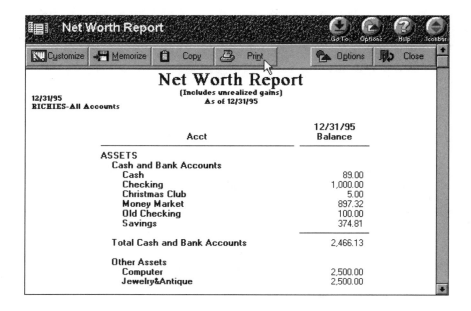

Figure 2-32. The Net Worth Report is also accessible from HomeBase through the Reports & Graphics button. Click the Print button for a hard copy of the Richies' Net Worth Report.

You can see part of the Richies' Net Worth Report in Figure 2-32. As you look through the report on your computer, you see each Account and the current balance in that Account. Each area of assets and liabilities is subtotaled. For example, the Cash and Bank Accounts section lists each Account and a subtotal of all of those Accounts. Under liabilities, totals are given for Credit Cards and Other Liabilities. At the bottom of the report, you can see the overall total of assets less liabilities, or net worth.

Load your data file and print out a copy of your Net Worth Report. It's time to determine what positive aspects are there and where there is room for improvement. Let's analyze your position.

ANALYZE YOUR POSITION

Everyone's position is unique. It's important for you to evaluate your assets and liabilities. Consider the value of each asset and the cost of each liability. Then you can determine if you should make any changes in your financial position. Let's look at the Richies' assets and liabilities. Use them as an example to analyze what is positive about their situation and where there's room for improvement. Due to space restraints, we cannot fully analyze their position, but let's take a brief look at it.

POSITIVE ASPECTS

We will use the Richies' Net Worth report as an example of things to look for as you analyze the positive and negative aspects of your current position.

First, it is positive that Sam and Sally have cash in the bank. They have a total of $2,466.13 in cash and deposit account assets. This is actually better than most Americans. The average American probably has $1,000 or less actually available to them in cash and deposits. The Richies have a money market "checking account" with a mutual fund. There are at least three positive aspects to this:

1. Mutual fund money market checking accounts generally do not have any service charges.
2. The Richies are earning a competitive rate of return on their money. It's not just sitting around in the typical non-interest-bearing checking account at their local bank. Mutual fund money market funds typically pay market rates. Those rates are usually higher than bank or savings-and-loan interest-bearing checking accounts.
3. Mutual fund money market funds generally require you to write checks of at least $250. Having to write larger checks deters people from using their money for frivolous expenses, and this inhibition helps people build a larger net worth.

Sam and Sally set up a new personal checking account. They will be able to manage it properly with Quicken and will not lose track of their account balance.

Finally, Sam and Sally have a Christmas Club. It is amazing how Christmas sneaks up on people every year. Then they resort to using their credit cards to pay for Christmas gifts. They spend the rest of the year paying off the credit cards, just in time to begin using their cards again next Christmas.

Now let's consider their other assets. The most important financial step Sam and Sally have taken so far is to begin their retirement program. Although the account values are small, they plan to make monthly contributions to their IRA and 401(k).

Another important item is the family home. Although home ownership is less important to creating wealth today than it was in the '70s or '80s, it is still an important consideration. Eventually, the cost of owning a home should be less than the cost of renting a similar structure. We will explore this issue in greater depth in Chapter 8. Since many homeowners would not live in the same type of house they're living in now if they were renting, this is not an apples-to-apples comparison.

ROOM FOR IMPROVEMENT

As we consider Sam and Sally's assets from the standpoint of creating wealth, we should note that jewelry and antiques are not something that most people should purchase as investments. Jewelry and antiques are typically personal possessions with sentiment attached. I have no problem with people owning these types of assets, as long as they do not consider them investment assets.

MONEY MATTERS

Has a jewelry store sales clerk ever tried to convince you of the investment value of a beautiful article of jewelry? The probability of ever selling a piece of jewelry again is remote. I have

seen signs in shopping malls proudly proclaiming that the jewelry store is willing to give you 40 percent of an item's value, if you need cash. Buy jewelry for beauty and love, not profit!

Finally, let's consider the Richies' investment assets. As we mentioned a moment ago, they have done a good job in establishing an IRA and a 401(k) plan. Both of those plans, as they add to them over time, will become significant assets in wealth creation. The problem is the IRA's investment vehicle. CDs are savings vehicles, not investments. The CD is paying a relatively low rate of return compared to other investments that are available on the marketplace.

The Richies' U.S. Savings Bonds, although they were a gift from Grandma, also pay a relatively low rate of return. Sam and Sally need to consider redeploying those assets into other investment opportunities that will give them a better rate of return. They should consider a good growth fund for their IRA and 401(k) accounts. The money in the bonds would yield a much higher return if they were to cash them in and use the proceeds to pay down a credit card.

Speaking of liabilities, we saw in Chapter 1 that debt, especially credit cards and other non-deductible forms of debt, can be devastating to one's financial welfare. Sam and Sally have $6,322.28 in credit card debt. The average credit card collects between 15 and 21 percent interest. That can be very detrimental to one's financial health. One of the best investments they could make at this time would be to pay off those credit cards. Unfortunately, they have very little cash available, and the bonds are not worth much. We will continue to tackle this problem in Chapter 3.

Once the Richies reduce their credit card debt to zero, they need to review their other liabilities. After paying off their credit cards, their next task should be to pay off their auto loan. After they pay off their auto loan, they should concentrate on making additional principal payments to their home mortgages. First, they should pay off their home equity loan, and then they should work on their first mortgage.

As with the average American, there is a lot of room for improvement in the Richies' debt situation. In fact, average Americans, if they concentrate on it, can pay off all of their consumer debts within two years of creating and implementing a debt elimination plan. Most people get excited about paying off their debts for a short period of time. Then something distracts them, and they stop following their plan. We will discuss a solution to this problem in Chapter 3. If you are an enlightened individual in debt, you will appreciate the following five-step plan for getting out of debt.

FIVE STEPS TO REDUCING DEBT

During the past decade, I have met and spoken to hundreds of individuals and couples who desire to reduce or eliminate all of their debts. We have found that almost anyone with a steady income can pay off all of his or her consumer debts within 24 months of beginning to follow a very easy five-step plan to get out of debt. Here are the five simple steps:

1. You must change your lifestyle and attitudes from debt-oriented to cash-oriented. This will be a continuing process. You will work on achieving this goal as you implement the following steps. It will probably be necessary to reorder your priorities and habits.

2. Determine where you are. If you haven't already entered all of your assets and liabilities into Quicken, do it now! An important aspect of knowing where you are is managing your cash flow. We will discuss this in greater detail in Chapter 4.

3. Stop going into debt. This is easier said than done. Most people find the cold turkey method is best. Lock all of your credit cards away. Better yet, destroy them!

MONEY MATTERS

Create a credit card collage with your credit cards. Preheat your oven to 450 degrees. Place all of your credit cards (and your ATM cards, if you have trouble with taking too much money from your friendly ATM) on an aluminum foil-covered cookie sheet.

Carefully watch the cards as they melt together in the oven. They will turn black if they bake too long. Remove the collage from the oven and let it cool. Most people find it best to hang their collage where they will see it a couple of times each day. It reminds them of their goal and commitment to stop using debt. You may consider hanging your masterpiece over the porcelain throne in your bathroom!

4. Develop a written repayment plan and stick to it. Your plan should include many if not all of the following parts:

    a. Sell assets. Almost everyone has accumulated valuable items that are of little use to them. Have a garage sale or advertise your excess assets in the paper. Sell your neighbors the extra bike that they have been eyeing in your garage. One rule of thumb is to sell anything that you have in storage and haven't used in the past six months to a year.

    b. Use your savings. This is a radical idea to many people because they have struggled so long to accumulate a meager savings account. Some people object to using their savings to pay off their debts because they want to keep the money in savings for emergencies. This is necessary only if you have destroyed your credit and your creditors will no longer allow you to make additional charges. If you do use your savings and need the money in a pinch, you can always charge it or get a cash advance from a credit card. Your credit card issuer will gladly send you a new card if you have transformed your old one into a work of art, a credit card collage. You will save a lot of money on interest until you have an emergency—hopefully you won't!

    c. Increase your debt payments. Pay off the card or loan with the highest interest rate first. One exception is to pay off some or all of your smallest loans immediately. The advantages are: You will save money on postage each month; you will have to deal with a smaller number of creditors; you will benefit from the immediate satisfaction of knowing that you have already paid off one or more debts!

d. Keep your total debt service payments constant. If you start with $500 a month in payments on six loans and cards, continue paying $500 or more each month even though the loans require smaller monthly payments as the outstanding balances decrease. As you pay off cards, use the money you formerly sent to those cards to increase your remaining payments.

e. Reduce your living expenses. Virtually everyone can reduce the cost of their lifestyle. One idea many people use is canceling their cable TV, magazine, and newspaper subscriptions. Limit the number of times you eat out and then go to less expensive restaurants. Begin brown-bagging your lunch when you go to work. Lunches out during the work week add up quickly.

f. Reduce your income tax withholdings, if you expect to receive a refund when you file your income taxes. Use the additional money to increase your debt payments. Be careful when you adjust your withholding. You could end up owing the IRS.

g. DO NOT get a consolidation loan. Most people who consolidate their consumer debt or pull equity out of their homes end up going back into debt because they haven't adjusted their attitudes and lifestyle.

h. Get help. Even if you feel as though you are being swallowed in a swamp full of debt, it can be very worthwhile to pay a financial counselor for assistance. Consumer Credit Counseling Services is a non-profit organization with locations in most metropolitan areas in the United States. They generally offer a free consultation and a low-cost program to help you get out of debt.

They are often able to negotiate lower interest rates and payments with your creditors if you are really struggling.

5. Become accountable to someone. Everyone needs someone to encourage them through their struggles. If you are married, getting out of debt must be a team effort. Absent that effort, you may end up like the couple rowing the rowboat who wanted to go opposite directions. They each rowed toward where they wanted to go. They paddled around and around in circles—until they learned to cooperate.

Freeing yourself from the quagmire of debt will not be easy. It will take time, so don't get discouraged when you seem to be slipping further into debt's clutches. You will have setbacks. You can do it!

PRACTICAL APPLICATIONS

If you haven't already done so, enter all of your assets and liabilities into Quicken. Generate a Net Worth Report. Analyze each of your assets. Can you use any assets more productively? Could you better use an asset to reduce your debt or reinvest it at a higher rate of return? Do you have credit cards at high interest rates with balances you could transfer to other credit cards or personal loans with lower interest rates? Are you using your credit cards to increase your debt, or have you stopped using them in that way?

Begin to develop a library of resources to assist you on your financial journey. After you finish reading *The Richest Man in Babylon*, which we recommended in Practical Applications in Chapter 1, read *The Debt Squeeze* by Ron Blue, published by Focus on the Family Publishing.

You're ready to move on to the next chapter, where we lay the foundation for optimizing and maximizing your cash flow!

CHAPTER 3

QUICKEN FUNDAMENTALS

ANNUAL INCOME TWENTY POUNDS, ANNUAL
EXPENDITURE NINETEEN NINETEEN-SIX, RESULT
HAPPINESS. ANNUAL INCOME TWENTY POUNDS,
ANNUAL EXPENDITURE TWENTY POUNDS OUGHT
AND SIX, RESULT MISERY.
—CHARLES DICKENS' MR. MICAWBER

You can't fool me. I know what you're thinking. You're wondering if you can skip the next couple of chapters. The last thing people want to hear is someone else telling them how to manage their cash flow properly. But I promise you, when you read through these chapters, you will probably learn things you've never heard and understand concepts you've never considered before—that is, if you're an average person. Surely, though, many of you are far above average.

You may be asking, "Why do I need to manage my cash flow?" That is a very good question. I met with the Board of Directors of a high-tech corporation that is one of the best in its field of expertise. They have just about everything going for them. Their competitors refer business to them on an ongoing basis—that's how good they are. The only problem is, they're in bankruptcy! Why? It is because the very intelligent people who manage this company lost track of the very foundation that makes a business run—money.

It takes only a few bad decisions to totally destroy your cash flow for many years to come. Conversely, if you make a few wise decisions, you'll be able to manage your cash flow in an optimal manner for many years to come. That's what this chapter is about. We will help you lay a foundation that will enable you to optimize and maximize your cash flow and create wealth beyond your wildest dreams. Well, maybe not your wildest dreams, but at least more than you could ever honestly expect to have!

In this chapter, we see how Quicken keeps track of our money by categorizing our expenses. Finally, we will learn how to use Quicken's Registers effectively by trying some real-life examples.

SETTING UP AND USING CATEGORIES AND TRANSFERS

One key to wealth creation is to keep accurate records of every financial transaction. When you track every penny you spend, you will care more about each penny spent. It is only when you carefully categorize each transaction that Quicken can properly assist you along the road to financial success. In addition to an increased awareness of your cash flow, you will have meticulous records that will help ensure your successful survival of any IRS audits you encounter.

The process of categorizing your records will take a little time. Once you finish the process, you will quickly complete your bookkeeping chores. Don't settle for half-complete financial records. You will spend significantly less time and have greater financial control with Quicken than you could hope for with a manual system. You will be extremely pleased when your tax records are complete on January 1 next year! After confirming your records with year-end statements in January and spending about five minutes in Quicken producing a complete report of your tax-related transactions, you will be ready to complete your tax return!

If you already have records in Quicken, you will learn how to manage them more efficiently. If you read this before you initially set up your Quicken data files, you will spend the least amount of time setting up Quicken. At the end of this section, we provide a sample list of categories and descriptions and the tax form or schedule to which each category relates.

If you watch your pennies, your dollars will take care of themselves!

THE BASICS

On the second line of each Quicken Register entry is a field for entering the category of each transaction. This field is the heart of your record-keeping endeavor. This is where you track each tax deduction, income source, and expense item. When your cursor is in this field, choose from the handy drop-down list of available transaction categories. Simply pick the category that best describes your transaction and then tab to the next field. If your transaction doesn't fit the description of an available category, you can add a new category name to the list. It is also easy to rename your categories and reorganize them in the list.

Quicken is powerful and easy to use. A well-thought-out category list is a key component to optimizing Quicken. In the next section, we will discuss how to set up and optimize your category list.

SETTING UP USEFUL CATEGORIES

Most users find Quicken's predefined categories interesting to learn from. After perusing them, they delete and edit them to meet their own needs. Many of the predefined categories do not pertain to most users. In previous versions of Quicken for Windows and in all versions of Quicken for DOS, several categories are specifically for Canadian users, while others are for U.S. users only. When you first install Quicken 5, Canadian users can mark a checkbox to install categories that include categories unique to Canada. If you have an existing data file, delete any categories you do not use. This will save you time scrolling through the drop-down list.

Since you just set up a new file for the Richies, their category list is empty, assuming you followed our directions to not install Quicken's predefined Home and Business categories when you set up the file. Press Ctrl-C to open the Category & Transfer List window. When you set up your first Investment Account, Quicken sets up eight categories, even if you don't want it to. These categories are hard-coded to investment-related transactions. Quicken preassigns tax Forms and schedules to these categories. Unfortunately, Quicken severely limits your ability to edit these category names. Figure 3-1 shows the eight investment categories and the edit window that appears if you attempt to edit one of them.

Before you set up an Investment Account, the Category & Transfer List window is empty, except for the names of any Quicken Accounts you have established. Use the New button to set up new categories in Windows. Select <New Category> in DOS. The Set Up Category window appears, as shown in Figure 3-2. Simply type in your category Name, Description, choose the Type, and mark the checkbox, if the category is Tax-related. Quicken 5 helps simplify matters by providing tabs for All Types, Income, Expense, and Transfer (Quicken Accounts) categories.

It is also easy to create subcategories to keep greater detail in your records. Mark the "Subcategory of:" checkbox and, in the drop-down list, choose the category for which you want a subcategory, as shown in Figure 3-3.

The Category & Transfer List includes any Quicken Accounts you set up. These Accounts appear at the end of the list.

Figure 3-1. When you set up your first Investment Account, Quicken adds eight predefined categories to your Category & Transfer List. Limited editing ability is available for these entries. You can only edit the category descriptions and assign tax forms or schedules. We show the drop-down list to indicate some of the Form choices available.

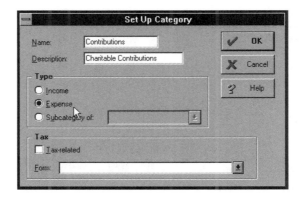

Figure 3-2. Add categories to the Category & Transfer List using the Set Up Category window.

Figure 3-3.   It is easy to set up income and expense subcategories. Be careful to assign tax Forms and schedules only to the categories and subcategories you want to transfer to your federal tax return.

NAMING CATEGORIES

Quicken limits each category name to 15 characters. Use names that make sense to you and that you will remember. You can set up multiple levels of categories with subcategories, as shown in Figure 3-4.

In this example, Contributions is the main category. Cash and Non-cash are the first-level subcategories. Cash has Boy Scouts, Church, and Homeless Shelter as second-level subcategories or sub-subcategories. Finally, Church has third-level subcategories also. When Quicken lists a category, colons separate each category and subcategory name, as in **Contributions:Cash:Church:Missions**. Before continuing, take a minute to set up the Contributions category and the subcategories shown in Figure 3-4.

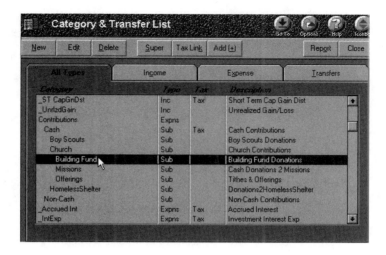

Figure 3-4. Notice how each level of subcategory is indented slightly more than the level above it. Only assign Tax Forms and schedules to the category levels you want to transfer to your federal tax return at the end of the year.

Another category-naming limitation is a 30-character maximum extended-name length. Quicken for Windows 5 checks the total name length, categories plus subcategories, as you set up subcategories. As soon as the total name length of the category plus subcategories plus separators (":") equals 30 characters, Quicken for Windows does not allow you to add more subcategories to a subcategory. Quicken for DOS 8 and prior versions of Quicken for Windows do not check total name length as you set up subcategories. Unfortunately, Quicken for Windows does allow you to give the last subcategory in the hierarchy a name that exceeds the 30-character limit—resulting in problems when you attempt to use it.

When you exceed the 30-character name length limit, Quicken truncates the subcategory name on the category drop-down list, even though it appeared in the Category & Transfer List window. Continuing with the above example, you may want to track how much money you give to the church's Building fund. When you enter **Building** as a subcategory to Contributions:Cash:Church, you exceed the 30 character name length limit. As we saw in Figure 3-4, Building Fund appears on the Category & Transfer List without indicating any problems. Open one of the Richies' Registers and attempt to use Building Fund. You will discover that it appears as Build on the drop-down list, as you see in Figure 3-5. Also, notice that Quicken truncates the names of some of the other categories in Figure 3-5 as well.

When you press Tab or Enter to accept the category, a warning window opens and advises you that the "Selected category is too long to fit field." You have two choices. You can edit the name to make it shorter in the category field in your Register, but the old Building category will still remain in your Category & Transfer List. It is more efficient to edit your Category & Transfer List entries. By comparing the edited entry with other subcategories, you can also eliminate the same problem with other subcategories that are too long. The following instructions demonstrate how to edit your Category List.

1. Click the OK button in the warning window; press Esc in DOS in the Set Up Category window.
2. Open the Category & Transfer List window by typing Ctrl-C.
3. Find and highlight Contributions.

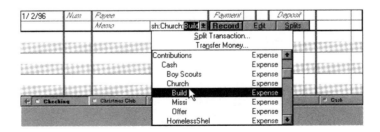

Figure 3-5. When we try to use one of the subcategories we set up in the Category & Transfer List, we discover that some of the names are shorter than we expect.

4. Click the Edit button; press Ctrl-E in DOS to open the Edit Category window.
5. Change the category name to **Contribs**, then click OK to accept.
6. Return to the Account Register you want to use and complete the transaction using the shortened category name.

Keep Quicken's naming restrictions in mind as you set up your own categories. Consider using logical abbreviations whenever you expect to use multilevel subcategories.

ASSIGNING TAX FORMS TO CATEGORIES

One of Quicken's strengths is its ability to assign a tax form to a category. When you install the software, the default setting is to assign tax forms to categories.

Q-TIP

You can change the default setting if you do not plan to assign Tax Forms to categories. To change this setting, click the Options icon on the icon bar, then click the General button to open the General Options window. Uncheck the Use Tax Schedules with Categories check-box to turn off this option.

DOS users always have tax forms available. Simply press F9 to select a form. This opens a list of forms and schedules without line-item descriptions. Select the category you want to assign to a form or schedule and press Enter. This opens a window that describes the tax categories available on that form or schedule. Select the proper description and press Enter.

Quicken supports the forms and schedules listed in Table 3-1. The purpose of assigning tax forms and schedules to categories is to export the information to TurboTax or another tax preparation package that supports the Tax eXchange Format, TXF. The following sample category list provides appropriate tax forms or schedules for each category.

Form/Schedule	Official Name
Form 1040	U.S. Individual Income Tax Return
Schedule A	Itemized Deductions
Schedule B	Interest and Dividend Income
Schedule C	Profit or Loss from Business
Schedule D	Capital Gains and Losses
Schedule E	Supplemental Income and Loss
Schedule F	Farm Income and Expenses
Form 2106	Employee Business Expenses
Form 2119	Sale of Your Home
Form 2441	Child and Dependent Care Expenses
Form 3903	Moving Expenses
Form 4137	Social Security Tax on Unreported Tip Income
Form 4684	Casualties and Thefts
Form 4952	Investment Interest Deduction
Form 6252	Installment Sale Income
Form 8815	Exclusion of Interest From Series EE U.S. Savings Bonds Issued after 1989
Form 8829	Expenses for Business Use of Your Home
Schedule K-1	Beneficiary's Share of Income, Deductions, Credits, Etc. (Form 1041) Partner's Share of Income, Deductions, Credits, Etc. (Form 1065)
Form W–2	Wage and Tax Statement
Form 1099R	Statement for Recipients of Total Distributions From Profit-Sharing, Retirement Plans, Individual Retirement Arrangements, Insurance Contracts, Etc.

Table 3-1.   United States Tax Forms Supported by Quicken and Their Official Names

As a tax practitioner, I find that the way the software keeps records is less than adequate for taxpayers whose returns are of above-average complexity. You may find it easier simply to create financial reports based on your categories than to assign tax forms or schedules to each category and create reports based on the assignments. Even an average taxpayer's figures only take a few minutes to enter into a good tax software program. Most individuals will find it less time-consuming to manually enter the information directly into their tax software instead of assigning tax forms and schedules to their categories.

My contacts at Intuit's tax software division tell me that the TXF standard is evolving and that none of the financial record-keeping programs fully implement the standard. The last version of TurboTax, for filing 1994 returns, even bypassed the TXF format in favor of directly interacting with your Quicken data.

A SAMPLE CATEGORY LIST

This list is only a sample of the types of categories and descriptions you may use in your own situation. We use the **boldface** entries in the exercises throughout the book. We have tried to keep the category names here consistent with how they are used in the text, but you may need to abbreviate longer category names as you enter them. You will also need to abbreviate many of the descriptions as you enter them in Quicken.

Please feel free to adapt this list to suit your own requirements. Quicken sometimes provides more details than the average taxpayer needs. When more form choices are available than the categories listed, you should choose the tax form or schedule item that best fits your situation. Don't forget to establish categories for each tax situation. When a Form or Schedule is not provided, there are usually no tax consequences associated with the category. To avoid double deductions, it is advisable to assign tax forms only to categories at the same level, as illustrated by the Contributions:Cash entry.

Category	Description	Tax Related	Type	Quicken Form Description
Income			Inc	
Alimony	Alimony	*	Sub	1040:Alimony received
Awards & Prizes	Awards and Prizes	*	Sub	1040:Prizes, awards, gambling
Bonuses	Bonus Income	*	Sub	Varies by individual
Commissions	Commission Income	*	Sub	Varies by individual
Gifts Received	Gifts Received		Sub	Usually non-taxable
Home Sale	Gross Home Sale Income	*	Sub	2119:Selling price of old home
Interest Income	Interest Income	*	Sub	B:Choose appropriate

**Set up a separate category for each type of interest you receive.

Category	Description	Tax Related	Type	Quicken Form Description
Lottery & Gambling	Lottery and Gambling Inc.	*	Sub	1040:Prizes, awards, gambling
Reimbursements	Reimbursements		Sub	
Business Meals	Business Meals Reimbursement	*	Sub	2106:Emp. meal reimb.
Business Expense	Business Expense Reimbursement	*	Sub	2106:Emp. expense reimb.
Moving Reimburse	Moving Expense Reimbursement	*	Sub	1040:Moving exp. reimb.
Personal Reimbrs	Personal Non-taxable Reimburse		Sub	
Refunds	Refunds		Sub	
Federal Tax	Federal Income Tax		Sub	Non-taxable
State & Local Tax	State & Local Tax Refunds	*	Sub	1040:State and local refunds
Salary	**Gross Salary Income**	*	**Sub**	**W-2:Salary**

Category	Description	Tax Related	Type	Quicken Form Description
Other Income	Other Income	*	Sub	1040:Other Income—Misc.

**Other Income includes hobby income, election judge, and executor pay.

Category	Description	Tax Related	Type	Quicken Form Description
Pension Income	Pension Income	*	Sub	1099R:Choose appropriate
Rebates Recvd	Rebates Received		Sub	Usually non–taxable
Rental Income	Rental Income	*	Sub	E:Rents received
Social Security	Social Security Benefits	*	Sub	1040:Soc. Sec. Income
Tips—cash	Cash Tips Not Employer Reported	*	Sub	4137:Cash tips not yet reported
Unemployment	Unemployment Compensation	*	Sub	1040:Unemployment compensation
_DivInc	Dividend	*	Inc	B:Dividend income—choose appropriate
_IntInc	Investment Interest Inc	*	Inc	B:Interest income—choose appropriate
_LT CapGnDst	Long-Term Cap Gain Dist	*	Inc	D:LT gain/loss—security
_RlzdGain	Realized Gain/Loss	*	Inc	D:Choose appropriate
_ST CapGnDst	Short-Term Cap Gain Dist	*	Inc	D:ST gain/loss—security
_UnrlzdGain	Unrealized Gain/Loss		Inc	
Alimony		*	**Expns**	1040:Alimony Paid
Automobile	Automobile Expenses		Expns	
Fuel	Auto Fuel		Sub	
Parking & Tolls	Parking and Tolls		Sub	

Category	Description	Tax Related	Type	Quicken Form Description
Rentals	Auto & Truck Rentals		Sub	
Service	Auto Maintenance & Repairs		Sub	
Bank Fees	Bank Fees & Charges		Expns	
Account Fees	Account Maintenance Fees		Sub	
Overdraft Fees	Bank Overdraft Fees		Sub	
Penalty	Early Withdrawal Penalty	*	Sub	1040:Early withdrawal penalty
Service Charges	Bank Service Charges		Sub	
Child care			**Expns**	
Baby-sitting	Baby-sitting Expenses		Sub	
Day Care	**Qualified Child Care expense**	*	**Sub**	**2441:Child care—day care**
Clothing	**Clothing Purchases**		**Expns**	
Contributions (use Contribs)	**Charitable Contributions**		**Expns**	
Cash	Cash Contributions	*	Sub	A:Cash charity contributions
Church	**Giving**		**Sub**	
Building	**Building Fund Donations**		**Sub**	
Missions	**Missions Giving**		**Sub**	
Offerings	**Tithes & Offerings**		**Sub**	
Mileage	Charitable Mileage @ $.12		Sub	

Category	Description	Tax Related	Type	Quicken Form Description
Non-cash	Non–cash Contributions	*	Sub	A:Non-cash charity contrib.
Dues	**Club Dues**		**Expns**	
Education	**Education**		**Expns**	
Employee Bus	Employee Business Expense		Expns	
Auto Business	Business Auto Expenses	*	Sub	2106:Automobile expense
Mileage	Business Mileage @ $.30 (1995)		Sub	
Parking & Tolls	Business Parking & Tolls		Sub	
Dues	Professional & Union Dues	*	Sub	2106:Other business expenses
Education	Job Enhancing Education	*	Sub	2106:Education expense
Entertainment	Business Entertainment Expense	*	Sub	2106:Meal and entertainment expense
Gifts—Business	Business Gifts	*	Sub	2106:Other business expenses
Job Search Expense	Job Search Expenses	*	Sub	2106:Job seeking expense
Licenses	Professional Licenses	*	Sub	2106:Other business expenses
Lodging—Actual	Bus Travel Lodging Expense	*	Sub	2106:Meal and entertainment expense
Lodging Per Diem	Business Travel Lodging Per Diem	*	Sub	2106:Meal and entertainment expense

**Use either actual costs or per diem amounts on a per trip basis.

Category	Description	Tax Related	Type	Quicken Form Description
Meals—Actual	Bus Travel Meal Expenses	*	Sub	2106:Meal and entertainment expense
Meals—Per Diem	Bus Travel Meal Per Diem	*	Sub	2106:Meal and entertainment expense
**Use either actual costs or per diem amounts on a per trip basis.				
Office Expenses	Office Expenses	*	Sub	2106:Other business expenses
Publications	Publications & Subscriptions	*	Sub	2106:Other business expenses
Supplies	Supplies	*	Sub	2106:Other business expenses
Telephone Business	Business Telephone Expense	*	Sub	2106:Other business expenses
Tools 4 Job	Tools for Job Use ONLY	*	Sub	2106:Other business expenses
Travel Expense	Air, Bus, Taxi, Train Fares	*	Sub	2106:Travel
Uniform Expense	Employee Uniform Expenses	*	Sub	2106:Special clothing expense
Entertainment	**Entertainment Expenses**		**Expns**	
Dining Out	**Dining Out**		**Sub**	
Fast Food	Fast Food		Sub	
Recreation	Recreation Expense		Sub	
Gift Expenses	**Gift Expenses**		**Expns**	
Anniversary	Anniversary Gifts		Sub	
Birthday Gifts	**Birthday Gifts**		**Sub**	

Category	Description	Tax Related	Type	Quicken Form Description
Christmas Gifts	Christmas Gifts & Wrapping		Sub	
Other Gifts Given	Other Gifts Given		Sub	
Wedding Gifts	Wedding Gifts		Sub	
Groceries	**Groceries**		**Expns**	
Home	Home Ownership Expenses		Expns	

**Mortgage interest and points are under Interest Expense.

Category	Description	Tax Related	Type	Quicken Form Description
Fixing-Up Expense	Fixing Up Expense At Time of Sale	*	Sub	2119:Fixing–up expenses

**Consult a tax advisor or tax guide before deducting Fixing-Up Expenses.

Category	Description	Tax Related	Type	Quicken Form Description
Home Repair	Home Repair & Maintenance		Sub	
Improvements	Home Improve-ments (Capital)	*	Sub	Not in Quicken, use cost of new home
Purchase Home	Capitalized Costs of Buying Home	*	Sub	2119:Cost of new home
Sale Expenses	Expenses of Selling Your Home	*	Sub	2119:Expense of sale

**Tax information related to home ownership is covered in Chapter 8.

Category	Description	Tax Related	Type	Quicken Form Description
Household	**Household Misc. Expense**		**Expns**	
Insurance	**Insurance**		**Expns**	
Auto	**Automobile Insurance**		**Sub**	
Disability	Disability Insurance		Sub	
Homeowner's	Homeowner's Insurance		Sub	

Category	Description	Tax Related	Type	Quicken Form Description
Life	**Life Insurance**		**Sub**	
Medical	**Dental Health Vision Ins.**	*	**Sub**	**Not in Quicken use A:Doctors, dentists**
Renters	Renters' Insurance		Sub	
IntExp	**Interest Expense**		**Expns**	
Consumer	**Consumer Interest**		**Sub**	
Auto Loan	**Auto Loan Interest**		**Sub**	
Credit Card	**Credit Card Interest**		**Sub**	
Other Interest	Other Consumer Interest		Sub	
Investment Interest	Investment Interest Expense	*	Sub	4952:Investment interest
Mortgage	**Mortgage Interest**	*	**Sub**	**A:Home mortgage interest (1098) A:Home mortgage int. (no 1098)**
Points	Deductible Points Paid	*	Sub	A:Points paid
Invest Expense	Investment Expenses		Expns	
Advisor Fees	**Investment Advisor Fees**	*	**Sub**	**A:Investment man. fees**
Fees	Investment Fees		Sub	
Account	Investment Account Fees	*	Sub	A:Investment man. fees
Transaction	Transaction Fees	*	Sub	A:Investment man. fees
Office Expense	Phone, Postage, Supplies, etc.	*	Sub	A:Investment man. fees
Publications	Publications & Subscriptions		Sub	

Category	Description	Tax Related	Type	Quicken Form Description
Trustee Fees	Investment Trustee Fees		Sub	
Lottery & Gambling	Lottery & Gambling Losses	*	Expns	A:Gambling losses
Lunch@Work	**Lunches Bought At Work**		**Expns**	
Medical	**Medical, Dental, Vision** Expense		**Expns**	
DDS & MD	Dentist & Doctor Fees	*	Sub	A:Doctors, dentists, hospitals

**Medical Insurance is listed under Insurance:Medical.

Category	Description	Tax Related	Type	Quicken Form Description
Mileage	Medical Mileage @ $.09	*	Sub	A:Med. transport/ lodging
Rx	**Prescriptions**	*	**Sub**	**A:Medicine and drugs**
Miscellaneous	Miscellaneous Sched A Expenses	*	Expns	A:Misc. (Subject to 2%)
Other Expenses	**Other Personal Expenses**		**Expns**	
Other Ded Expense	Other Deductible Expenses	*	Expns	A:Not in Quicken
Publications	Personal Publica-tions Subscriptions		Expns	
Taxes	**Taxes, Taxes & MORE Taxes**		**Expns**	
Auto License	Auto License Registration	*	Sub	A:Other taxes
Federal Income	**Federal Income Taxes**		**Sub**	
Fed. Est. Tax	Federal Estimated Taxes	*	sub	1040:Fed. estimated tax

Category	Description	Tax Related	Type	Quicken Form Description
Fed. Tax w/held	Federal Taxes Withheld From Pay	*	sub	W–2:Federal withholding
Local	**Local Taxes**		**Sub**	
Local Tax Paid	Local Taxes Paid by Check/Cash	*	Sub	A:State and local taxes
Local	Local Taxes Withheld From Pay	*	Sub	W-2:Local withholding
Medicare	**Medicare Withholding**	*	**Sub**	**W-2:Medicare tax withholding**
Other Taxes	Miscellaneous Deductible Taxes		Sub	A:Other taxes
Personal Prop.	Personal Property Tax	*	Sub	A:Other taxes
Real Estate	Real Estate Taxes	*	Sub	A:Real estate tax
Social Security	**Social inSecurity Tax**	*	**Sub**	**W-2:Soc Sec tax withholding**
State Income Tx	**State Income Tax**		**Sub**	
State Est. Tax	State Estimated Taxes	*	Sub	A:State and local taxes
State Tax W/held	State Taxes Withheld From Pay	*	Sub	W-2:State withholding
Tax Preparation	Tax Preparation Expenses	*	Sub	A:Tax preparation fees
Utilities	**Electric, Gas, Water, etc.**		**Expns**	
Cable TV	**Cable TV Fees**		**Sub**	
GarbageDisposal	**Garbage Disposal Fees**		**Sub**	
Gas & Electric	**Gas and Electricity**		**Sub**	

Category	Description	Tax Related	Type	Quicken Form Description
Sewer	Sewer Expense		Sub	
Telephone	Telephone Expense		Sub	
Water	Water		Sub	
Vacation Expenses	Vacation Expenses		Expns	
_Accrued In	Accrued Interest		Expns	
_IntExpense	Investment Interest Expense	*	Expns	4952:Investment interest

USING REGISTERS AND MEMORIZED TRANSACTIONS

Once you have set up your categories, you are one step closer to properly using Quicken's Registers. The Account Registers are Quicken's central feature that enables the software's functionality.

Quicken tends to be very user friendly. One of the built-in features that contributes tremendously to this ease of use is Quicken's ability to remember actions that we repeat over and over again, like paying our monthly bills. Quicken can actually memorize many of your transactions for repeated use. These naturally become, in Quicken parlance, Memorized Transactions.

To fully realize Quicken's ease of use, before using the Financial Calendar, learn to create Memorized Transactions. Begin by choosing the Richies' Personal Checking Account from their Account List. So far, you have only entered the Richies' opening balances in their Registers. Now, we will enter some transactions for Quicken to memorize.

Most people make payments to and receive income from the same people or companies over and over again. When you have Quicken memorize a transaction, the next time you begin to type that Payee's name, the

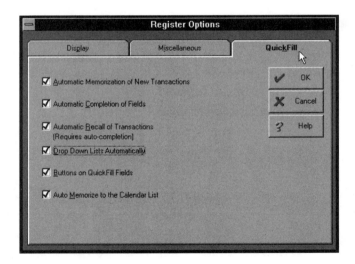

QuickFill feature will finish typing the entry for you. Quicken creates a list of Memorized Transactions for future use. You can edit entries so that only the information you want appears in your Register.

First we need to check the settings for QuickFill. From your Checking Account Register click the Options button at the top of the Register window to open the Register Options window, shown in Figure 3-6. This window has three file-folder tabs running across the top. Select the QuickFill tab. For now, click on any unchecked boxes to make sure all check-boxes are selected, as shown in Figure 3-6. If, by the way, you do not want to have all transactions memorized, you can manually memorize a transaction in a Register by highlighting it and pressing Ctrl-M. **NOTE:** If you click the Display tab, you will be able to choose several different options to adjust the way the

Figure 3-6. **Enable and disable QuickFill and automatic memorization of transactions by clicking the Options button in a Checking Account Register window. The Register Options window allows you to customize many other default settings.**

Register is laid-out. We prefer the Date to be placed to the right of the Number and for the Memo to appear before the Category.

Change QuickFill's default settings by choosing Set Preferences on the Main menu and then choosing General Settings on the next menu. Choose "Y" to activate QuickFill. The DOS version is currently unable to memorize transactions automatically. You can manually memorize a transaction by highlighting it in the register and pressing Ctrl-M.

Q-TIP — **By the way, you can change the default setting that moves you from field to field in the Registers from Tab to Enter by selecting the Miscellaneous tab in the Register Options window and choosing the desired setting. The DOS version does not allow you to change this setting.**

Sam and Sally Richie are entering information into their Quicken Checking Register on January 2, 1996, the day after New Year's Day. Please change the date of the current entry accordingly.

Intuit patterned Quicken's Registers after the paper variety that most people keep in their checkbooks. Here is a quick rundown on how it works; an example follows. To open a Register, double-click on its name in the Account List. Your cursor appears in the date field of a new entry. Change the date, if necessary. The default date is your computer's system date. One nice feature in the Windows version is the miniature calendar that is available in the date field, shown in Figure 3-7.

Tab to the Num field, which is next. A customizable drop-down list appears in the Windows version (DOS users should read the DOS Instructions that follow before continuing). Enter a check number, or choose an item from the list. Tab again to the Payee field. Another drop-down list appears, showing the names of Payees in your Memorized Transaction List. Type the name of the Payee. If you memorized a transaction with this

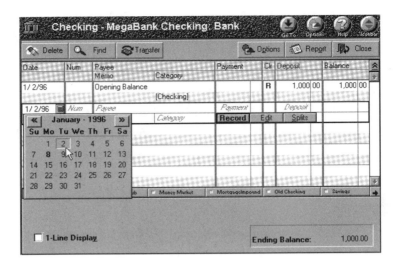

Figure 3-7. Register dates are easy to change with the handy pop-up calendar in the Quicken Registers.

Payee, QuickFill will finish your typing for you. When you tab to the next field, QuickFill will enter any other memorized information into the remaining fields. Enter the amount of your deposit or payment in the appropriate field or accept QuickFill's entry by tabbing past it to the Memo field. Enter a short memo to jog your memory about this transaction in the future, like when the IRS sends you an audit request.

Remember, the Category field assists us in tracking every penny we spend, when we enter those expenditures into Quicken.

 Intuit has chosen to keep the DOS version of Quicken slim enough to run on millions of older IBM-compatible PCs with early processors and less memory than most Windows users' computers. Thus, the DOS version does not have as many drop-down lists and other helpful goodies as the Windows version. Keep the following caveats in mind when using the above instructions. QuickFill works in the DOS version but doesn't offer a list. Instead, you type the first character of the name of the Payee and press Ctrl-+ or Ctrl-− to scroll up or down the portion of the list beginning with the same character. To assign a category, begin typing the category name, QuickFill will complete an entry for you, but maybe not the one you expect. You can't scroll through the Category List from the Register, either. Alternately, if you want to choose from the list, you have two choices. You can either: 1) type a category name not on the list, or 2) Quicken will ask you to either add the category or choose an existing category from the Category List. The simpler solution is to press Ctrl-C to open the Category List, then choose the proper category. Either way, once you choose the proper category, press Enter to Use it in the transaction you are creating or modifying.

The Richies are a fairly typical family. They enjoy spending their money. Therefore, they have a fair number of Quicken transactions. Don't let that intimidate you. It is to your benefit to follow the Richies through each step of managing their finances with Quicken. It amazed our quality assurance testers how much more they learned about Quicken when they actually did each Quicken step than when they just read through a chapter. The hands-on experience is quite enlightening.

Sunday, December 31—Richie Standard Time, the Richies went to church and then took the kids out for burgers. They put a $100.00 check in the offering and paid $14.73 for lunch. Let's begin with the offering:

1. Open their check Register by double-clicking on it.
2. Is your computer's internal date January 2, 1996? If the date is incorrect, please change it. You may obtain different results with Quicken if your computer's clock is set for a different date. See Chapter 2 for details on changing your system date. You can easily

verify your computer system's date by looking at the date Quicken displays in the Register when you open it for the first time each day.

3. Enter 12/31/95 for the date, then press [Tab] and enter the check number 101.

4. Press [Tab] once more and enter the payee: Community Church.

5. Press [Tab] to reach the Payment field, and enter 100.

6. Tab to the Memo field and enter **Offering**.

7. Press [Tab] once more to activate the Category field. I will assume that you have already entered the Categories listed earlier in this chapter. Choose **Contribs:Cash:Church:Offerings** from the drop-down list (main category Contribs, subcategory Cash), DOS users press [Ctrl]-[C] to open the Category List, shown in Figure 3-8. Otherwise, Quicken will ask you to set it up; see Figure 3-2. The IRS considers the Richies' offering a tax-deductible charitable contribution. This is an important distinction for those taxpayers who are able to itemize their deductions—even though we are not attaching a tax form or schedule to the category.

8. The Windows version automatically memorizes transactions, unless you change the default setting. DOS users press [Ctrl]-[M] to memorize this transaction. We will be using it again for long-range planning.

9. Press [Enter] to record this entry, which should now look like Figure 3-9.

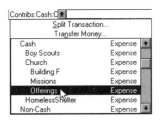

Figure 3-8. Your category drop-down list should look like this if you entered the categories provided in this chapter.

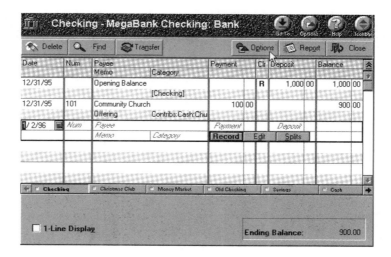

Figure 3-9. This is how the Richies' MegaBank Checking Register looks after you enter the first check. Note that you may adjust the size of most Quicken for Windows windows if you have QuickTabs turned off (use the Options icon then choose the General button to access the QuickTabs setting). You may decide to keep your Registers in larger windows than the default size.

TAX TIP The 1993 Tax Act makes it a little more difficult to claim charitable contributions as itemized deductions. For any single cash contribution, including contributions given by check or credit card, that equals $250.00 or more, the charity must provide you with a official receipt. Your canceled check or credit card payment receipt will no longer be sufficient evidence for the Internal Revenue Service if you are audited. To be on the safe side, we recommend that you obtain a year-end statement from the charity if your *cumulative* contributions during a tax year equal or exceed $250.

Now open the Cash Account Register (DOS users press Ctrl-A to open the Account List first.) Create an entry for the $14.73 the Richies spent on lunch at the Burger Basket. Use **Entertainment:Dining Out** as the expense category. The Payee field has a drop-down list available, which includes your Memorized Transactions and transactions from your Register entries. Quicken's default Preference settings cause drop-down lists to appear in QuickFill fields automatically. The completed entry should look like the one shown in Figure 3-10. The drop-down Payee list includes the entry made in the previous Register entry.

Q-TIP

While the cursor is in the date field, you can press + or − to advance or set back the date. You can also press T for today's date to appear. ("Today" is the date to which your computer's system clock is set.) Press M to go to the first day of the current month or H to go to the last day of the month. To go to the first day of the year, press Y. Similarly, R, takes you to the last day of

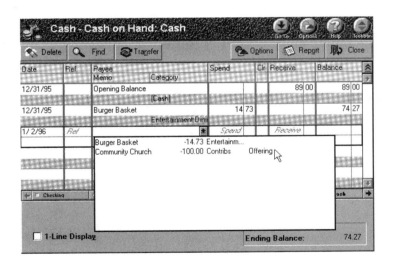

Figure 3-10. The Payee list contains entries from all of your Accounts, making it easy when you pay someone from multiple Accounts.

the current year. Finally, you can change the date by simply typing in a new one. In Quicken for Windows, a handy pop-up calendar simplifies the task of changing dates, as shown in Figure 3-7. Access the pop-up calendar by clicking on the down arrow that appears on the right side of the Date field.

You can also use the category field to transfer money between Quicken Accounts. All of the Accounts appear at the bottom of the category list. Simply enter a transaction into the Register that you want to transfer money from. The receiving Account name is the category name. Let's run through an example using the Richies' Accounts.

1. Open the Richies' file, if it isn't open.
2. Sam and Sally want to pay their Mega-Stores Card from their Old Checking Account. We will enter the check to pay the card in their checking Account Register. Open the Account List using the Accts icon, Accounts QuickTab, or Quick Key combination Ctrl-A. DOS users choose Use Register from the Main menu. The last Register you used will open; if it is not the Old Checking Register, please open it.
3. The default date should be 1/2/96. Press Tab to go to the Check number field. A drop-down list appears. This list has a number of preprogrammed choices and functions. For example, Next Chk# will automatically fill in the next check in the series in the Check number field. If the last check in the Register is 890, Next Chk# will insert 891 into the Register for you. Since we just created this Account, Next Chk# will insert 101. Quicken assumes new Registers start with check number 101. None of the other preprogrammed functions meet our needs, so manually type **891**. You may have noticed that one of the preprogrammed functions is Transfer. We did not use this option because we are making a

payment with a check. Quicken's intent is to reserve this option for electronic transfers between accounts, like when you transfer money between two accounts over the telephone or from an automatic teller machine.

4. Press Tab to go to the Payee field. Another drop-down list appears. Type **Mega-Stores** as the Payee and press Tab.

5. In the Payment field, type **20** and press Tab again.

6. For the Memo, you can type any short note that will remind you about this transaction. Since we make a payment on the Mega-Stores account each month, we'll type **Due - 1/5, Ck 891**. We like to type the check number in the memo since Quicken doesn't show the reference (check) number of the sending Account in the receiving Account.

7. Press Tab to go to the Category field. Another drop-down list appears. Scroll down the list until you highlight [Mega-StoresCard] or beginning typing **Mega-Stores** until QuickFill highlights it for you, as shown in Figure 3-11. Press Enter to select it and press Enter again to complete this transaction.

After you complete the transaction, return to the Account List and open the Mega-Stores Card Account Register. Quicken automatically entered the payment from the Old Checking Account and updated the Mega-Stores Card's Account balance, as shown in Figure 3-12. Just make sure that you write out the paper checks and mail them after transferring money between Accounts in Quicken!

Q-TIP

The Transfer button at the top of the Register window is a handy feature. Although Quicken intends Transfers to be between accounts in the same financial institution, you can use it for any transfers between Accounts. When you click Transfer, the Transfer Money Between Accounts window opens, as shown in Figure 3-13. Simply fill in a Description of the transfer and the

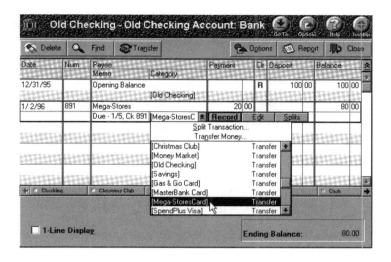

Figure 3-11. Choose the Account you want to transfer funds to, Mega-Stores Card, from the Category & Transfer List.

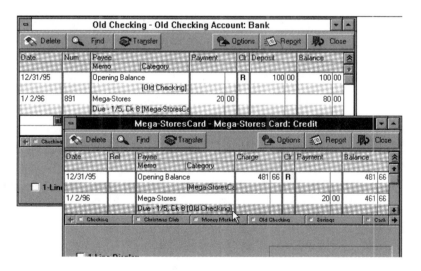

Figure 3-12. Quicken automatically updates the Mega-Stores Card Register with the payment from the Richies' Old Checking Account. Notice that the category field lists the originating Account's name, so you know where the money came from.

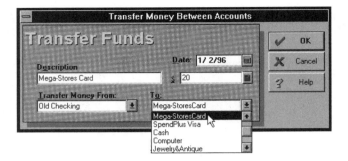

Figure 3-13. The Transfer button allows you to quickly transfer money between two Quicken Accounts. You may want to properly document the transfer in your Account Registers by adding a note in the Memo field.

amount, and select which Accounts you want to transfer funds between.

Not all is as it may seem at first blush. The Description, whose default value is "Transfer Money", becomes the Payee in your Registers. Quicken automatically fills TXFR, for transfer, in the check Num(ber) field, so you may need to open your Register and manually enter the paper check number. You may also want to include a Memo about the transfer in your Register after completing it and note the check number of the sending Account in the receiving Account.

We have found that using an Account name as the category can cause difficulties in certain circumstances. Should you ever decide to delete an Account, all transfers to and from the deleted Account are also deleted. This causes chaos and throws the remaining Accounts out of balance. It can be very time-consuming to manually re-enter the Transfer transactions. We prefer to create a new category called Transfer and use the Account names as the subcategory name, i.e., Transfer:Checking.

We also like to use Memorized Transactions to record recurring transfers. We will discuss Memorized Transactions in a moment.

When you first use Quicken, it will take more time to enter transactions because you will have so many new transactions for Quicken to memorize. When you have a list of transactions to enter, it can be faster over the course of time to enter them all as Memorized Transactions than to enter them individually into your Quicken Accounts. Sam and Sally made lists of their usual monthly transactions. We will enter the items on their list as Memorized Transactions. When we finish, we will use those items to demonstrate the power of the Financial Calendar.

We will begin by entering their paycheck information into Quicken. Considering the amount of information a pay stub contains, it may seem like a daunting task to enter all of it into the computer every payday. It would be, if we had to enter each piece of data each time we were paid. Fortunately, we simply need to enter a series of short steps into Quicken once as a Memorized Transaction. Then we don't need to bother with it again—until our deductions change. As your pay and deductions change periodically, just update your Memorized Transactions. Let's walk through Sam's paycheck together, and then you can enter Sally's.

We are going to enter the paychecks as Memorized Transactions, not as Register entries, because payday is still a few days away. We will actually enter all of the information for Sam's pay stub as one entry, taking advantage of the power of Splits. Splits give you the ability to break down complex transactions into a series of simple transactions, each of which can be categorized. The DOS and Windows versions of Quicken share similar Quick Key combinations but have very different menu structures, so we will use the key combinations to simplify and speed up the process. Many users prefer shortcut key combinations to mouse actions. See Appendix A for a list of Quick Keys. To make the pay stub entry, complete the following steps:

1. Press Ctrl-T to bring up the Memorized Transaction List window, shown in Figure 3-14. Notice that Community Church, Burger Basket, and the Mega-Store payments are already on the list. DOS users must access the Memorized Transaction List window from a Register.

   You should recognize the purpose of most of the columns in the Memorized Transaction window. The two columns at the right side of the list are new to our discussion. The next to last column contains little padlocks when the transactions are locked. This signifies that the transactions will not change if you subsequently use the same Memorized Transaction and update the values in your Register. For example, Sam and Sally put $100.00 in the offering at church. If they use the Memorized Transaction to record a $25.00 contribution next Sunday, the Memorized Transaction itself will not adjust to the new amount if it is locked, as shown in Figure 3-14. If the transaction were not locked, Quicken would update it to reflect the most recent use—$25.00. Quicken automatically locks any transactions imported from an older version of the software. It also locks new transactions as you manually create them. To change the lock status of an entry, simply

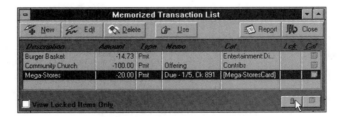

Figure 3-14. The Memorized Transaction List window keeps track of all of your Memorized Transactions. You can edit transactions and select individual entries for inclusion in the Financial Calendar. Notice the two columns on the right. The first column holds little padlocks, which indicate locked transactions, and the other contains miniature calendars.

click the lock column for that entry. The lock function is not available in the DOS version of Quicken.

The final column has miniature calendars in it. These calendars indicate that the transaction will appear in a list of transactions available for use with the Financial Calendar. You will learn more about the Financial Calendar in Chapter 4. DOS users will learn to simulate this function in Step 7.

2. Windows users, click on the New button, Ctrl-N, to bring up the Create Memorized Transaction window. DOS users, press Ctrl-Ins to open the Edit/Set Up Memorized Transaction Window.

3. DOS users, skip to Step 4. Windows users need to select a transaction Type. A drop-down list allows you to choose the type of transaction, as shown in Figure 3-15. Checks written by hand are Payments. Checks Quicken prints are Print Checks. Since we are depositing Sam's paycheck into his checking account, this is a Deposit.

4. Tab to the Payee field and type **El Construction Co.** Tab again and type **Sam's Paycheck** for the Memo. Your window should look like Figure 3-16. Now, click the Splits button to open the Splits window.

5. Enter Sam's pay stub information from Figure 3-17. Notice that Sam's gross pay is a positive number and each of the deductions are negative numbers. You may not find Social Security on your paystub; most payroll services list it as "FICA."

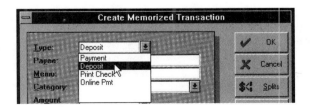

Figure 3-15. Choose the transaction type from the drop-down list. Your choices are Payment, Deposit, Print Check, or Elec Payment (Electronic Payment).

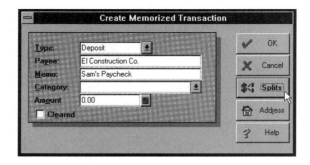

Figure 3-16. Begin entering paychecks in the Create Memorized Transaction window. Since most people have multiple deductions taken from their pay, we use the Splits window to account for each deduction.

After you enter each deduction, Quicken recalculates the net pay and displays the total in the bottom right corner of the Splits window as the Splits Total. If we had entered the Amount of Sam's net pay in the Create Memorized Transaction window, the net pay

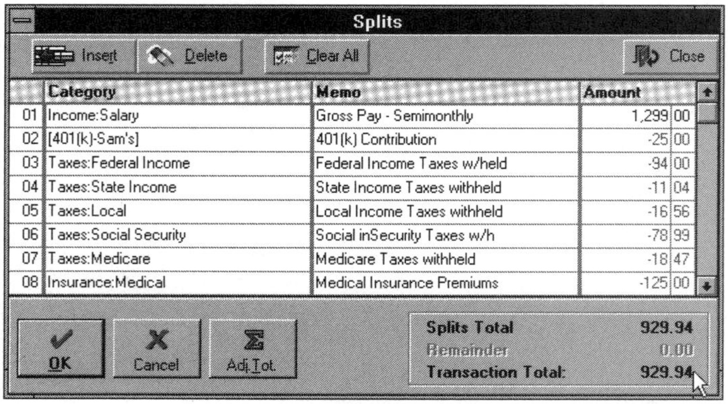

Figure 3-17. This is Sam Richie's pay stub information for January 5, 1996. You can copy the information from this figure into your software. As you enter these transactions, remember to enter the payroll deductions as negative numbers.

would appear as the Transaction Total, and the Remainder would tell you the amount of deductions required to equal Sam's net pay. The calculated amounts in the lower right corner of the Splits window do not appear in the DOS program. When you finish, click OK to return to the Create Memorized Transaction window.

6. When you return to the Create Memorized Transaction window, notice that Sam's net pay now appears in the Amount field in light gray print (you can't change it here) and that the Category field says "--Splits--" in gray, shown in Figure 3-18. Click OK to return to the Memorized Transaction List window.

7. You have successfully completed Sam's complex paycheck! Notice in Figure 3-19 that the Memorized Transaction List window shows the paycheck as El Construction Co. This ia a locked item since it's manually entered.

Q-TIP

Your Memorized Transaction List can become quite lengthy. Quicken 5 for Windows includes a new feature that could be useful. You can have Quicken automatically delete a Memorized Transaction after a designated number of months of non-use. For example, if one of those pesky long-distance carriers calls in

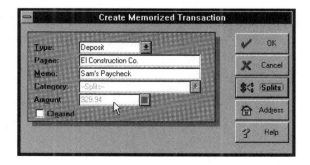

Figure 3-18. Your Create Memorized Transaction window should look like this after you enter Sam's splits.

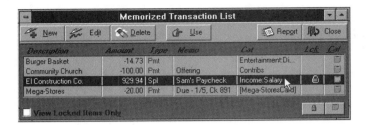

Figure 3-19. Your Memorized Transaction List window should look like this after you enter Sam's Paycheck as a Memorized Transaction. Notice that the Category column lists Income:Salary, the first transaction in the Splits window.

the middle of dinner and actually convinces you to switch, you can tell Quicken to delete your old phone company from the list.

To activate this new feature, click the Options icon then the General button. Put a ✓ in the box for Remove Memorized Transactions Not Used in Last ☐ Months. Be sure to put a number of months in the box or you may wonder why your Memorized Transactions keep disappearing (the default is zero)!

Be careful how many months you choose. Since this choice affects all of your Memorized Transactions, most people will not want to set the number of months to anything less than 14. Fourteen months would allow annual transactions to remain undisturbed, assuming that you pay early one year and late the following year. I personally need to set the number of months a little higher than 24 because one of my professional licenses renews bi-annually. This option would be much more useful if you could designate a number of months for individual transactions.

DOS users have one more step to complete. Highlight El Construction Co. in the Memorized Transaction List and press Ctrl-J to open the Scheduled Memorized Transaction window. Add this transaction to the Scheduled Transaction List.

You have all of the data required to complete this window, except you need to use the MegaBank Checking Account for all of the transactions. Note that the memo field for Income:Salary tells how often Sam and Sally are paid. Accept the default values for the remaining entries.

Completing this quick, simple step now will save you time later when we begin using the Financial Calendar. Take a minute to highlight Community Church and add it to the Scheduled Transaction List, too.

Q-TIP

PC users can memorize transactions already in a Register by highlighting the entry, then pressing Ctrl-M. You can also include future transactions in the Register by entering a future date. You may find this course of action dangerous and confusing, as it affects the Balance your Account List displays. Delete transactions by pressing Ctrl-D. Deleting a transaction from a Register will not affect a Memorized Transaction.

Now that you have entered the information from Sam's pay stub, you can enter Sally's through the same sequence of steps. Sally works for Professional Service Corp. She will receive her first biweekly paycheck of the new year on January 5. Use the data provided in Figure 3-20. Sally has $45.00 directly deposited to her Christmas Club account by her employer. To transfer the money from her paycheck to her Christmas Club Account in Quicken, use [**Christmas Club**] as the category. You will find [Christmas Club] near the bottom of the category list where Quicken lists all of the Account names.

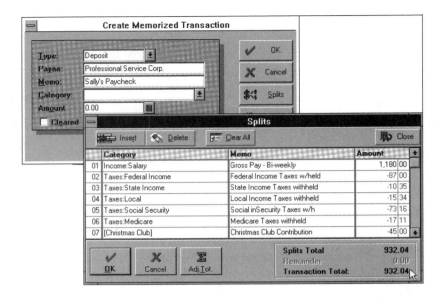

Figure 3-20. This is Sally Richie's pay stub information for January 5, 1996. Use this information to complete a Memorized Transaction for her paycheck.

Q-TIP

If you have multiple recurring transactions that are similar, you may not be thrilled about retyping all of the details over and over again into Memorized Transactions. For example, Sam is paid twice a month. Suppose that he only has medical insurance premiums deducted from one of those monthly checks. There is an easy method to copy the splits from his first paycheck to the second and delete the insurance premiums from the second.

First, open a Register. It doesn't matter which one you open because we will delete the transaction when we finish. Begin typing El Construction Co. in a Payee field. QuickFill will complete the entry for you. Press Tab to move to the next field. You will see that Quicken automatically fills in the amount of Sam's net pay, the Memo field and the Category fields for you. Click the Splits button to open the Splits window. Find the Medical Insurance Premium transaction and delete the entries on that line by highlighting the entry and pressing [Ctrl]-[Del]. Click the Adjust Total (Adj.Tot.) button to recompute Sam's net pay. Then click OK to close the Splits window. Press [Shift]-[Tab] a few times until you are back in the Payee field. Press [End] to move your cursor to the end of El Construction Co. Press the spacebar and type (2nd check). Press [Ctrl]-[M] to memorize the second paycheck Sam receives each month. Finally, press [Ctrl]-[D] then [Enter] to delete this transaction from the Register.

MONEY MATTERS

Does using Sam and Sally's net pay instead of their gross pay plus all the splits in their Registers tempt you? Even worse, you may

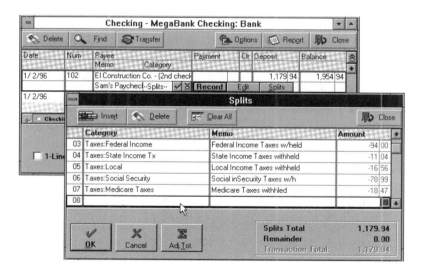

Figure 3-21. You can quickly modify an existing Memorized Transaction and save the new entry as another transaction as we demonstrate with Sam's second paycheck.

want to use your net pay in your own Register! The net pay is all you really need for simple cash flow projections, but you need all of your tax-related transactions to simplify your tax planning. Those additional figures are indispensable for tax-planning purposes. Minimizing your tax bite can do wonders if you are serious about creating additional wealth!

The Richies are not setting up Memorized Transactions for their monthly receipts from their interest- and dividend-paying accounts because the amounts are so small that they don't really affect their cash flow projections. Quicken for Windows will automatically memorize those transactions as they occur. DOS users must manually memorize transactions by pressing Ctrl-M.

Now that their income is accounted for, Sam and Sally are ready to enter their monthly expenses as Memorized Transactions. They plan to pay all of their bills out of their new checking account because they suspect that they spend a lot more cash than they should. They are also trying to cut down on using their credit cards.

Rather than breaking down each expense, they are listing general items and amounts. When an amount fluctuates, they use a high-average figure. Their utility bills are a good example. The central heating and air conditioning system is more expensive in the winter and summer than in the spring and fall, when temperatures are more moderate. Their most expensive bills run about $125, while the milder months cost about $60. An even $100 seems like a fair figure to them. Note: We want to lock these transactions in the Memorized Transaction list.

As Sam and Sally put their list together, they found an asset they overlooked! Their mortgage company set up an impound account for their homeowners' insurance and real estate taxes to accumulate in each month. Their lender then pays those bills as they are due. The Richies live in a state that requires lenders to pay interest on mortgage impound account balances, and so they receive interest income on the account.

They called their lender and obtained their current impound balance. Set up a new Savings Account (Bank Account in DOS) called **Mortgage-Impound** with a balance of **$1,074.59** on **December 31, 1995**. If you need assistance setting up the Account, see the examples in Chapter 2 or use Quicken's excellent Help function.

The printouts they made of their loans' payment schedules gave them the approximate principal and interest amounts payable on their next minivan and mortgage loan payments (see Chapter 1 for instructions). Therefore, it will not be necessary for you to create loan schedules for the Richies; you need only enter the payments.

You may notice that the credit cards listed in Table 3-3, do not have Accounts listed for Splits. You may set up Splits by using **IntExp:Consumer:CreditCrd.** Sam and Sally decided to edit those transactions as their statements arrived, a couple of weeks after they wrote the checks to pay their credit card bills. Quicken is unable to calculate interest that is compounded daily on a fluctuating balance, the method credit card issuers use. You will need to account for the interest when your credit card statements arrive and bill you for the interest paid. You must use this information to Reconcile your Accounts, or they won't balance!

Q·TIP

Recon

Balancing your checkbook is a breeze with Quicken's Reconcile command. Use the Reconcile icon on the Windows button bar (or the Reconcile item on the Activities menu in all program versions) to access this feature. In the DOS version, the Activities menu is available only from a Register. Use the Clr field between Payment and Deposit to mark reconciled items with your bank statement. Reconcile works with the Credit Card Account, also. If you need help reconciling your Register, Quicken Help will guide you through the process.

MONEY MATTERS

The loan schedule Quicken creates for you may not exactly match payment figures calculated by your lender. It is useful to

update the amounts you enter into your Accounts for principal and interest paid with the amounts actually reported to you by your lender. If you do not receive a statement showing how each payment is applied, plan to periodically call your lender to obtain the exact figures.

Some items, like lunches at work, clothes, and entertainment, occur on a regular basis but represent money spent at various places. You can set up a Memorized Transaction without a Payee, but when we begin to use the Calendar for those transactions, Quicken is unable to schedule them without Payees. To work around this difficulty, Sam and Sally set up these transactions with Payee names beginning with AAA so that they appear at the top of the list.

Like most people who take some time to sit down and determine how they are spending their money, Sam and Sally could hardly believe how much their lifestyle costs them. Even after spending an hour examining their check register and bills, they are remembering more items to add to the list.

Create Memorized Transactions for the items in Tables 3-2 and 3-3. For your convenience, we show the Create Memorized Transaction and Splits windows for the Richies' first mortgage in Figure 3-22. The Quick Key to open the Memorized Transaction List is Ctrl-T. Click New to add your first transaction.

Q-TIP

Several data entry windows in Quicken, such as the Create Memorized Transaction window, allow you to enter the payee's address. This option is available only when the Type of transaction is a Print Check. A Print Check is a check printed by Quicken. Checks that you write by hand are Payments. Use Print Check for any Type of Payment with an address, phone number, or account number you would like to store in Quicken. The Address button brings up the Printed Check Information window shown in Figure 3-23.

Payee	Item (Memo)	Category	Amount ($)	Date	Frequency
Home Mort Co.	Mortgage Payment		$1,005.42	1/25	Monthly
	Principal	[First Mortgage]	$266.32		
	Interest	IntExp:Mortgage	575.10		
	Impounds	[MortgageImpound]	164.00		
Steve's Bank	Home Equity Loan		$63.35	1/25	Monthly
	Principal	[Equity Line]	$44.83		
	Interest	IntExp:Mortgage	18.52		
Jumbo Credit Union	Minivan Loan		$283.53	1/5	Monthly
	Principal	[Auto Loan]	$234.12		
	Interest	IntExp: Consumer:AutoLoan	49.41		

Table 3-2. This is the Richies' best estimate of their normal monthly expenses that require split transactions. The Date column shows the date that the payment is automatically withdrawn from their MegaBank checking account or the date that they must mail the payment for it to arrive by the due date. You'll find the Date and Memo columns necessary in an exercise we complete later in Chapter 4. Do not memorize split transactions as percentages. If you want to create loan amortization schedules for these loans, you need the following information: The mortgage is a 15-year loan with a 9.625 percent fixed rate. The beginning balance was $80,000 on January 4, 1993. The equity line is a variable rate loan amortized over seven years. The beginning balance was $4,000 on January 13, 1994. The current interest rate is 8.5 percent. The minivan loan is a 7.95 percent fixed-rate five-year loan. The beginning balance was $14,000 on April 16, 1993.

Payee	Item (Memo)	Category	Amount ($)	Date	Frequency
Credit Cards					
Mega-Stores	Dept. Store Card	[Mega-StoresCard]	$20.00	1/5	Monthly
Gas & Go Co.	Gas Card	[Gas & Go Card]	45.00	1/25	Monthly
MasterBank	MasterCard	[MasterBankCard]	50.00	1/5	Monthly
SpendPlus, Inc.	Visa	[SpendPlus Visa]	25.00	1/10	Monthly
Utilities					
Big Eye TV	Cable TV	Utilities:Cable TV	36.45	1/8	Monthly
ElectroGas	Gas & Electric	Utilities:Gas&Electric	100.00	1/10	Monthly
AmeriWaste	Garbage	Utilities:Garbage Disposal	12.50	1/17	Monthly
CountyServices	Sewer & Water	Utilities:Sewer	17.87	1/10	Monthly
CallTel	Telephone	Utilities:Telephone	85.00	1/13	Monthly
Insurance					
Premium Ins.	Auto	Insurance:Auto	$567.49	1/8	Quarterly
Family Earning & Retirement Ins Co	Cancer–family	Insurance:Medical	27.95	1/15	Monthly
Monolith Life	Life–Sam	Insurance:Life:Sam	150.00	1/12	Monthly
Premium Ins.	Life–Sally	Insurance:Life:Sally	75.00	1/5	Monthly
Miscellaneous					
AAA Clothes	Clothes	Clothing	150.00	1/28	Monthly
AAA Charity	Charity	Contributions:Cash	250.00	1/30	Four Weeks
AAA Fun	Entertainment	Entertainment	40.00	1/7	Weekly
FreshRex	Food	Groceries	150.00	1/8	Weekly
Kidlet Kare	Day Care	Childcare:DayCare	125.00	1/5	Weekly
Weeds B Gone	Gardener	Household	65.00	1/27	Monthly
Atlas Club	Health Club	Dues	225.00	1/24	Quarterly
TidyClean	Housekeeper	Household	75.00	1/27	Monthly
StealthyNinjas	Karate Lessons	Education	45.00	1/31	Monthly
AAA Lunch	Lunch— both @ work	Lunch@Work	10.00	1/3	Work Days
AAA Misc.	Other	Other Expenses	50.00	1/6	Weekly

Table 3-3. This is the Richies' best estimate of their normal monthly expenses that do not require split transactions. The Date column is the date the payment is automatically withdrawn from their MegaBank checking account or the date they must mail the check for it to arrive by the due date. You'll find the Date and Memo columns necessary in an exercise we complete later in Chapter 4.

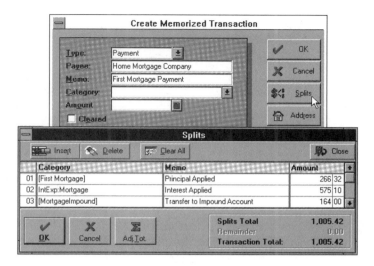

Figure 3-22. Use the information in the Create Memorized Transaction window to create a Memorized Transaction for the Richies' first mortgage. Click the Splits button to enter each of the Richies' mortgage payments which include the three transactions shown above. Use this figure to set up the Richies' mortgage Splits.

PRACTICAL APPLICATIONS

It is important that you begin using Quicken to track your cash flow. Enter all of your checks and deposits in your checking Registers. You should also keep track of all of your cash transactions, even little ones, in a Cash Account. One day, when you have some extra time, enter all of your year-to-date checking account transactions into their appropriate Registers. If you need to prepare last year's tax return, you should enter all of last year's tax-related transactions into a different data file. It is easy to create a new data file from your current data file by using Quicken's Copy command on the File Operations submenu of the File menu. In the DOS version, Quicken's Copy File command is on the File Activities submenu of the Main menu. All of the categories in your current file can be copied into the new file.

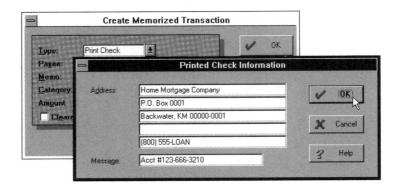

Figure 3-23. To use the Address button in the Create Memorized Transaction window, you must classify the Type of transaction as a Print Check. After changing the mortgage payment from a Payment to a Print Check, we are able to enter the address and other information in the Printed Check Information window.

Continue feeding your mind with positive material that will encourage you to become a wealth creator, not just a cash consumer! I highly recommend *The Wealthy Barber* by David Chilton. It contains a wealth of ideas and easily understood financial concepts. It is very easy to read and quite enjoyable.

As we went to print, we were putting the finishing touches on a home page for *The Computer Connection*, my weekly radio program, on the World Wide Web. We have a section there about *Create Wealth with Quicken*, and we plan to publish updated financial and Quicken information not contained in this book. Please visit our web site at http:// www.c3rn.com.

PART II

PLOT YOUR PATH TO WEALTH

CHAPTER 4

THE CASH FLOW CONUNDRUM

I AM INDEED RICH, SINCE MY INCOME IS SUPERIOR
TO MY EXPENSE, AND MY EXPENSE IS EQUAL TO MY
WISHES.

—EDWARD GIBBON

Now that we have laid a foundation of some basic Quicken functions, we will explore some methods for managing cash flow with Quicken. The first is the Financial Calendar coupled with Quicken's forecasting tool, both of which are available in the last two DOS and last three Windows versions. If you don't have Quicken 7.0 or 8.0 for DOS, or Quicken 3.0 or later for Windows, then you can fall back on the second method, the Budget Worksheet, which is found in all present versions and most prior versions of Quicken. (Please note that the instructions given in this text are for the latest versions of Quicken. Each update tends to have changes in the steps required to carry out similar tasks.) Even if you have an old version of Quicken that does not support the Financial Calendar, we recommend that you read that section—and update to the current version. It contains many useful concepts, strategies, and tips. Many of the methods for using the Calendar apply to other areas of the program as well.

We will also give you an excellent reason to watch your cash flow later in the chapter. This secret may well motivate you to new heights of personal cash flow management!

CASH FLOW PROJECTION MAGIC

The last two Windows and DOS versions of Quicken include the Financial Calendar, which makes cash flow projections a cinch. The DOS version of the Calendar is not as powerful as the Windows version, but you will still find the information helpful. At the end of this section, we will tell DOS users how to simulate much of the Windows' Calendar cash flow projection finesse.

You can benefit from the power and simplicity of the Financial Calendar, Figure 4-1, to project your cash flow into the future. The concept

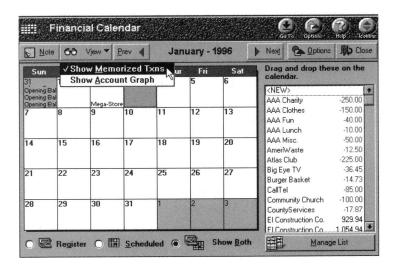

Figure 4-1. Quicken's Calendar will help you plan your future cash flow.

behind the Financial Calendar is really quite simple: You spend and receive money on a periodic basis. Every month, you pay your mortgage or rent. You more than likely make a car payment and, of course, have regular living expenses. You receive income at certain times during the month (once a month, bi-weekly, or every week). You receive a paycheck on a regular basis, unless, of course, you work for commissions, in which case your compensation is paid when you sell something.

Back in the old days before computerization, people would sometimes pull out a paper calendar and plot out financial events. They might think, "On the first of each month, I get paid, and again on the 15th. I need to mail off my mortgage payment on the 25th for it to arrive by the 1st, when it's due. The telephone bill and other utilities should be in the mail by the 17th." By marking these items on a paper calendar, they could keep track, in a very tedious manner, of their cash inflows and outflows. Unfortunately, because it is difficult to keep track of things manually, very few people track their cash flow. The Richies were considering employing their large wall calendar until they discovered Quicken's Financial Calendar.

To use Quicken effectively, you need to know your income (how much and when you receive it) and your expenses (how much and when due). If you are a new Quicken user, gather your check registers and your outstanding bills. Sort your bills by their due date. Now, you are ready to compare the information you've gathered with your Account List. Your Account List should include all of your open credit accounts, most of which will have payments due each month. If you find a bill for which you didn't set up a Quicken Account, then set it up now. If you are already a Quicken user, then you will also want to print your last few months' Register entries for your spending Accounts—checking, credit, and cash.

USING THE FINANCIAL CALENDAR

Most of the Richies' normal living expenses are in the Memorized Transaction List. Few people know exactly where they spend all of their money;

inevitably, most of us will remember additional expenses. We are now ready to schedule the transactions Sam and Sally did remember in their Financial Calendar. The shortcut key for accessing the Calendar in DOS and Windows is Ctrl-K. You may also access it through the Calendar icon or the Activities menu. In the DOS version, you must be in a Register to access the Calendar. Open the Financial Calendar now.

Sam and Sally put in a full day learning to use Quicken and entering their Memorized Transactions. They are continuing their planning on January 3, 1996. Check the default date in your Quicken Register. Please set your system date if it doesn't show January 3, 1996, or you will not get the results shown. See Chapter 2 for instructions on changing your system date.

As you saw in Figure 4-1, the Financial Calendar has Note, View, Prev(ious), Next, Options, and Close buttons across the top.

You will be pleased at how easy the Calendar is to use and understand. When you initially open your Calendar, it should look like Figure 4-1. If a graph area is visible at the bottom of the Calendar, click the View button and select the option shown in Figure 4-1 so that the Calendar fills the Calendar window from top to bottom. The transaction list to the right of the Calendar should be visible. If it isn't, click the View button and then click Show Memorized Txns (Transactions) to open the list. This list contains the Memorized Transactions and Register entries in your Quicken data file. At the top of the column is the item <NEW>. You can use <NEW> to schedule any transactions that are not on the list.

Q-TIP

Using <NEW> enters transactions into the Calendar but not into the Memorized Transaction List. When the due date occurs for an item you schedule, Quicken enters the item into the appropriate Register as a payment or deposit. You may then manually memorize it by pressing Ctrl-M. You may find it easier to enter the transaction into the Memorized Transaction List initially.

In Chapter 3, you learned to create Scheduled Transactions. You must create the Scheduled Transactions list to use the Financial Calendar in DOS. It is easy to create this list from your Memorized Transaction list. To access the Memorized Transaction list, press Ctrl-T. **The Memorized Transactions List window will pop up. Highlight the transaction you want to memorize, then press** Ctrl-J **to schedule the transaction. Enter the requested information in the Schedule Memorized Transaction window.**

Q-TIP

If your transactions do not appear on the Calendar, Checking is not selected.

To simplify the process of using the Calendar, we will have all of the Richies' income and expenses run through their Checking Account. Therefore, to analyze their cash flow we need only keep an eye on their Checking Account transactions. Near the upper right corner of the Calendar is the Options button. When you click it, the Calendar Options window shows a list of all the Richies' Accounts under the Accounts tab. When you open this window, all of the Accounts are marked, as shown in Figure 4-2. We want to include only the Checking Account. Click on the Clear All button once. You will see check-marks disappear in the left column. Click Checking, and a check-mark will appear in the left column. Click OK to continue. The DOS version places all Scheduled Transactions on the Calendar.

We are ready to schedule our first Calendar transaction. Coincidentally, Sally remembered that her dear friend, Wendy, has a birthday on January 19. Sally wants to buy her a $15 to $20 gift when she goes shopping at the mall on the 14th. Let's use <NEW> to schedule this expense.

Move your cursor off the Calendar into the transaction list area—your cursor transforms from an arrow into a hand. Move the hand to <NEW> and hold down your primary mouse button (probably the left button, if

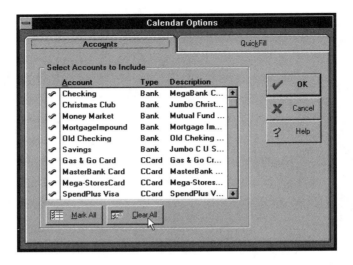

Figure 4-2. Your Calendar Options window should look like this before you select the Checking Account as the only selected Account.

you're right-handed). Drag the hand to the 14th on the Calendar. As you drag the hand onto the Calendar, the pointer becomes a miniature Calendar. Release the mouse button. When you release the button, the New Transaction window appears. If the Register Transaction option is marked (in the upper-left corner of the window), you are attempting to schedule a transaction for the current date or a date in the past, as determined by your computer's internal date. The Calendar will not show a Register Transaction until the transaction appears in the Register.

In the upper-left corner of the New Transaction window, you can choose between scheduling a Register Transaction or a Scheduled Transaction.

The New Transaction window assumes we are creating a Scheduled Transaction when you choose a future date. We will set up a future transaction using the information in Figure 4-3 but will explain some of the elements in the New Transaction window as we go. Sally will pay for the gift from their checking account, so choose Checking from the drop-down list in the Account field.

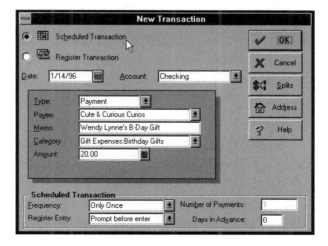

Figure 4-3. Schedule Calendar transactions from the transaction list using the New Transaction window. When you attempt to schedule a transaction to a date that is past, the information requested is different than shown in this figure.

We encounter a couple of handy new fields in the New Transaction window when Schedule Transaction is selected. In the Schedule Transaction section at the bottom of the window, we must tell Quicken the Frequency of Payment. We have several choices: Only Once, Weekly, Every two weeks, Twice a month, Every four weeks, Monthly, Every two months, Quarterly, Twice a year, and Yearly. Choose Only Once, the default setting, because Sally would like to make, not buy, Wendy a gift next year. The "1" in the Number of Payments field is greyed out due to the fact that we chose Only Once for the Frequency.

For the Register Entry field, we have two choices. The first is "Automatically enter," which will automatically enter the transaction into the Checking Register without our intervention. This option is appropriate for set payments and deposits. Sally doesn't know exactly how much she will spend, so we want Quicken to prompt us before using the transaction information. By using "Prompt before entry," we can adjust the entry to the actual amount Sally spends. The number of days in advance we want the Billminder to warn us is zero because we do not need advance warning for a check we will write at a store.

Now click on OK to schedule the event on the Calendar. Congratulations, your first item is on the Calendar. The 14th should look like Figure 4-4. That was fairly easy, right?

1. Type Ctrl-J to open the Scheduled Transaction List window.

2. Type Ctrl-Ins to open the Set Up Scheduled Transaction window.

3. Fill in the information using Figure 4-3. As you complete a window, press Enter to continue to the next window until you enter all of the requested data.

4. The Scheduled Transaction is added to the Scheduled Transaction list and highlighted. Press Enter or select Use. The Record the Following Transaction window opens.

5. Accept or edit the data provided and press Enter to add this transaction to the Calendar.

6. Quicken returns you to the Calendar and places the cursor on the date you scheduled the transaction. A "T" also appears on that date. Double-click the date to confirm that the transaction is properly scheduled. The

14		
	Transactions	
Cute & C	Note	Alt+N
	Previous Month	Alt+P
	Next Month	Alt+T
	Options	Alt+O

Figure 4-4. Posting notes on your Calendar can be quite helpful. Click your right mouse button anywhere on the Calendar as a short-cut to opening this handy drop-down list.

Scheduled Transaction List window appears and allows you to modify the transaction. If you double-click the date, one of the transactions will appear for editing, but any other transactions scheduled on that date will not be available.

Sally is also going to a surprise birthday party for Wendy on the 19th. She wants Sam to remember this, so let's add a note to the Calendar, too. Click on January 19 and then click on the Note button on the Calendar's icon bar or click the right mouse button while on the Calendar (press Ctrl-N in the DOS version). Type a note about the party and click Save (see Figure 4-5). Double-click on a note to retrieve it from the Calendar.

The Windows version of the Financial Calendar is much more robust than the DOS version. Many of the features we discuss in the following pages are simply beyond the DOS version. We had expected that many features in the Windows-version Calendar would appear in future DOS releases but we have been told that DOS development has stopped. To learn how to simulate some

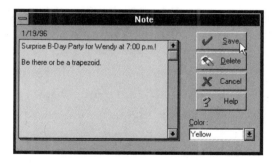

Figure 4-5. You can easily add notes to the Financial Calendar using the Note button. You can even post a rainbow of colors on the Calendar. Try attaching meaning to the various colors; e.g., red notes can alert you to a critical message. Note: DOS notes are not color-coordinated.

of the Windows Calendar's power, see the Q-Tip at the end of this section. Meanwhile, we suggest that you consider upgrading to Quicken for Windows. The added features in the Calendar alone justify the added expense. Intuit had claimed that the DOS and Windows data files were interchangeable. This is no longer true, but your DOS data can be imported to the Windows version. Please back up your data files before opening them with another version of Quicken.

Q-TIP

DOS users can follow the following steps to edit transactions in the Register from the Calendar:

1. Double-click on T in the date you wish to edit.
2. Edit the information.
3. Press Enter to return to the Calendar.

We will now take advantage of all the effort we put into creating Memorized Transactions for the Richies' pay stubs and bills. Let's begin with Sam's paycheck. Drag the $929.94 "El Construction Co." on the transaction list to the 5th. When you drop it on the 5th, the New Transaction window opens. Sam's employer pays him twice a month, electronically depositing his check into his MegaBank checking account. Sam's paychecks have slightly different deductions, as we saw in Chapter 3. This transaction is for the first check Sam receives each month. Click on OK after completing the New Transaction window using the information in Figure 4-6. Schedule Sam's other paycheck on the 20th of January. Schedule Sally's paycheck from Professional Services on the 5th and choose Every two weeks for the Frequency.

As you use the Calendar, you will eventually notice that the Calendar schedules a transaction that would normally occur on a weekday on a weekend or holiday. Many banks do not process payments or deposits on weekends or holidays. The transaction will probably post to the

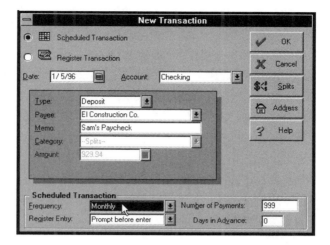

Figure 4-6. Set up the first paycheck Sam receives each month using this information. We recommend using Prompt before Enter with electronic deposits so you can confirm any changes in your pay or deductions.

account on the next workday. Situations like this rarely cause problems, unless the account is underfunded.

Q-TIP   The Financial Calendar is very powerful, but you may still need to figure some things out for yourself. For example, Sam and Sally attend the Sacramento PC Users' Group meetings on the third Wednesday of each month. They always go out to dinner before the meeting. If you try to schedule the cost of dinner on the Calendar, you will find that Quicken schedules the transaction for the same date each month. To schedule for the same day of a certain week each month, you will need to schedule each transaction manually.

Please schedule the remaining entries from Tables 3-1 and 3-2 for Sam and Sally. Use the date column to determine which date to schedule the transaction and the frequency column to determine how often the transaction occurs.

Scheduling Hints: Together, Sam and Sally spend $10 total each workday on lunch. Weekdays is not a choice for the Frequency of Payment field. Schedule Lunch@Work each weekday for a week as a weekly expense. Double-click on any weekday that is a holiday and delete Lunch@Work. Transactions now cover Sam and Sally's Calendar, as shown in Figure 4-7.

Q-TIP To edit a Calendar entry, simply click on the date the entry is scheduled. A small window appears that lists all of the transactions scheduled for that day. To get the Edit Scheduled Transaction window, highlight the entry that requires adjustment. Now you can edit any of the entries for that transaction. You can also change the transaction date.

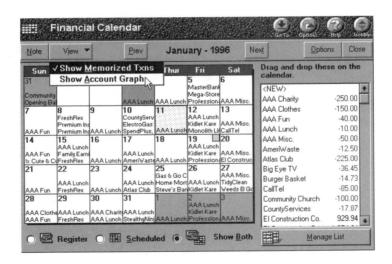

Figure 4-7. Your Financial Calendar should look like this after you schedule the Richies' transactions.

How does the Calendar help us in a practical way? The Windows version of Quicken offers a graphical representation of your day-to-day financial situation. Click the View button near the upper-left corner of the Calendar window. Click the Show Account Graph option on the menu. A graph of scheduled income and expenses will appear below the Calendar, as shown in Figure 4-8.

The graph shows you the amount of money available or how over-drawn the selected Accounts shown on the Calendar will be for each day shown. You can also move to a previous month and view a graph of your previous cash position or to a future month. Move ahead a few months and see how the Richies' projections look. Their bank balance will seldom be equal to their Quicken Account balance, since it normally takes a few days after you write a check for it to clear your bank account. The graph in Figure 4-8 shows negative balances from January 30 through February 3.

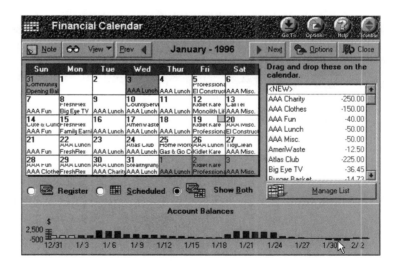

Figure 4-8. Your Financial Calendar should look like this after you schedule the Richies' transactions. Is their month longer than their money? How about next month or the month after that?

We have all of the Richies' income and expenses running through their Checking Account. Therefore, to analyze their cash flow, we need only graph their Checking Account transactions. When we first began scheduling transactions on the Calendar, we set the Calendar to include only Checking Account transactions. Therefore, when we graph the Richies' cash flow, the graph will only show the Checking Account's balance. It is important to know what you are graphing. If you include another Account in your cash flow projections graph, you may not realize that you will overdraw your account, and you could begin bouncing checks! If you include all of your Accounts in the graph, then you can see how your net worth fluctuates over time.

Let's see how the Richies' Checking balance will look over a longer period of time. We will use Quicken for Window's Forecasting feature to see longer term projections. Click the Forecast icon to open the Forecasting - Base Scenario window.

If the Forecast icon isn't on your icon bar, click the Options icon, then the Iconbar button to open the Customize Iconbar window. Press the New button to open the Add Action to Iconbar window. Select Quicken Forecasting from the Icon Action list, then choose OK, then Done to add the icon.

Clicking the Forecast icon will also open the Automatically Create Forecast window. Enter **1/96** and **12/96** as the From and To dates, then click the Advanced button to open the Advanced AutoCreate window. In the Forecast Items to Create section check Known Items (From Scheduled Txns). Confirm that From Register Data is checked in the Create Estimated Amounts section. Click Done, then choose OK to go to the Forecasting–Base Scenario window, shown in Figure 4-10. If your figure looks different than ours, click the Accounts button to confirm that Checking is the only Account selected.

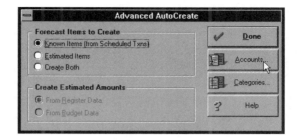

Figure 4-9. The settings in the Advanced AutoCreate window are essential to creating an accurate graph forecasting the Richies' finances.

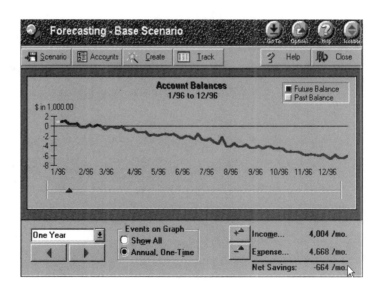

Figure 4-10. The Richies were very surprised to see how much more money they want to spend each month than they earn. If your graph looks different, confirm your graph's date range.

1. Go to the Main menu.
2. Select Forecast.
3. Type ⑤ to choose Selected accounts and press ⎡Enter⎤ to continue.
4. Press ⎡F9⎤ to Select All of the Accounts listed until the word Include is not shown in the right column.
5. Use the arrow keys to highlight Checking then press the spacebar to Include it.
6. Press ⎡Enter⎤ to open the Projected Cash Flow Graph.

Their future prospects don't look very promising, do they? It doesn't require an MBA to see that if Sam and Sally expect to create any wealth, they will need to satisfy their champagne tastes with a generic soda budget. We will discuss managing cash flow in Chapter 5.

Forecasting has a couple of interesting options that are beyond the scope of this book. We are confident that your knowledge of how Quicken works is broad enough for you to explore Forecasting's other features on your own.

Q-TIP

If your version of Quicken lacks a Calendar, you can simulate many of the features. Set up Scheduled Transactions for a dummy Account, i.e., a Checking Account called Dummy Account. Use your real checking Account's current balance as the Dummy

Account's opening balance. Set all of the transactions to schedule without prompting. Turn on Quicken's Billminder if it is off. Exit Quicken. Reset your computer's system date to some point in the future, say six months from now. Start Quicken. Billminder will automatically enter all of the Scheduled Transactions for the Dummy Account into the Register. Scroll through the Register while you keep an eye on the Balance column.

THE CASH FLOW SECRET

"Eat, drink, and be merry, for tomorrow may never come." This is the philosophy on which many individuals base their cash flow management priorities. These people pay little attention to their future since, after all, they may not be here to enjoy it!

All of us need to enjoy life, but we must be careful not to spend our future prosperity on today's pleasures. In my mind, the purpose of cash flow management is to create a stable stream of money that we can use to purchase our future prosperity. A survey of 65-year-old Americans that I once saw found that only two percent were financially independent. Twenty-three percent were still working, while 45 percent had to depend on their relatives for at least a portion of their finances. Almost a third of those surveyed, 30 percent, were forced to depend on charity for a portion of the financial resources required for survival.

My goal is to live in financial freedom when I am 65 but to achieve that freedom long before then! (I'm now in my mid-30s.) To which class of 65-year-olds will you belong?

Several surveys I've seen show that financial security during retirement concerns more Americans than any other financial issue. As a rule of thumb, many people estimate that they will need about 80 percent of their pre-retirement income to maintain their pre-retirement lifestyle as retirees. Today's retirees are healthier and living longer than ever before. Their expectations are rising, also. Ask yourself what kind of retirement lifestyle you desire. Do you want to travel, see the world, and take cruises? Do you plan to spend more time on the links, or less? Will you have grandchildren who you want to spoil a bit—after all, that is one way to get back at your kids for the grief they caused you as teenagers!

Almost every United States resident who works for a living either has Social Security taxes deducted from his or her paychecks or pays them along with federal income taxes each year. (Certain government and railroad employees have a separate pensions and do not participate in the Social Security system.) Are you depending on Social Security to provide for your retirement? Recent estimates show that low-wage earners may collect as much as 60 percent of their retirement income from Social Security. Higher-wage earners (in the $50,000 per year range) can expect the government to provide less than 30 percent of their retirement needs. A recent study by the Social Security Administration found that the average person collects 36 percent of their retirement income from Social Security. The balance of post-retirement income comes from savings and investments (24%), earnings (18%), pension plans (18%), and other sources (4%). These figures are for today's retirees. What do you expect from the government? Table 4-1 shows the history of the maximum monthly benefits available to 65-year-old retirees. Remember, most people do not qualify for maximum benefits!

In 1935, during the Great Depression, the government started the Social Security Administration. The original intent was to provide funds for supplemental retirement income. The government sold Social Security to the public as a "trust fund"—put your money in today and the government will give it back to you with interest when you retire. Many people have come to anticipate that Social Security will provide all of their retirement income. The original intent of Social Security was to act as a safety net to protect Americans from retiring into poverty. Figures 4-11 and 4-12 illustrate this point. Most current retirees will collect the amount they paid in taxes, if not

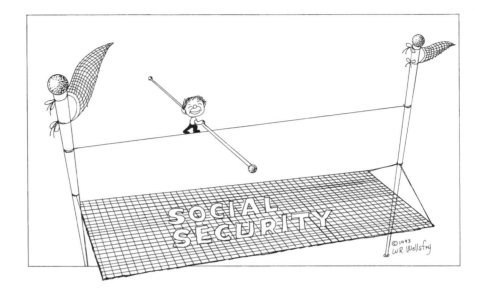

Figure 4-11. Social Security was originally intended to act as a safety net.

Figure 4-12. Today, many people erroneously believe that Social Security will provide adequately for them during their golden years.

Year	Maximum Monthly Retirement Benefits at Age 65
1996	$1,248
1995	1,199
1994	1,143
1993	1,128
1992	1,088
1991	1,022
1990	975
1989	899
1988	838
1987	789
1986	760

Table 4-1. Source: Social Security Administration

more, in retirement benefits before they die (based on current life expectancies).

What about the rest of us younger citizens? The Social Security Administration and other groups have produced studies that show the number of workers per Social Security recipient has been steadily declining. Experts expect this trend will continue or even accelerate as we live longer than our predecessors. As the retired population increases, the number of wage earners per retiree decreases. It really gets scary when you consider that a larger percentage of U.S. residents are on public assistance, food stamps, welfare, etc. than at any time in our country's history!

The number of people collecting benefits and amount of benefits being collected is mind-boggling. In October 1995, I visited the Social Security Administration's web site (http://www.ssa.gov) and learned that about one in six U.S. residents, 42.9 million recipients, collected some form of Social Security at the end of 1994. A total of $284.1 **Billion** in various benefits were paid in 1994 ($23.68 **Billion**/month). That was a significant increase from the $248.6 **Billion** paid in 1990 ($20.72 **Billion**/month). The Social Security Administration's executive summary of their annual report states that the total trust-fund assets were slightly higher than $413 billion at the end of 1994. That sounds like a lot of money, but, at 1994 rates, there were only 17.4 months' benefits payments available in the Social Security Trust Funds! No wonder I affectionately call this the Social **In**-Security System in my financial planning seminars.

Don't consider my concern about the future solvency of the system to come from an extreme viewpoint. The Trustees for the Social Security and Medicare Trust funds agree and have the inside information to substantiate their concerns. The Need For Action: During the past 5 years there has been a trend of deterioration in the long-range financial condition of the Social Security and Medicare programs and an acceleration in the projected dates of exhaustion in the related trust funds. To some extent, this has been predictable because when doing annual 75-year projections, an additional deficit year in the 2060s is being added with each new projection. But to some extent, the increasingly adverse projections have come from unforeseen events and from the absence of prompt action in response to clear warnings that changes are necessary. These adverse trends can be expected to continue and indicate the possibility of a future retirement crisis as the U.S. population begins to age rapidly. We urge that concerted action be taken promptly to address the critical public policy issues raised by the financing projections for these programs.[1]

Anyone born after 1960, including yours truly, will be unable to collect full retirement benefits until they reach age 67. Also, consider that the government is increasing the amount of earned income that is subject to

---

1. Social Security Administration, *Status of the Social Security and Medicare Programs: A Summary of the 1995 Annual Reports*, accessed from the Social Security Administration web site on October 23, 1995.

Social Security taxes each year. In 1992, the first $55,500 of earned income was subject to 7.65 percent combined Social Security and Medicare taxes. That amounted to $4,207.50 taken out of your paycheck. Your employer paid an additional $4,207.50 in matching contributions on your wages! For 1996, the Social Security wage base is $62,700, for a combined Social Security and Medicare tax bill of $4,796.55 for the employee, and again your employer pays a matching amount. Under current law, all covered employees pay an additional 1.65 percent on **all** wages earned in excess of the Social Security wage base (and people wonder why their boss can't raise their pay). See Table 4-2 for more information.

If you think that is heavy taxation, you must remember that you also will pay state and federal income taxes on your gross wages—the amount you earn BEFORE your employer deducts Social Security and Medicare taxes from your wages! The self-employed have the greater privilege of paying both the employee's and employer's shares.

Even with such a huge chunk of our pay going to fund Medicare, the 1995 annual report on the system states that Medicare will run out of money in seven short years. The report stresses the need for Medicare reform:

> We strongly recommend that the crisis presented by the financial condition of the Medicare Trust Funds be urgently addressed on a comprehensive basis, including a review of the program's financing methods, benefit provisions, and delivery mechanisms...[2]

The first Republican Congress elected in 40 years and the Republican-controlled Senate have taken this bull by the horns and, as we went to press, passed reforms that aim to create a sound Medicare system for years to come. Entrenched and ultra-left-wing special interest groups are battling for the status

2. *ibid.*

quo. I agree with Paul Harvey, who said that the government provides some useful services, but none of the services are worth enough to go into debt.

That's not the end of the story. When you retire, the government will likely pay you back only a portion of what it took out of your after-tax pay. Then it will require you to pay income taxes again—remember that you pay into the system with after-tax dollars, on an ever-increasing share of your "benefits!" Social Security benefits were first subject to income taxes in 1984. Effective January 1, 1994, 85 percent of the Social Security benefits of "wealthy" Americans are subject to income taxes. The "wealthy" are singles with $32,000 and couples with $44,000 in provisional income, as described in Chapter 6. This is an increase from the prior level, taxing 50 percent of Social Security benefits.

Even with increasing Social Security and Medicare taxes on wages, the government predicts that the Social Security Trust Fund will be broke around the year 2015. If you look a little closer, the only real assets the Social Security Trust Fund owns are U.S. Government Bonds. The United States of America is about $4 trillion in debt now. How confident are you that the government will pay adequate returns on the Social Security Trust Fund investments to keep the system afloat?

Signs of tax relief are here at last. Most of the Republicans elected to Congress in 1994 signed the Republican *Contract with America*. After the Republicans won majorities in the House of Representatives and the Senate, Republican leaders made a number of promises. As we went to press, these leaders were sending legislation to President Clinton to cut our income taxes, send billions of dollars in federal programs to state and local governments to administer, and phase out the increased taxes on Social Security enacted in the Clinton Tax Act of 1993.

MONEY MATTERS

You can receive a projection of your retirement benefits by contacting the Social Security (contact information is available in

Year	Maximum Wages Taxed	Employee & Employer Tax Rate (% Each)	Total Employee/ Employer Taxes (Maximum)
1996	$62,700 Social Security in excess of 62,700 Medicare	7.65 1.45	$9,593.10 unlimited
1995	61,200 Social Security in excess of 61,200 Medicare	7.65 1.45	9,363.60 unlimited
1994	60,000 in excess of 60,000	7.65 1.45	9,180.00 unlimited
1993	57,600 57,600 to 135,000	7.65 1.45	8,812.80 11,057.40
1992	55,500 130,200	7.65 1.45	8,491.50 10,657.80
1991	53,400 125,500	7.65 1.45	8,170.20 10,261.10
1990	51,300	7.65	7,848.90
1989	48,000	7.51	7,209.60
1988	45,000	7.51	6,759.00
1987	43,800	7.15	6,263.40
1986	42,000	7.15	6,006.00

Table 4-2. This table shows a brief history of rising Social Security wage levels and tax rates, courtesy of the Social Security Administration.

Appendix B). Ask for form SSA-7004, "Request for Statement of Earnings Card." When the card arrives, complete it and mail it back to Social Security, which will prepare a report of your earnings on which you paid Social Security taxes. The report will also project your future retirement benefits, disability benefits, and how much money your family will receive if you die.

You should "audit" your Social Security earnings records at least once every three years by following the instructions in the above Money Matters. You may discover that the government has not included all of your earnings in its computer. If you do not dispute a mistake within three years, they may not correct it. An error could result in a reduction in the potential retirement, disability or survivors' benefits that you or your family may eventually collect (contact information is available in Appendix B).

Are you or is someone you know about ready to celebrate a 65th birthday? You must contact Social Security within three months of your birthday and sign up for Medicare, or you will have the privilege of paying higher Medicare premiums for the rest of your life. Call Social Security at (800) 772-1213. Ask for the Medicare booklet, Publication No. 05-10043.

You can trust the government to keep its promises to you, the same way it fulfilled its promises to Native Americans.

If the government is unable to provide for your retirement, who will? It will either be you, your family, or charity. I do not expect that those reading this book would choose anyone but themselves to be responsible for their own future financial well-being.

The best way to prepare for your own fiscal future is to begin setting aside a little bit of money each month. As you accumulate little by little, invest, and wisely manage what you put away, your savings will grow tremendously.

The best time to plant a shade tree is twenty years ago. You could enjoy its many benefits today if you had. The second best time is today. If you are currently spending everything you make (and then some), the odds are that you will never reach the goal of financial freedom. What you can't do today, you are unlikely to find the strength to accomplish tomorrow.

Let's play pretend for a minute (my three children still watch Mr. Rogers and Barney incessantly, so please forgive me). Your employers are struggling financially but are certain the company will survive and then thrive. They must trim expenses to get through the current rough times. You are a valued employee and well-liked by management. They hate to do it, but they want to give you the choice. You are free to go find another job or to accept a ten percent cut in pay and maybe work a little harder so that the company can survive. If you are willing to stick with them, they will share a portion of the future profits with you! What would you choose? Almost everyone would choose to continue with their current position if they thought the company would succeed. In these troubling times, many have no choice. Some people couldn't find another job if they wanted a new one.

I propose you do the same thing with your personal cash flow. Set aside a tenth of your income today, so that you can thrive financially tomorrow. What if you have to take a ten percent pay cut? What can you cut from your budget? Could you pack a lunch to take to work one or two more days a week? Do you really get your money's worth from cable TV? Where is the fat in your budget?

The average family that consults with me for financial planning can cut five percent without even noticing it. Most can cut ten without much trouble. Many could go to fifteen or even twenty percent, if necessary.

What are we going to do with this newly freed cash? At first, I recommend that it be devoted to paying off your consumer debt—auto loans, credit cards, signature loans—as well as beginning an investment program. Use half to pay off your debt and half to invest. After you repay your liabilities, use the entire ten percent to build your wealth!

Some people struggle with reducing their debt. Give yourself six months to apply half of the tenth you are setting aside toward reducing your debts. Still, some people can not learn to live on 90 percent of their income. If you are continuing to charge more than you can repay without using your investment money, then we need to adjust the strategy. Put all of your tenth toward investments—at least your investments will offset some of your debt.

We discussed how to pay off your debt in Chapter 2. In Chapter 5, we will discuss strategies to increase your cash flow by managing your income and expenses wisely. We will launch our discussion of investments, one of my favorite topics, in Chapter 6.

PRACTICAL APPLICATIONS

The actions the government takes or refuses to take have tremendous impact your future prosperity. I recommend that you begin to actively inform your elected representatives of your position on various issues.

For example, do you know that the government is using your Social Security "trust funds" to make disability payments to thousands of substance abusers and incarcerated criminals because they are unable to earn a living to support themselves? Is that how you want your "trust funds" spent? If you want the system to be able to provide any benefits to you when you retire, you need to take action today. Let your voice be heard in your elected representative's offices. Write or phone your Congressional Representative and Senators today. Refuse to reelect any representative, conservative or liberal, who votes to squander your hard-earned tax dollars. They are not wasting the government's dollars—they are wasting YOUR MONEY!

Contact your Congressional Representative at:

   (Your Congressperson's Name)

   U.S. House of Representatives

   Washington, DC 20915

   (202) 224-3121

Contact your Senator at:

   (Your Senator's Name)

   U.S. Senate

   Washington, DC 20510

   (202) 224-3121

Additional contact information, including World Wide Web addresses, is in Appendix B. Your involvement in the political process will stimulate your mind and maybe raise your blood pressure a bit.

Most people know that the United States tax code attempts to level the economic playing field by imposing higher taxes on those who achieve greater financial success. This is known as a progressive tax system—progressively taxing higher incomes at higher tax rates.

At first glance, Social Security appears to treat everyone equally. The 7.65 percent combined Social Security/Medicare tax rate is the same for employees earning $12,000 or $62,000 per year. Most people do not realize that the Social Security system is also progressive. Lower wages accrue greater benefits than higher wages.

Congress created a system that rewards wage earners with lower benefits for each dollar in taxes paid as wages increase. Social Security uses a formula to determine your Primary Insurance Amount, PRI. In 1994, 90 percent of the first $422 in monthly earning accrued future benefits. Thirty-two percent of the next $2,123 in monthly earning wages accrued benefits. Only 15 percent of the amount in excess of $2,545 (up to the maximum wage base, shown in Table 4-1) accrued benefits. The result is that someone earning $4,000 per month doesn't receive ten times the benefits of someone earning $400 per month. The bottom line is that each dollar in taxes paid doesn't result in equivalent benefits—the result is an invisible, progressive tax on an unsuspecting populace.

The story doesn't end here. When you retire, the same system penalizes you by reducing your trust fund benefits if your retirement wages exceed a fairly low threshold. Furthermore, as

we discussed earlier in this chapter, a portion of your benefits are subject to income taxes when your taxable income is "too high."

Take time to use the Financial Calendar and Quicken's other tools to manage you money properly. It will take awhile to initially set up Quicken, but it will certainly be worthwhile in the long run.

Take a few minutes to call Social Security or hop on the World Wide Web and get a Request for Statement of Earnings Card (http://www.ssa.gov). Fill it out, send it in, and in a couple of weeks you will have an estimate from the government of your future Social Security retirement income. That should motivate you to get serious about planning and investing for your own retirement!

Now that you have your cash flow scheduled on the Calendar. How can you manage it better? Chapter 5 will give you a few ideas.

CHAPTER 5

CASH FLOW CONSERVATION

In Chapters 3 and 4, you learned the mechanics Quicken offers to help manage cash flow. In this chapter, you will learn how to manage cash flow in a practical manner. We will complete this pragmatic discussion with a few tips and tricks for outfoxing the financial foxes—your friendly bankers!

As discussed in Chapter 4, the reason to manage cash flow is to create a stable stream of excess income to invest for the future. I don't know anyone who wants to retire with a lower standard of living than they have while they're working. Most Americans consider preparation for retirement their primary investment goal.

In addition to creating cash flow for investment, you probably want to manage your cash flow to increase your savings. Saving is setting aside money that you intend to spend in the future. It can be in the near or more distant future, but it's definitely money you intend to spend, not invest. Our investments are funds we intend to accumulate. The goal is to create enough wealth to live off the income that the accumulated assets generate. The ultimate goal is an increasing stream of retirement income during the golden years.

Another distinct advantage of managing cash flow is that it enables you to live better with less money. It may seem strange, but it is true. If you plan your purchases and expenditures, you will pay more attention to sales and getting the most from the money that you spend. By planning in advance, you have the opportunity to shop for bargains. There is a distinct advantage to not waiting until the last minute to make purchases at the price *du jour*.

Yet another benefit of proper cash flow management is reduction and eventual elimination of debt. When debt is gone, all of the money now paid in principal and interest will be available to create wealth or increase your standard of living. When you repay your debts, you will notice a big difference in your cash flow.

REVIEW YOUR CASH FLOW

How did your cash flow graph look when you completed Chapter 4? Did you run out of money before the month ran out, or were you still solvent when your next paycheck arrived? It is absolutely astonishing how many very intelligent, well-paid people, in one- or two-income families spend more money than they make each month. While Johnny Carson was still host of *The Tonight Show*, a Hollywood star once lamented, "I used to dream of making the money I can't survive on today!"

We saw how the Financial Calendar allows you to create a basic graph showing daily Account levels. We also learned to use Forecasting, which gives even more detail than the Financial Calendar's graph. Quicken also creates income and expense, or cash flow, graphs that give even more historical detail information than Forecasting does for projections. For a unique twist, we will show you how to project your income and expenses using these historical cash flow graphs. Follow these steps to create a three-month graph of the Richies' projected income and expenses, as scheduled on the Calendar. DOS instructions follow.

1. Set your computer's date to **4/1/96**.
2. Start Quicken. If you were already in Quicken, load the Richies' data file. If you are already in that file, close the file and then reload the Richie file. Step 3 will not work properly unless you do this.

Q-TIP

If you want to make projections using your own data, we recommend that you copy your data to a temporary file and use the temporary file to do your projections. Windows users will find the copy function by choosing File from the menu-bar. Select File Operations, then Copy. In DOS, choose File Activities from the main menu, then File Copy.

 Record

3. When you first load the Richie file after changing the system date, the Scheduled Transactions Due window appears. Figure 5-1 shows an example of the Scheduled Transactions Due window. We want to post the transactions to a Register by clicking the Record button. Since there are a number of transactions, it would take a long time to record each one separately. Fortunately, the Windows version of Quicken uses common Windows mouse actions that allow us to select more than one transaction at once. Unfortunately, the final copy of Quicken 5 that we received limits the number of transactions that appear in the Scheduled Transactions Due window to 50, so we will need to repeat the following process a couple times, unless Intuit removed this feature from your copy.

   To select all of the transactions, confirm that the first entry is highlighted. Use the scroll bar to the right of the transaction list to scroll to the bottom of the list. Press (Shift) then click the last entry

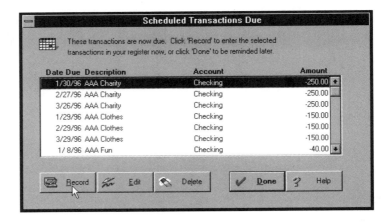

Figure 5-1. The Scheduled Transactions Due window assists you in entering scheduled transactions into the appropriate Registers. You have an opportunity to edit each transaction before it is entered.

on the list with your primary mouse button to highlight all of the transactions due. (There may be times when you don't want to highlight all of the transactions due. You can hold down Ctrl while clicking individual transactions to select or deselect them.) After the transactions are highlighted, click the Record button.

After the first set of Scheduled Transactions Due properly record, you will notice a flashing ToDo sign in the lower-left corner of your screen. Click ToDo to open the Quicken Reminders window, pictured in Figure 5-2. You can also check for Reminders from the Activities menu. Choose the Scheduled Transactions Due... button open another window of Scheduled Transactions Due. Repeat this process until no more transactions are due.

4. Now we are ready to graph the Richies' income and expenses for January through March. Go to HomeBase. Choose Graphs from the Reports & Graphs graphic to open the Create Graph window. You could also use the Graphs icon to open this window. If your iconbar

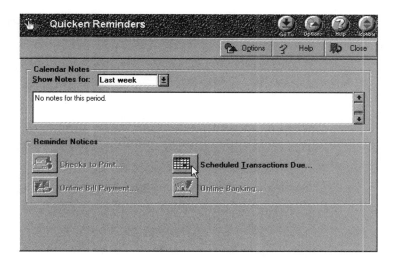

Figure 5-2. The Quicken Reminders window acts like a tickler file and allows you to retrieve your Scheduled Transaction Due list.

does not have a Graphs icon, use the Options icon to get to the Iconbar button, which opens the Customize Iconbar window. Choose New, then select Open Graphs from the list of available icons.

5. Your first task in the Create Graph window is to set the graph dates from **1/96** to **3/96**, as shown in Figure 5-3.

6. Choose Income and Expense Graph in the Graph to Create section of the Create Graph window.

7. Click the Accounts button in the Income and Expense Filters section to open the Select Accounts to Include window.

8. Click the Clear All button to deselect all of the Accounts. Mark the Checking Account as the only Account to include, then click OK. Remember, we ran all of the cash flow through the Checking Account to simplify the process in Chapter 4.

9. Click the Create button to generate the Income and Expense Graph windows.

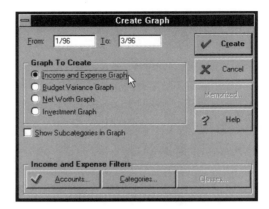

Figure 5-3. Set the dates to graph. Choose Income and Expense Graph, then click the Create button in the Create Graph window.

10. The Income and Expense Graph window opens, as seen in Figure 5-4. The default settings draw two graphs in this window. The Monthly Income and Expenses graph is on top. It is a bar chart of total income and expenses for each month. The Expense Comparison graph is a pie chart showing expenses broken down by category. The legend lists ten expense categories, plus Other, and the percentage of total expenses that each category contains. If you have more than ten categories, like the Richies, click the Next 10 button, near the lower left corner, to update the legend.

1. Set your computer's date to 4/1/96.
2. When you open the Richies' file, or when you go to a Register if the Richies' file was that last one you used, the To Do List for File Richie window appears. The To Do List indicates that there are Scheduled Transactions due.
3. Press [Enter] to open the Select Scheduled Items to Record window. The far right column in this window is the Action column. Press [F9] until Record appears beside the transactions in the Action column. Press [Enter] to record the

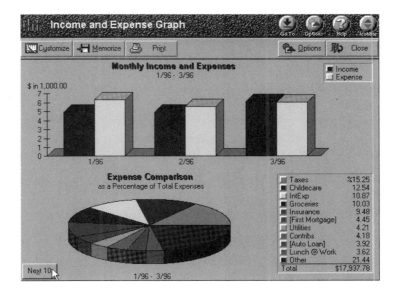

Figure 5-4.   The Richies' projected expenses regularly exceed their income, as shown in these graphs. Your graph should be similar to this one but may vary if you did not enter all of the Richies' transactions.

scheduled transactions due. If you do not want to record all of the transactions in the future, highlight the transaction and press the spacebar to change the action to Defer, Edit, or Skip.

4. Go to a Register, then select Graph from the menu-bar. Choose Income and Expense from the Graph menu. Select Monthly Income and Expense to open the Monthly Income and Expense window.

5. Change the dates to 1/1/96 through 3/31/96. Press F9 to open the Income and Expense Filter window.

6. Skip to the final item in the window, and select S for Use Current/All/Selected accounts. Press Enter to open the Select Accounts to Include window.

7. Press F9 to deselect all of the Accounts and then choose Checking by highlighting it and pressing the spacebar. Press Enter several times to create the graph.

8. To create the Expense Composition Graph (Expense Comparison Graph in Windows) click on the Expenses box in the legend. If you do not have a mouse, repeat steps 4 through 7, except choose Expense Composition instead of Monthly Income and Expense in step 4.

In Windows, you can change the options for graphs so that Quicken draws each graph in a separate window. Use the Options button in the Income and Expense Graph window to open the Graph Options window. Check Create All Graphs in Separate Windows. Close the Graph Options window and the Income and Expense Graph window. Recreate the graphs from HomeBase to draw them in separate windows. Notice there is also an option for the graph to be drawn 2D, which is faster.

After you view the graphs, you may find the Cash Flow Report even more helpful. DOS users have the advantage here. They simply click the Report button near the lower-right corner of their graphs. In Windows, create a Cash Flow Report of the income and expenses we just graphed using these steps:

1. Click the Reports icon on the iconbar to open the Create Report window.

2. In the Create Report window, select the Home tab. Cash Flow report should be highlighted. The beginning date is already **1/1/96**. Change the ending date to **3/31/96**. The completed screen is shown in Figure 5-5. Click on the Customize button at the bottom of the window to open the Customize Cash Flow Report window when you finish.

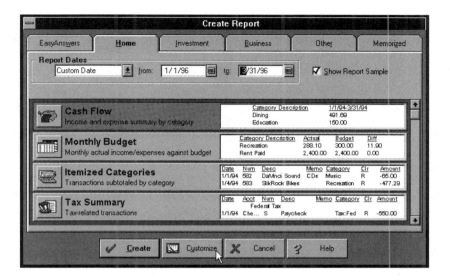

Figure 5-5. Use the above settings in the Create Report window to generate a Cash Flow Report.

3. In the Customize section of the Customize Cash Flow Report window, confirm the report dates you selected select the Accounts tab. Quicken marks all of the Bank, Cash, and Credit Card Accounts as the default setting. Click the Clear All button once to unmark all of the Accounts. Click on Checking at the top of the Account list to mark it, as shown in Figure 5-6. When you finish, click Create to open the Cash Flow Report window.

4. The Cash Flow Report is much longer than the window, as shown in Figure 5-7. You may wonder why the Richies' income is so high on the report. Remember that we entered their gross pay as their income and also entered all of their payroll deductions in the Splits window. Thus the net pay ended up in the Register. Please notice that the higher income is offset by the deductions in the Cash Flow Report. Use the scroll bar to view the report. If you are satisfied that the report shows the information you need, click the Print button to

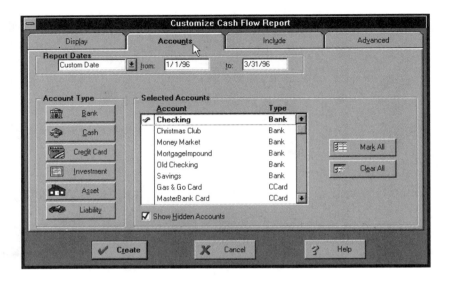

Figure 5-6. Customize the Cash Flow Report to only include Checking Account transactions.

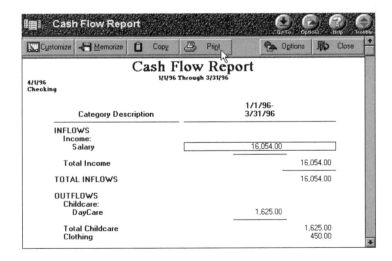

Figure 5-7. View the report by moving the scroll bar on the right side of the window. Click the Print button to print.

print. To tailor the report to your needs, click the Customize button. The Print Report window is self-explanatory.

Like many of us, the Richies live on the brink of financial calamity. What would they do if their home or car needed major repairs? Will their furnishings and appliances last forever? They know they would be in deep financial trouble if they spent all the money scheduled on the Financial Calendar. As intelligent people, they know they must make adjustments to their expectations to survive and thrive financially. They must cut out the excess spending and even cut back on some of the things they really enjoy. They know things will be tight for a while, but once things are under control, they will live better on less. They will attain their goals if they persevere. Will you?

Even if you're coming out even at the end of the month, are you investing for your future prosperity? Are you saving money to replace items that wear out, such as your car? Will you have enough money available to pay for those items with cash? Are you the type of person who saves for a vacation and spends cash on it, or do you charge your vacation and take the following year to pay it off? If you are the latter type, perhaps you would consider a less expensive vacation this year and use the money you normally pay off your travels with to build a vacation fund for next year. If you are not saving for your future, you certainly need to make some adjustments to your cash flow.

How do you go about reviewing your cash flow? First of all, you need to keep track of the money you're spending. That is why you probably bought Quicken—to keep track of your cash. Enter all of your checks and deposits into your Quicken Registers. Enter all of your cash transactions in your cash Register. It is amazing how much cash people spend, even in today's cashless society. Credit cards and ATM transactions are extremely important to enter into your Registers, too. When you use your ATM card, you want to use the Cash Account as the category in your bank Account's Register.

Q-TIP If your bank charges for ATM transactions or visits to a live teller, don't forget to record those costs in your Register. Many people live so close to the edge that a few minor fees could cause overdrafts which result in additional fees. Our bank doesn't charge us monthly fees and pays interest with a $600 minimum balance. We maintain the minimum balance by adding a Minimum Balance transaction in our Registers. We simply date the entry for the last day of the current year with the Payee being Minimum Balance. The Account List always shows us how much spendable money remains in our Account. The current date in the Register always shows the actual Account balance.

Credit cards are a problem area for many Americans. Few people keep track of how much money they spend on their credit cards until their bills arrive in the mail. Some people don't even review their bills for accuracy. Whenever you charge something on a credit card, put the receipt in your pocket or purse and record it in the proper Credit Card Account in Quicken. If you record all of your transactions, you will always know exactly where you are, from a cash flow perspective.

After you record your cash, credit card, and checking account transactions for one month, you will get a pretty good idea of how you spend your money. Most expenditures occur sometime during the course of a month. Some items only occur once per quarter, six months, or year, but most events happen once each month.

Do you set aside money for annual or semi-annual events? If you pay your auto insurance semi-annually, are you setting aside one-sixth of the premium every month so that the money is available when it's time to pay the premium? You could receive substantial discounts by paying your insurance premiums annually or semi-annually instead of monthly. Most insurance companies charge between six and eight percent more for monthly premiums than for annual premiums. Many insurers also add a one-or two-dollar billing charge per payment.

Most people have multiple insurance policies with different insurance companies to cover their car, home or apartment, boat, and other property. It is often possible to save ten to fifteen percent on your insurance bill by consolidating your property and casualty coverage with one reliable carrier.

Parents with children living away from home can often benefit from lower auto insurance rates when the children only occasionally drive the family vehicles. The prime example is a college student living on an out-of-town campus who only returns home for school holidays. Even when the child takes a family vehicle to school with him, the family can often significantly reduce its premiums when the school is in an area with lower rates than the area where the parent's home is located.

Unlike a hypothetical situation such as the Richies' finances, it is difficult to limit a real financial situation to one Account. When you create your own financial reports and graphs, include all of your Bank, Cash, and Credit Card Accounts that have income or expenses.

Remember, every dollar you save is a dollar you can invest. Another way to look at it is that every dollar you save is $1.50 to $2.00 less income you must earn. As you enter all of your transactions into Quicken, begin to optimize your cash flow and form new spending habits.

CREATE AND OPTIMIZE A NEW SPENDING PLAN

Change does not occur without reason. You must desire change for constructive change to occur, otherwise the events in your life propel you along. You must be proactive, not reactive, to achieve financial success. One of the most important steps is to grab the cash flow tiger by the tail and tame it. You need a spending plan. Then you need to optimize the plan to maximize your benefits. This will take time. You cannot expect to sit down and say, "This is my spending plan," and have everything go perfectly from the first day. This process will take you months, or even years, to master. You will experience setbacks. You will need to revise and optimize again and again. The first step is to establish goals.

ESTABLISH GOALS

Goals are essential to achieving financial results. If you don't have a goal, you're sure to achieve it! If you have a goal and you set it high, even if you don't meet it, you will more than likely be better off than if you never established the goal in the first place.

There are two types of goals: long-term and short-term. Set long-term goals first. What are your long-term goals? Have you written them down? After you set each long-term goal, establish a series of short-term goals that work together. This will enable you to attain the long-term goal.

After setting long-term goals and their attendant short-term goals, many people want to set short-term goals for short-term desires. Consider how these near-term desires fit into your long-range plans. If satisfying an immediate desire will take cash you need to meet a long-term goal, you must decide what is more important. Watch out— satisfying immediate desires impedes many people's progress on the road to riches.

Studies prove that Americans are more concerned with financing their retirement than with any other financial issue. What are your retirement goals? How long do you have until you want to retire? How much income will you need? What other long-term goals do you have? In Chapter 1, you learned how to use Quicken's Financial Planners. Use the planners to determine how much it will cost to finance your retirement and meet other financial goals.

Set reasonable, achievable goals. Set short-term goals, goals as short as a day, a week, or a month. Keep your short-term goals under two or three months. Make them achievable and measurable. If you can't measure your goals, there is a lower probability of success. As you meet your goals, you will have a feeling of accomplishment and success. As you establish a pattern of success, set higher but still achievable goals. In time, you will find yourself achieving results you would have previously considered unattainable. Continue this process for the rest of your life.

What are your short-term financial goals? Which credit card will you pay off first? How much additional principal will you send in with your mortgage payment this month? When will you be ready to start investing? How will you pay for your next computer upgrade?

In addition to setting goals, you need dreams. A dream is a goal that is beyond your actual reach—a goal that you do not necessarily expect to actually accomplish. Dreams are long-term. If you shoot for the moon in the short-term and miss, you will tend to become discouraged. You can reach your dreams one step at a time. Determine how you can break down each of your dreams into a series of attainable goals. It may take longer than you initially planned, but you can make your dreams come true.

Several years ago my wife and I determined that we want to live a debt-free life. We found it necessary to acquire a mortgage on our home, though. We originally set a dream goal of paying off the mortgage in four years. Four years have past and although the house still has a mortgage, we've managed to pay down a significant portion of the loan. We broke the dream into a series of simpler steps. The first step was to finance the mortgage for only 15 years instead of the usual 30. That cuts the normal 30-year time to attaining the goal in half. The 15-year payment is a couple hundred dollars a month more than a 30-year loan. The second step was paying extra principal each month.

How has it worked so far? We bought our first home about five years ago. Sure, there were one or two tight months where the mortgage company only received the minimum payment. Except for the one or two tight months, we have always paid extra principal on the loan and several chunks of principal were quite large. According to Quicken's Loan

Planner, the minimum required payment will pay the loan in full in about six years! By continuing to pay extra each month, we can realistically pay the house off in three or four more years.

Meanwhile, our family became larger and we outgrew that house. We just bought another house. Unfortunately, real property prices have plummeted in California. We never would have thought that real estate values in our area would drop so much. Even financial planners like myself have foggy crystal balls. Since they plunged, we are renting the house out until prices recover. The depressed housing values in our area would cause us to lose some serious money if we were forced to sell now. The current market did allow us to buy a much larger home in a nicer neighborhood for slightly more than we paid for the old home in 1990. When values recover, we can sell the old house and should be able to use the proceeds to pay off most of our new home's mortgage! Then we will realize one of our major financial goals—total freedom from debt— within a few years!

SETTING PRIORITIES

Once you establish goals, you need to set everyday priorities.

It is very important to maintain balance in your approach to managing cash flow. If we only play and indulge ourselves, we will not have any excess cash flow to invest. If we do not allow ourselves to enjoy life, we'll end up like Scrooge in Dickens' *A Christmas Carol*. Neither end of the spectrum is healthy. We need to find a happy medium. It's up to each family or each individual to determine what is healthy for them.

When you examine your monthly expenses, see how they fit within your priorities. Prioritize your cash flow. If you have only $1,500 per month, how will you spend it? Most people tend to make their house or rent payment first. Then they pay their bills and buy groceries. Finally, they spend their discretionary money.

If you want to create wealth, make it a high priority to set aside ten percent of your gross pay, or at least ten percent of your net pay, *before* you pay anyone else. Some people call this the Ten Percent Solution. We will discuss this again in Chapter 7. If ten percent is too much today, start smaller. Perhaps you can invest only two or three percent now. As the months progress, increase your investing by an additional percent each month or two. Determine a reasonable amount of money to save each month. Go back to Chapter 1, review how to use the Financial Planners for savings and investments, and do some projections as to how that amount of money, compounded on a monthly basis at a reasonable rate of return, will grow over time. Print out a schedule and tape it to your mirror or somewhere you'll see it every day. After we set our priorities, we need to begin making adjustments in our actual spending patterns.

Before seriously considering an investment program, make certain you are standing on a firm financial foundation. Part of that foundation is having funds available for opportunities and crises that can arise in our lives. Many people want to jump into investing. It is glamorous to invest. If you do not have adequate cash reserves, "invest" ten percent of your income into a reserve fund. As your reserves begin to build, slowly begin investing a portion of the ten percent. When you have adequate reserves, invest the full ten percent for your future.

A lot of people call these savings "cash reserves," but an important fact that many people who attain wealth begin to understand early in their quest is that your cash reserves don't have to be cash. You can use a line of credit as your opportunity fund or your crisis fund. If you have a number of credit cards with no outstanding balances, you can use the credit available on those cards to meet opportunities and needs in a crisis situation.

It is not wise to have all your cash reserves in the form of a line of credit because you can lose your line of credit. Your bank can take away your credit card. You can lose a line of credit very easily, especially if the institution that you're dealing with falls on hard times, itself. At times, lenders review all of their accounts and sometimes require new credit information. It is possible, especially if you are in a position of financial weakness, that the bank will limit or remove your access to funds.

Many people are unsure how much money they should have for an opportunity or a crisis. The rule of thumb that most financial planners use is that you should have between three and six months' expenses on hand to meet those needs. Now, the term "expenses" is very important. Some people spend more money than they make. Most people have certain periods in their life when they spend more money than they make. Make sure that you have at least three to six months' expenses on hand in case of a crisis or for cash that you could use to seize an opportunity—*Carpe Diem!*

WHAT CAN YOU ADJUST?

Let's look at some of the items you can consider. This is not an inclusive list. We just want to pass on some ideas as you examine your spending habits to determine where you may be able to cut. Don't even overlook the little ways to save some money. Ben Franklin said it well, "Beware of little expenses; a small leak will sink a great ship."

First of all, do you have cable TV? It sounds kind of strange, but I know many people with cash flow problems who refuse to give up their cable. They can't live without their television. Americans waste a tremendous amount of time sitting in front of the television. How much does cable cost each month? Even if it only costs $10 per month, that's $120 per year for the privilege of watching television. You would probably spend less money renting videos every month. And you would probably enjoy the selection more, too.

Where else are you spending money unnecessarily? Do you subscribe to magazines you don't read or could borrow from a friend? Could you cancel the subscriptions and get a refund?

Are you paying more than you should for your auto insurance? Do you have unnecessary auto coverage? Auto insurance differs from state to state. In my state, there are several ways the average driver can save money. Auto insurance policies I've reviewed typically apply ten to twenty percent of the premium to unnecessary items. When was the last time that you shopped around for auto insurance? You should compare rates on your auto insurance at least once a year. It doesn't take long to make a few phone calls.

How much do you spend on life insurance? First, do you have enough life insurance? Most people do not have enough life insurance to cover their survivors' needs if they meet with an untimely demise. Are you buying the right type of insurance for your situation? I firmly believe that there is a place for each type of life insurance. Some people should own term insurance, while others should have cash value policies. Typically, life insurance agents try to persuade you to purchase cash value insurance. Most younger people do not even need life insurance unless they have a family or are planning to start one. They should buy term insurance, because they cannot afford to purchase an adequate amount of coverage with a cash value plan. Read Chapter 6 before you make any life insurance decisions.

Do you have disability insurance? What would happen if you lost your ability to work due to illness or injury? How would you support yourself? Would you become a burden to your family or to society? It is amazing how many people spend $1,000 or more per year to insure their car yet don't consider insuring their ability to earn a living. The potential benefits disability insurance can offer are usually much greater than those offered by auto insurance, yet disability coverage often costs the same or less than car insurance.

What type of lifestyle do you want in the future? What type of image are you trying to project today? Does the image you're trying to project sync with the amount of cash you have to spend? Many young couples, especially career-oriented professionals, try to project an affluent image when they can only afford a middle-class lifestyle. They have champagne tastes but a generic soda budget. This causes trouble for many people.

Another area where people spend a lot of money unnecessarily is eating out. In the last chapter, we scheduled $10 per workday for the Richies to eat lunch out. It is amazing how many people will purchase lunch every day at work. Sure, it's a lot more convenient. The peer pressure is substantial when all of your coworkers go out to lunch. But, how much is it costing you? How much of your future prosperity are you literally eating away? It may be a little bit more trouble to fix yourself a lunch in the morning, but consider the economic benefits.

Housing is another major area where people spend money. Should you reconsider how much money you spend every month on rent or a house payment? Should you move to lower-priced accommodations? Some people even find it best to sell their house and move into a rental while they establish a firm financial foundation.

No matter how well you plan, something unexpected can come along and throw a monkey wrench into the works.

BUDGETS MADE SIMPLE...AND EVEN FUN!

Now that you understand the importance of setting goals and priorities and you have considered what you can adjust in your spending patterns, it is time to commit your plans to an electronic ledger. Quicken has long offered a traditional option to planning your spending—budgeting.

Yes, we really must discuss the awful "B" word—the dreaded budget, before we move on to investments. Whoever made budgets a nasty topic should be shot at dawn. A proper budget is not constraining or painful. You have the advantage of being able to keep records on your income and spending with greater ease than any previous generation in modern history. With the power and ease of Quicken, you can put a budget together in no time flat. If you have been using Quicken a while, it can even create a budget for you. Can it get any easier?

If you are using the Financial Calendar, you already have a budget. You just need to keep it up-to-date. As your expenses change, adjust the entries to reflect reality. If your version of Quicken doesn't include the Calendar, you can use Quicken's budget worksheets. The worksheets are easy to use, but the Calendar allows better control over your cash flow.

 Q-TIP   **If you are using an old version of Quicken that doesn't include the Calendar, you should run to the store today and buy the upgrade. As stated earlier, we recommend the Windows version—especially since DOS development has stopped. The value the Calendar adds to the software is tremendous and well worth the price of upgrading!**

Even without instructions, you should be able to set up a budget in a few minutes. The following DOS and Windows instructions should make budgeting almost irresistible. You may actually **enjoy** budgeting!

  1. Go to HomeBase. Choose the Budgeting graphic to open the Budget worksheet window. DOS users need to choose Activities from a Register menu bar and then choose Set Up Budgets.

 2. Use the Budgets button to open the Manage Budgets window.

3. Budgeting with Quicken works best when you have been using the product for awhile and you have a few months of data entered. Our budgeting example works well with the Richies' data because we took time to automatically enter three months' income and expenses to do Forecasting in Chapter 4. We simply need to Click

 the Create button (in DOS, choose Edit from the menu then Auto-Create All) to open the Create Budget window.

4. Name this budget **Richie Budget 1** and type **The Richies' First Budget** as the Description. Confirm that Autocreate Budget is

marked in the Create Budget Options section, as depicted in Figure 5-8 then press (Enter) or click OK.

5. The Automatically Create Budget window appears. Confirm that your transaction dates are from **1/96** to **12/96** and that Use Monthly Detail is selected in the Amounts section. The completed window should look like Figure 5-9. Choose OK to create the Richies' budget.

6. Quicken creates the Richies' budget, shown in Figure 5-10, based on their past spending patterns in their Registers.

You can edit the numbers Quicken provides to reflect any changes you plan to make to your anticipated spending habits. If you are a new Quicken user, begin filling in the rows and columns in the Budget window with the amounts you plan to spend.

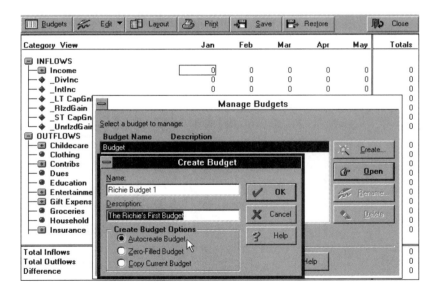

Figure 5-8. You must step through several windows before you can create a budget. This figure was captured with QuickTabs turned off.

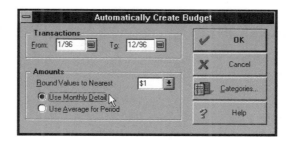

Figure 5-9. To accurately duplicate the Richies' budget, you need to check Use Monthly Detail in the Automatically Create Budget window.

The left column is the list of categories that appear in your Category and Transfer List. If the left column is empty, you should review Chapter 2 and learn about Categories and Transfers before you begin creating a budget. You can change the numbers in the budget by simply

Richie Budget 1 - The Richies' First Budget				
Category View	Jan	Feb	Mar	Totals
INFLOWS				
Income	4958	4958	6138	16054
_DivInc	0	0	0	0
_IntInc	0	0	0	0
_LT CapGnDst	0	0	0	0
_RlzdGain	0	0	0	0
_ST CapGnDst	0	0	0	0
_UnrlzdGain	0	0	0	0
OUTFLOWS				
Childcare	-500	-500	-625	-1625
Clothing	-150	-150	-150	-450
Contribs	-250	-250	-250	-750
Total Inflows	4958	4958	6138	16054
Total Outflows	-5184	-4372	-4789	-14505
Difference	-226	586	1349	1549

Figure 5-10. The Richies' budget only takes about a minute to create and provides a wealth of information.

clicking on one and typing in a new one. You now have enough experience with Quicken that you should be able to learn all you need to know by playing with the budget commands. If that isn't enough, use Quicken's excellent online Help system and manuals.

Without a plan to control your cash flow, financial setbacks could devastate your future plans.

If you prefer less detail on your Budget reports, you can use a handy Quicken feature called SuperCategories. SuperCategories allow you to group individual categories into logical groups. They also eliminate some of the details, which can be good or bad depending on the situation. You can implement SuperCategories by clicking the Super button in the Category & Transfer List window.

DEALING WITH SETBACKS

Everyone has little, unexpected surprises that come into their lives. Many of them cost money. You should plan for these, expect them, and not be discouraged when they occur.

Do you remember Richard and Laura, the first couple we met in Chapter 1? When they began the process of eliminating their consumer debt, it equaled one-half of their gross annual pretax income. In less than two years, they planned to have all of that debt repaid in full. About 18 months in to the plan, Richard called me and said, "Chris, our refrigerator stopped working. It's three days before Christmas and we don't have any money because we spent all of our money on Christmas presents. What should we do?" I asked him, "Well, you paid down your credit cards, right?" He said, "Yes." So I responded, "Charge it, but pay it off as soon as you can." That's exactly what they did.

They had a few other unexpected surprises, like car problems. Even with the unexpected events in their lives, they still were able to repay all of their consumer debt in two years. They had a plan, they stuck to their plan, and they met their goal. Richard and Laura experienced an unexpected benefit of being debt-free. Richard was offered the opportunity of going into business in another city. With no debts weighing them down, the decision was easier and they have moved on to greener pastures! As discussed earlier, almost anyone with consumer debt can pay it off within two years.

The key to dealing with setbacks is knowing that you can overcome them. They may slightly delay you reaching your goal, but stick to the plan and you will eventually succeed! To ensure success, you must evaluate your progress periodically.

EVALUATE YOUR PROGRESS

Most people tend to have problems managing their cash flow because of a lack of discipline. It's just too easy to be lazy. It takes a lot of personal effort to control your spending habits, and it is best if you do this in partnership with your spouse or a friend you can trust. Be accountable to someone. If you go on a spending splurge, you have someone who can say, "I don't think you should do this," or, "Is this really how you want to spend your money?"

What are your weaknesses? I love to drink Slurpees. It sounds silly, but I'm addicted. A frozen slush really hits the spot during Sacramento's scorching summer days. A Slurpee only costs $.96 with tax, but those pennies add up fast. What little things do you buy? Can you economize a bit?

One thing that will help us create a new habit is to monitor our progress, and we should do this on a monthly basis. One of the wonderful things about Quicken is how efficiently it can track our spending. As we saw earlier in this chapter, it is easy to create monthly reports. Every month, you should produce a Cash Flow Report to review your progress for the month and to review where you spent every penny that burned a hole in your pocket.

In addition to the monthly review, you should evaluate your progress quarterly. Each month, you should review your cash flow and see how you're doing. Every three months, you need to review your net worth and tax situation, too. You already know how to create a net-worth report, as described at the end of Chapter 1. Place your monthly cash flow reports and quarterly net-worth printouts in a binder. Compare your new reports with your older ones. It is encouraging to see yourself make progress.

Now let's turn to a few financial tips, tricks, and traps for dealing with financial foxes.

OUTFOXING FINANCIAL FOXES: TIPS, TRICKS, AND TRAPS

Your banker wants you to believe he or she is your friend. This may be true on a personal level—many bankers are very friendly. When it comes to business, however, your banker has one goal—PROFIT! Don't misunderstand, I am all for honest profits. The problem is that many people don't know how the banks are profiting from them. With a little effort, you can keep some of the precious dollars the bank is so easily transferring from your pocket into their coffers!

BANKING TIPS

Over the years, I have banked with a wide range of financial institutions. Each type has advantages and disadvantages. Since various institutions have strengths and weaknesses, I usually keep accounts in a variety of places. The following tips are certainly not comprehensive or without exception.

Almost everyone has a checking account. Your checking account should pay interest and not charge any fees. Does this sound like Utopia? My bank pays more interest on my personal and business checking accounts than the large commercial bank down the street pays on many of its certificates of deposits! I must simply keep a minimum of $600 in each account throughout the month. They charge no account or per-check fees, provide free cashier checks, and even give me a free order of checks when I need a new account. Even though my bank is in a large metropolitan area, the branch manager and tellers know most of the customers by name. If there is a problem with my account, as there seldom is, they call me at home or at the office.

MONEY MATTERS

Banks typically charge fees for business accounts that they do not charge on individual accounts. Banks like to charge per-check deposit fees, per-check written fees, and fees based on your account balance. Over the years, I have had accounts at several banks and types of banking institutions. As a self-employed businessman, I have always been able to set up a personal account dba—doing business as—my business name.

The discipline of maintaining a minimum account balance serves me well in other ways, too. With Quicken tracking my checking balance, I don't bounce checks. That saves me $10 to $15 for each overdraft I avoid. My wife and I need multiple checking accounts because we each have businesses. Therefore, I know that we have cash reserves of at least $600 per account. If things get tight, I can use those reserves to pay my mortgage and put food on the table without tapping other resources.

Where can you find a bank like mine? My bank is a former savings and loan that converted to a savings bank. Technically, savings banks are different than commercial banks, but the difference is unlikely to matter to the average person. Your small, local bank is where you will probably find the best service at the lowest cost. After all, your local bank must survive with large commercial banks as competitors!

Credit unions are popular financial institutions that are owned by their members and typically pay higher interest rates than banks or savings and loans. Credit unions also offer their members many attractive reasons to do business with them, such as lower-than-average loan rates, free or low-cost traveler's checks, and free or low-cost cashier's checks. Many people have their checking accounts at a credit union. I have yet to find a credit union that returns canceled checks to their account holders. This makes credit unions a potentially expensive place to bank. See the accompanying Financial Alert.

FINANCIAL ALERT

Do you get your canceled checks back? If not, you may be in store for a surprise. If the Internal Revenue Service audits you, they can, and often do, require you to provide them with canceled checks or copies of the front and back of your canceled checks. Your friendly banker normally charges for check copies. The average cost in our area is five dollars per check, with no volume discounts. I know of at least one small business owner who spent more than $3,000 in check copying fees for an IRS audit! Save all your canceled checks for a minimum of three years after you file that year's tax return. Canceled checks are important tax documents.

TAX TIP

Credit unions usually call the interest they pay their members "dividends." Report any dividends received from a credit union as "interest," not "dividends," on Schedule B of your federal income tax return. This could save you the trouble of answering a friendly letter from the IRS! Note: Mutual-fund money market funds also pay interest as dividends, but you should report these to the IRS as dividends, not interest. Who said the tax code wasn't confusing?

Many mutual fund families and stock brokerage houses offer money market funds. As a college student in the early '80s, I deposited my interest-deferred student loans into a money market fund and received high double-digit annual interest rates until my tuition was due. My money market checks were from an institution on the opposite side of the U.S., so I earned interest on the money for about a week after paying my school bills while waiting for the check to travel across this great land!

In today's low-interest-rate environment, many money market funds pay almost the same rates as banks. Most money market funds return your canceled checks or at least provide free copies with your monthly statement. My money market fund currently requires a $1,000 deposit to open an account and a $50 minimum balance. It charges no fees and provides free check copies any time I need them. The only potential hitch is that the minimum amount you can write a check for is $250, but it is easy to write a check to your local checking account to pay small bills. This isn't the type of account the average family would use to buy groceries. Not all money market funds are created equal, so check out several before opening an account.

Banks like for you to deposit your money with them, and they really love it when they can lend your money back to you when you use their credit card!

Q·TIP

Unless you are Rip Van Winkle, you have seen all of the hoopla in the media about electronic banking and the Internet. Quicken has offered online transaction processing for some time now through the Quicken credit card and Checkfree Corporation's CheckFree. Intuit is inaugurating its web site (`http//:www.intuit.com`) with the release of Quicken 5 for Windows and is starting its own electronic bill-paying service that will only work with Quicken 5 for Windows. Also, more than twenty banks have announced plans to offer some form of electronic banking for Quicken users.

CheckFree allows you to schedule checks or electronic fund transfers to anyone with a bank account or who will accept a check. If your are a busy or forgetful person, having someone else send out your bill payments could save you hundreds of dollars a year in late payment penalties and could even help you earn more interest on your money, since the payments occur on their due dates. Appendix B contains contact information for CheckFree.

You may want to check out IntelliCharge, the Quicken credit card. This card allows you to download your credit card transactions or receive them by mail on a floppy diskette. Your Quicken manual has contact information for IntelliCharge.

The Internet took off in 1995. It seems like everyone has or is getting a home page (you can look me up on *The Computer Connection's* home page at `http//:www.c3rn.com`, which has areas of particular interest for Quicken users and readers of this book). Few people are totally comfortable with the security of financial transactions over the Internet. I expect some significant advances in the security of electronic transactions in 1996. Meanwhile, doing business on the Internet is still for the adventurous.

CREDIT CARD TRICKS AND TRAPS

Credit cards are probably one of the most profitable businesses banks have. Most bank cards charge you an annual fee, usually from a low of $15 to highs in excess of $75. Many banks are able to charge you interest, even if your card has a grace period. This occurs when you have an existing balance on your credit card. A grace period is the amount of time from when your credit card statement closes until when your payment must arrive without incurring interest charges. Banks also make a lot of profit from late charges. If your payment arrives late, the bank will usually charge a late fee of $5 or more, usually around $15. Furthermore, they will charge you interest! Credit card interest rates are normally outrageous, with a national average around 18 percent.

In addition to the profits banks collect from you, they also charge the merchants who accept your card transaction and processing fees. They usually base charges on a percentage of the amount of each charge, sometimes as much as four percent. There is usually a minimum charge per transaction, too. The banks can make out like bandits because they make money on both sides of most transactions.

If you are selective in choosing a credit card and careful with your money, you may never pay annual fees, interest, or late fees on a credit card again! Of course, you will need to pay your current balances in full before you can begin to realize this dream.

For several years, I avoided annual fees for our numerous credit cards. This includes some of those prestigious "Gold" cards. Many card issuers offer cards without annual fees. Here's a quick story about one of our bank cards with an annual fee. We received this card a number of years ago with an offer from the bank to waive the first year's fee. When the second year arrived, the annual fee magically appeared on our monthly statement. I simply called the bank's customer service number and gave the bank a choice—waive the fee or please close the account. They said they would be happy to waive the fee if I promised to use the card. This routine reoccurred like clockwork each year for several years until I no longer used the card!

Our family policy is never to carry a credit card balance. We follow Thomas Jefferson's advice, "Never spend your money before you have it." We never charge an item we can't afford to pay cash or write a check for at that moment. We also pay all cards in full by their due date, and so we avoid paying credit card interest. Unfortunately, the unexpected can and does happen.

Here are a few tips I've picked up over the years on dealing with the credit card company if you miss an occasional payment. If you find an overdue statement where it shouldn't be, promptly call the toll-free customer service number to explain the situation. Ask the representative if there is any way they can excuse the late charge and interest if you mail the full payment to them immediately. After reviewing your exemplary transaction history (lots of charges with payments made on time), the representative will probably agree to waive the charges and fees. If your history is less than stellar, you should not be calling anyway. After they agree to waive the penalties and interest, ask them to make a note in your file. You also need to note whom you speak with and what they agree to do. Include the date and time in your note in case they later refuse to forgive your obligation. Typically, you should call back in about a week. The representative who answers will see the note in your file and the date they received the payment. They will then remove the late fee and any interest charges! Occasionally, you will find additional charges or interest on the next statement. Simply call again and have them removed.

For this scenario to work, you need a good reason, not an excuse. You also need to be a good customer of the bank. They need to see that your account is profitable on the merchant's side, if you are not paying any fees or interest on their account. An immediate payment in full is also mandatory. You can't try this every other month, either. If the customer service person is unwilling to budge, ask for his supervisor. The supervisor usually has the authority to grant your request.

If all else fails, pull out the big guns—ask to have your account closed if they are unwilling to accommodate your wishes. Close the account if they won't comply. You may need them more than they want your business. In this case, just tell them you will stop using their card for six months to a year, and don't use it. At least you will have their credit line available, should you need it.

Credit cards are a Pandora's Box to many people, who open an account only to lose control and have their financial futures destroyed by an innocuous looking piece of plastic. Fewer people than you might imagine have the strength to use their credit cards properly without getting into trouble.

Properly used, a credit card is a mighty financial tool. As with any tools, you must carefully select the proper cards to fulfill your financial goals. Generally, you should accept only cards that have no annual fee and offer a 25-day grace period. Cards that offer rebates or other special benefits are preferable to those that don't. "Gold" cards are preferable to standard cards.

The credit card industry is very competitive. Most providers issue premium cards. These cards are usually gold-colored and are called gold cards. Gold cards normally offer several benefits lacking from standard cards. Typical gold card benefits include a lower interest rate (we don't care because we don't carry a balance), double the manufacturer's warrantee for up to an additional year, theft and breakage protection within a certain number of days of purchasing an item, rental car insurance coverage, and $250,000 or more in flight insurance for airline tickets bought with the card.

It is possible to produce spendable cash by using your credit card. Some cards offer up to one percent of your purchases in cash back. One of my clients, "Mr. Smith," frequently uses a cash-back card, Card A, that gives one percent back at the end of each month. Another of his cards, Card B, offered to pay a two percent cash rebate on any amounts transferred from another credit card for a limited time. This client charged his purchases on Card A and then paid Card A off with a transfer check from Card B. Card B charged interest from the day the transfer check arrived at the bank, so Mr. Smith sent a payment to Card B five days after mailing Card A's payment. The transfer checks usually arrived a day ahead of his payment check, so he incurred very little interest. Altogether, Mr. Smith paid less than $5 in interest and received over a $100 in rebates for writing a few checks during Card B's limited time offer!

A hot trend in credit cards is to offer manufacturers' rebates on cards bearing the manufacturers' names. The trend began with an appliance manufacturer, and two auto manufacturers are successfully implementing the strategy. It is actually possible to "earn" several thousand dollars in rebates toward the purchase of your next new major appliance or car. It is surprising how quickly the rebates add up. We received one of the auto cards in the mail a couple of years ago and earned the maximum amount of rebate dollars allowable in a year within a couple months. I hate to admit it, but I actually upgraded to the gold card because we can earn twice as many rebate dollars each year. At least this particular card gives its cardholders their annual fee back in rebate dollars.

I recently found an interesting book that reveals many of the tricks and traps banks have in store for you. Next time you are in a bookstore, take a look for *The Bank Book, 3rd. edition*, by Edward F. Mrkvicka, Jr.

FINANCIAL ALERT

Do you ever use your credit card to pay for tax-deductible expenses—charitable, employee business, or your own business expenses? You need to keep all of those pesky little credit card receipts and the credit card statements that include the tax-related charges with your tax records for the tax year in which you are claiming the deduction. If the IRS audits you, it can require these items to substantiate your deduction!

MONEY MATTERS

Many credit cards offer rebates and other special benefits, like frequent-flyer miles on your favorite airline. Rebates and other benefits can be very valuable to high-volume purchasers. Many people are able to generate a substantial amount of purchases on their personal cards by making purchases for their business, employer, or friends. A rebate is simply a refund of a portion of your purchase price and thus is non-taxable. Eventually, Congress and the IRS will figure out how to tax us on rebates and other special benefits credit card issuers offer. Until then, you can add this to your bag of non-taxable, wealth-producing tricks!

TAX TIP

The 1986 Tax Act phased out the deduction for consumer interest, including credit card interest. With careful planning, it is still possible for some employees and self-employed individuals to deduct credit card interest. The secret is to choose a credit card on which you charge only business expenses. You need to start out with a zero-balance card. If you mix any personal expenses with your business charges, the IRS will probably disallow the interest deduction as a business expense. Do not consider this tip a license to stay in debt!

PRACTICAL APPLICATIONS

As you have just read, it is possible to transform your credit cards from financial black holes into virtual "money trees." It is also possible to save hundreds of dollars in banking fees if you shop around a little and use Quicken to keep tabs on your accounts.

Your mission, should you choose to accept it, is to transform your financial practices. Begin by planning how you will reduce your expenses using the Financial Calendar or budget worksheets. In Chapter 4's Practical Applications, you scheduled your normal income and expenses on the Financial Calendar or in the Budget Worksheet. Take time to review your expenses in light of your goals and priorities. Do you have enough money to save and invest? How can you adjust your monthly cash flow to increase your funds and create wealth?

Remember the old saying, "A penny saved is a penny earned"? Well, that really isn't true in today's economy. Today, a penny saved is two pennies earned. A person of better-than-average means will have to earn two dollars for every dollar he or she has left over after taxes. Think about it for a minute. Under the Revenue Reconciliation Act of 1993, taxes are higher for the wealthy—that is, anyone making more than $20,000 per year. (Although income tax rates remain unchanged for the middle class, there are new energy taxes and other factors that raise the middle-class's tax burden.) Since a family making less than $20,000 per year is living in "poverty," that leaves a pretty small middle class!

Many people consider Cash Accounts a hassle. If you keep track of your entire cash flow for one month, you may find you're spending a lot of cash that you might not spend if you were keeping track of it. For many, part of their reduction in spending is a direct result of their unwillingness to prove to themselves that they are loose with their funds, so they spend less while they are recording their expenditures.

Next, develop a plan for converting your credit cards from profit-wasters into profit-producers. Then, do some market research on banks, savings and loans, and credit unions in your area. After you determine which institutions offer you the best return on your money and the most appropriate services, set up new accounts with them.

You are now ready to begin learning what to do with the precious cash flow that you have freed up for investment!

A dollar saved is two dollars earned!

CHAPTER 6

WEALTH CREATION OPPORTUNITIES

> IF YOU WANT TO BECOME REALLY WEALTHY, YOU MUST HAVE YOUR MONEY WORK FOR YOU. THE AMOUNT YOU GET PAID FOR YOUR PERSONAL EFFORT IS RELATIVELY SMALL COMPARED WITH THE AMOUNT YOU CAN EARN HAVING YOUR MONEY MAKE MONEY.
>
> —JOHN D. ROCKEFELLER

My favorite financial topic is investments. It is easy to write an entire volume on investments, and many volumes on the subject exist. In the next few pages, we will explore some of the viable opportunities for the average investor. We will set up Investment Accounts for some of these investments as we go. After examining the opportunities, we will explain and help you visualize some key investment concepts and strategies in the next chapter. We will use the Investment Accounts to explore how the concepts and strategies work in real life.

In this chapter we will strive to seek a balance. We will try to explain some technical investment concepts, opportunities, and strategies in language understandable to readers being introduced to the subject, yet we don't want to talk down to the initiated. You should find most, if not all, of the terms that are new to you defined in the Glossary. As we avoid language that is too technical, you may find some of the explanations of items or concepts factually correct although technically inaccurate. Our intent is to introduce you to investing, not to train you as an investment advisor. We hope that our discussion will whet your appetite to study additional materials on your own.

Although investments are my favorite financial topic, cash flow is the most important. If you skipped Chapters 3, 4, or 5, go back and read them before pursuing this chapter. The concepts and strategies of cash flow management are key to having money available to invest.

Now, let's talk about some investment opportunities in which you may want to participate.

AN INTRODUCTION TO INVESTMENT OPPORTUNITIES

Almost everyone wants to invest. There are many people who even have some money to invest. The question becomes, "Where do we invest?"

There are so many different opportunities that the average person can easily get very confused. Many potential investors just end up going with the recommendation of a friend or the first fast-talking salesperson who calls. Others are paralyzed by the vast number of choices and the stories heard from well-meaning friends and relatives. Almost everyone has heard of someone who made, or lost, a fortune in (<u>fill in your favorite type of investment here</u>). You do not want to take a haphazard approach to determining where to put your money to work.

As we discuss wealth-building concepts and strategies in the course of this chapter, we will need a few Accounts to experiment with. On Saturday, February 3, 1995, Richie Standard Time, about a month after Sam and Sally Richie scheduled their monthly income and expenses on the Calendar, they began thinking about putting their investment portfolio together. Sam, the dreamer of the two, put together a few Accounts to study how investments really work. We will establish Accounts with him to learn the financial principles he discovers.

First, he thought about winning the state lottery. After looking at the odds, he decided that he would have a better chance in Las Vegas or Atlantic City. After all, casinos return between 90 and 95 percent of gamblers' wagers. Lotteries typically return 30 to 40 cents for each dollar you "invest." Rule Number One for wealth builders is that you won't get rich gambling.

Finally, Sam determined that he would need to build his own nest egg or hope for long-lost, rich relatives to leave their fortune to him when they bite the Big One. Sam and Sally have heard that it is possible to begin investing with as little as $50 a month. We will discuss low-cost options in the next chapter. For now, they want to learn how investments work using larger sums. In Sam's dreams, he receives a $200,000 inheritance.

Use the instructions in Chapter 2 to change your system date to **February 5, 1996**. Now, set up a new data file for the Richies to learn about investments. Call this data file **Invest**. (See the beginning of Chapter 2 if you need a refresher on setting up new files and Accounts.) After creating a new data file, set up a Checking Account (Bank Account in DOS). Sam decided to call his **Dream Account**. He put all $200,000 in it for starters. Use the information in Figure 6-1 to set up this Account:

Intuit designed the DOS version to treat investments differently than the Windows version. Read through this section but do not try to follow the steps we outline. You will find complete instructions at the end of this section.

As we progress through the chapter, we will establish several Investment Accounts to use in the next chapter. You will need certain information as

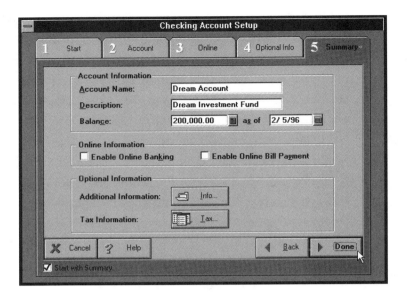

Figure 6-1. Use the above information to create Sam's Dream Account. Remember to check the Start with Summary checkbox at the bottom of the New Account Setup window when you reach the final setup screen.

you set up these Accounts. The easiest and fastest method is to prepare in advance. As we set up each Account, we will open it with a **$0.00** balance. In the Account Set Up window, you can ignore the questions about whether the Account contains a single mutual fund or is tax deferred.

We will use the Investment Accounts in the next chapter, where we discuss investment concepts and strategies. At that time, the Set Up Security window will ask for information about each investment: Name, Symbol (optional), Type, Goal (optional), Tax-Free Security and Estimated Annual Income (per share), as shown in Figure 6-2. To keep things simple, we will always assume that the Estimated Annual Income is zero.

To save time later, you can enter much of the information into lists that Quicken will use to track the investments. To illustrate certain concepts, we will set up Investment Accounts for some non-investment items in the

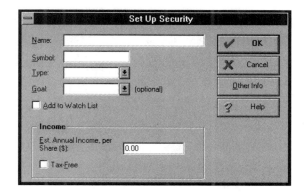

Figure 6-2. Use the Set Up Security window to create a profile for each investment you own or plan to track.

next chapter. We also use some odd abbreviations because of the limited number of characters Quicken allows. The non-investments and strange abbreviations will make sense when we use the items later in the chapter.

We will begin by setting up a temporary Investment Account. Call it **Temp**, as shown in Figure 6-3. When you set up the Investment Accounts we will use later in this chapter, you may delete this temporary Account or edit its Account name. If you do not establish this temporary Investment Account, the actions we take next will not work.

The quickest method of reaching the Investment Setup window is to choose the Portfolio Icon from the main iconbar. Quicken places the Portfolio icon on the iconbar after you open your first Investment Account. When the Portfolio View opens, click the Set Up Investment button in the lower-left corner of the screen.

Now that we have established an Investment Account, we will create a list of the Types of investments we will use. From the menu-bar, choose Lists; from the submenu, Security Type. A preprogrammed Security Type List window, Figure 6-4, will appear with the following entries: Bond, CD,

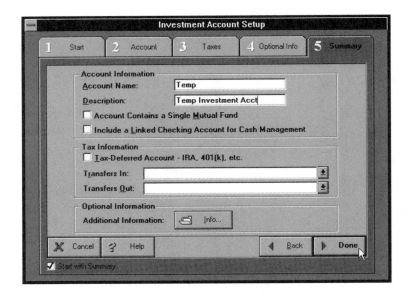

Figure 6-3.   We will use a temporary Investment Account as we create a hypothetical portfolio with the money in the Richies' Dream Account.

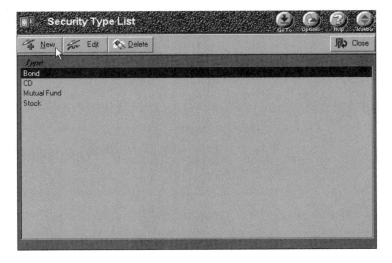

Figure 6-4.   Quicken comes preprogrammed with a few of the most common types of investments on the Security Type List.

Mutual Fund, and Stock. Click on New if you want to add items to the list, or highlight an item to edit and click the Edit button.

The Set Up Security Type window, Figure 6-5, requests the Type of security to set up. It also gives you the choice of Decimal or Fraction Pricing. Decimal pricing is the default. You will only price stocks and bonds in Fractions.

Set up the Security Type List with the security types shown in Figure 6-6. Include all of the provided entries in your Security Type List. You may edit or later remove unused default entries using the Edit and Delete buttons in the Security Type List window.

Quicken considers Investment Goals an optional item. We provide a list of goals that we specify for the investments we set up in this chapter. It is a good idea to assign a goal or objective to each of your investments. If all of your investments have the same objective, you may need to consider diversifying your portfolio. We will discuss portfolio diversification in detail in Chapter 7. Attaching labels to your investments can help you identify an obvious trend that you could otherwise easily overlook. Assign goals to your investments, as we describe next.

Choose Lists from the menu-bar again. Now choose Investment Goal to open the Investment Goal List window. Intuit preprogrammed

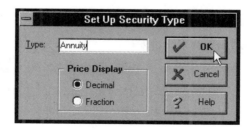

Figure 6-5.　It is easy to add new security types to the Security Type List.

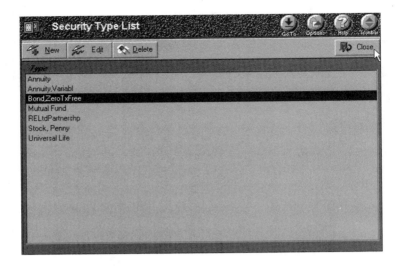

Figure 6-6. We will use the security types on this list to classify the Richies' investments in their dream portfolio.

Quicken with the following goals: College Fund, Growth, High Risk, Income, and Low Risk. Edit the list to include, instead, the goals shown in Figure 6-7. You may choose to leave in your list the investment goals we deleted from ours.

Now that you have lists of types and goals for our investments, we are ready to set up the investment list, which Quicken calls the Security List. Many investments are securities—investments with a paper certificate that provides evidence that you are the owner; e.g., stocks and bonds. Other investments are not securities, but Quicken considers all investments securities. Several of the investments on our list are not securities. Some are not even "investments," but they are all important for creating a sound investment strategy. In reality, we would not even call some of these items investments, but the name serves our current purpose well.

To access the Security List window, choose Security from the List menu or press Ctrl-Y. You will have an empty Security List. Click the New button to add investments. Use Figure 6-8 to create your Security List.

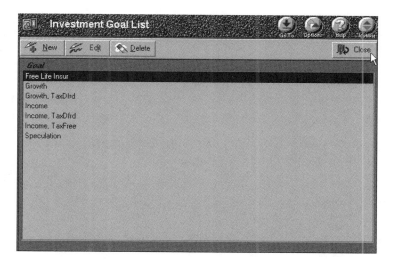

Figure 6-7. This Investment Goal List contains the Investment Goals we will assign to the Richies' investments.

Remember to leave the Estimated Annual Income at $0.00. We will use the investments on this list to illustrate important investment concepts and strategies in the next chapter.

Assuming you set your computer clock to February 5, 1996, and created the Dream Account, you will end up with the same result as the Windows users, but we must approach the task from a different angle due to the design of these versions of Quicken. Your version of Quicken organizes investments into related groups called portfolios. Each portfolio consists of various investments that have something in common. You will want to separate your personal investments along the following lines: personally owned taxable and tax deferred investments, your IRA, your spouse's IRA, your 401(k), your spouse's 401(k), et cetera.

Instead of setting up a temporary Investment Account called Temp, we want to set up a permanent Investment Account called

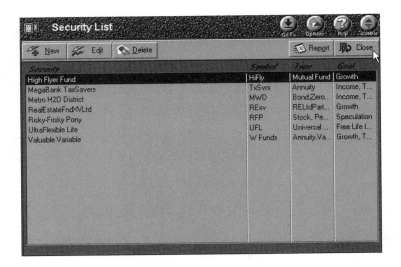

Figure 6-8. Use this Security List to create the Richies' Security List. Note that the Goal for MegaBank TaxSavers is Income, Tax deferred, while the Goal for Metropolitan Water District is Income, Tax Free.

Investments. **Create the Account Investments. Use the default settings in the Investment Account type and Description window. We will set up all of our investments in this one portfolio. Later in the chapter, when you are instructed to set up an Investment Account, you will set up another Security in your portfolio, instead.**

After completing the following instructions, you will not need to enter any more data until you get to Chapter 7. Nevertheless, you will want to read the remainder of this chapter. You should disregard the instructions to set up Investment Accounts for the investments in the tables in this chapter.

The following steps will produce a result equivalent to the instructions in the general text.

1. Go to the Investments Register. As the Register opens, you will encounter the First-time Setup window. Press [Enter] to continue. Go to the Shortcuts menu and select Security List or press [Ctrl]-[Y]. Highlight <New Security> and then press [Enter]. This opens the Set Up Security window.

2. Type High Flyer Fund for the security's Name (this is the first security we will set up in this chapter) and then tab to Symbol. Type HiFly and press [Tab].

3. A drop-down list will appear in the Type field. If the drop-down list does not appear, choose Set Preferences from the main menu. Then select General Settings. Change Automatic Pop-Up Diamond field to "Y". This will activate the drop-down list option. Choose Set Up New Type and press [Enter].

4. Using the Set Up Security Type window, set up the security types shown in Figure 6-6. The price of each security is either a Decimal or Fraction, see Figure 6-5. All of the securities we add are decimal except stocks and bonds, which are fractional. When you finish, choose Mutual Fund and press [Enter] to select it.

5. You are now in the Goal drop-down list. Edit this list to include the goals in Figure 6-7. Choose Growth and press [Enter].

6. Your cursor is now at the Estimate annual income field. Tab past the default setting of $0.00.

7. Tab to Display Mode. From the drop-down list, choose Open. Press [Enter] to complete setting up this security, or tab to any field you want to change. Pressing [Enter] will return you to the Security List.

8. Choose New Security and set up the rest of the securities listed in Figure 6-8.

Quicken for Windows Investment Accounts, like the DOS versions' Investment Accounts, can contain multiple investments. From a tax and planning perspective, I feel that it is better to set up separate Accounts for each investment. Feel free to use the approach you like best with your own data.

When you have money to invest, the first thing you want to determine is where you can get the highest rate of return with the least amount of risk.

IN SEARCH OF THE HIGHEST GUARANTEED RETURN

One of the first questions I ask new investment clients is, "Where can you earn the highest guaranteed rate of return on your money?" Most people immediately say their bank or credit union pays the highest guaranteed return on an investment. Typically, that answer is only half right. Your bank, credit union, or another finance company will pay you a very high rate of return on your investment if you owe them money and you pay it off. Where else can you earn a guaranteed yield of up to 21.9 percent or more? Bill Donaghue, noted financial advisor, calls paying off your credit cards an "absolutely foolproof" way of getting 15 to 20 percent return on your money.

Hopefully, you have already seen the light and have paid your consumer debts in full or are working at paying them down. There is absolutely no legal investment that can guarantee you as high a rate of return on your investments as what you currently pay on your credit cards, unless you own a finance company that issues credit cards. When someone does guarantee a very high rate of return, you must look at them very skeptically and wonder what they're doing to be able to offer such returns. Those opportunities typically expose you to a great amount of risk. So, paying off your credit cards and your other consumer debt typically will yield you the highest risk-free, guaranteed rate of return.

After you have all of your consumer debts paid off, you're really ready to begin building your investment portfolio. Until then, you need to work on reducing your debt. Meanwhile, let the following opportunities motivate you to reduce your debt.

BUSINESS OPPORTUNITIES

Many people believe that owning your own business is a sure path to financial success. Some studies show that family-owned businesses consistently out-perform corporate America in growth and profitability. Owning and running a business is certainly not an investment that suits everyone. Jumping into a business opportunity without an understanding of business, cash flow, taxes, and other important issues can result in a total loss of your investment capital.

With proper planning, having your own business can be an especially good investment for your future. Many successful entrepreneurs build companies that they eventually sell or milk as cash cows in their retirement years.

If owning a business interests you, your best opportunity is to start from scratch rather than to buy a company someone else is selling. Often, the reason a business is for sale is that it is suffering a hardship, struggling to survive, or the owners have built it from scratch and have a sizable amount of profit they can realize. Sellers usually want more than the business is really worth, especially when the business is a quality, growing business.

Although there are exceptions to the rule, you should never invest in a small business where you are a silent partner, not actively participating in the company's management. More than a few silent partners find that the active partners manage the business in their own interest, not in the best interests of all the partners. This is true even when you go into business with close friends or family members.

There are numerous wealth-creation opportunities available when you own your own business. One of the most popular seminars we present is call the *Small Business Success Seminar*. We also plan to discuss these opportunities in detail in a future book. Please register as a user of this book by completing the Reader Response Form at the end of this book, or send a request to the address in the Introduction. We will notify you when we release our book on wealth creation for business owners. You should also visit us on the World Wide Web. We will periodically publish financial material on our web site. Our address is `http://www.c3rn.com`. If you have questions about starting a business, I am available for on-site and telephone consultations. We have business and tax clients from coast to coast. Please consult our advertisement at the back of this book for additional information. For now, let's discuss opportunities that are more suitable for the typical investor.

LIFE INSURANCE AS AN INVESTMENT?

Traditionally, life insurance salespeople like to call life insurance "an investment for your future." In fact, many people do build up substantial amounts of cash inside their life insurance contracts. Unfortunately, the rates of return available on traditional life insurance policies are minimal at best. Most of the insurance products I've reviewed during the past decade have been very poor investment opportunities. Occasionally, you will see a product that actually does a decent job, but 90 percent of insurance policies are less than desirable as insurance products, much less as investments.

Life insurance comes in two basic flavors—cash value and non-cash value. Young people, singles and young parents, frequently purchase cash value policies to save for their future or their children's future. Cash value insurance is typically expensive and provides a lower amount of insurance coverage than young parents need to provide for their family's financial security, should they meet an early demise. (Have you noticed how hesitant people are to say "die"?). Singles without children usually should be investing their money for growth and probably have no real need for life insurance, anyhow.

Young parents want sufficient life insurance to provide for the family's needs at as low a cost as possible. Most of the young parents we see now need between $250,000 and $500,000 in life insurance each on both husband and wife. For a 30-year-old in good health, a $250,000 term life policy with one of the highest rated insurance companies in North America costs less than $25 a month. This rate is even guaranteed not to increase for ten years. Cash value insurance policies typically cost significantly more than $25 a month for only $50,000 of life insurance. A minimal amount of money to live on for a surviving spouse and one or more children.

In the early '80s, interest rates were high, and consumers realized that insurance companies were paying only about three percent interest on the money in their life insurance policies. Policy owners cashed in millions of dollars of life insurance policies. The insurance industry realized that it had to compete with the higher rates that consumers could find elsewhere. The insurance industry created universal life to offer higher and more competitive returns. A universal life insurance policy is basically a term insurance policy and a money market account wrapped up in one account. The policy owner deposits cash in the account. Some of the cash buys term insurance each month, and the remaining balance earns interest. Meanwhile, the owner of the policy doesn't have to pay any taxes on the interest he or she earns in the policy. The beauty of the system is that when you accumulate a large enough cash balance, the interest can pay all future insurance expenses with pre-tax dollars. The problem is that when interest rates are low—as they have been for the past few years—a fairly large cash balance is required to generate enough interest earnings to pay the ongoing policy expenses and cost of insurance.

People frequently ask me how much life insurance should they purchase on their children's lives. Your local life insurance agent may disagree, but the answer is almost always NONE!

The first concern is paying funeral and final medical expenses. Most people have the ability to pay for those expenses with savings, their credit cards, or by liquidating some investments if one of their children should die.

The other major reason the insurance industry gives you to purchase a policy on a child is so you can build up cash to pay for college expenses or to help them get started in life after they leave the nest. Life insurance is not an ideal investment vehicle. There are a number of far better ways to save for college or invest for your children's future.

The most important and final reason one may consider purchasing a life insurance contract on a child is to assure themselves that the children will be able to get insurance at a future date. The probability that a young person will become uninsurable is extremely small. If you believe your children may contract a life-threatening disease (including AIDS or another severe sexually transmitted disease), take illegal substances such as cocaine, or be convicted of a felony, you should seriously consider insuring your children while they are insurable.

In addition to life insurance, many life insurance companies sell annuities. An annuity is like a tax deferred certificate of deposit offered by an insurance company. In exchange for allowing an investment in an annuity to grow without current taxation, the government requires people under age 59½ to pay a ten percent early withdrawal penalty on their tax return. Young people can get around the penalty by having the insurance company pay the money out to them over the number of years remaining in their life expectancy. This is known as "annuitizing." A portion of each payment is taxable and a portion is tax-free because the IRS considers part of each payment principal, while the balance is interest. (There is another method of accelerating payments prior to age 59½, but it is too complex for this book. Contact your local insurance tax specialist or contact me at Vogt Financial Concepts & Strategies, Inc., for more information.)

As a rule of thumb, you want to keep your investments separate from your insurance. The introduction of variable life insurance and variable annuity products in the last few years challenges that rule of thumb. Variable products are basically mutual funds inside a life insurance policy or an annuity contract. Variable universal life is like a universal life policy, as just described, in that you are purchasing term insurance and investing your money in the same account. It is variable because the money is put in a mutual fund-type investment that can grow significantly or even lose value. We will discuss mutual funds in greater detail in a later section of this chapter.

One advantage some variable life and annuity products have over mutual funds is that the insurance company "insures" that at least the amount of money you invest will go to your beneficiaries at your death, even if the investments are worth less than the amount you invested. This feature is not available in all variable products. One well-known "no-load" vendor charges for the insurance yet gives the beneficiaries only the account value at death when the investment value declines.

The reason you may want to consider keeping some of your investments inside an insurance contract is the Internal Revenue Code. Congress blesses insurance with certain tax advantages that are unavailable with most other financial products. Did you realize that your money can grow inside an insurance policy without any current tax liability? Although you do not receive a tax deduction for money you put into an insurance product, there is no limit to the amount you can contribute. There are potential tax consequences if you exceed Internal Revenue Code premium guidelines. For example, you can't pay a $100,000 premium into a policy with a $50,000 face amount.

FINANCIAL ALERT

When you put more money into an insurance policy than the Internal Revenue Code allows, your policy becomes a Modified

Endowment Contract (MEC). Tax penalties may result when you withdraw or borrow money from a MEC. Your insurance company should warn you of the potential financial consequences prior to accepting a premium that could jeopardize a policy's non-MEC status.

Under current tax law, you can usually borrow your profits from your insurance policy without any tax liability, unless you let the policy lapse. If the policy lapses, the IRS will tax you on any profits that were included in the loan. When you borrow from your life insurance, the insurance company credits most of the interest you pay back into your policy. The most competitive policies credit your account with all of the interest you pay. Insurance companies call this a "zero net cost policy loan." If you can prove to the IRS that you used the life insurance loan money for investment purposes or to pay business expenses, you may even be able to deduct the interest on your tax return. You never need to repay most life insurance policy loans, although the policy may require you to pay the interest each year.

In addition to tax benefits while you are alive, there are tax benefits for your beneficiaries, too. They will receive the death benefit free from income taxes. If you set up your insurance properly, your estate, which ultimately means your heirs, will not pay any estate tax on the proceeds when you die, either. This can be very important because estate taxes can take up to 55 percent of the assets you leave behind when you die.

What the government gives with one hand, it often takes away with the other. Never forget the early withdrawal tax penalties imposed by the tax code. You also need to know that all taxable funds withdrawn from an insurance policy or an annuity are taxed as ordinary income. If you have a variable policy, you forfeit the benefits of long-term capital gains.

A number of issues relate to the taxation of life insurance. You should contact a competent professional with a thorough understanding of life insurance taxation for additional information. One of the problems with anything the government promises today is that it may rescind its promise tomorrow. That can trap us in a less-than-desirable situation. One recent example of this was enacted into law with the 1993 Clinton Tax Act. This outrageous law actually set a new precedent by retroactively increasing taxes on people after they had already died! The law achieved this by raising the tax rates on estate taxes.

In the 1970s and early 1980s, one of the strategies insurance companies used to encourage people to buy more insurance was leveraging life policies. The strategy required policy owners to borrow against an existing policy and use the borrowed funds to purchase a new policy. The policy owners would then deduct the policy loan interest on their tax return. This was fabulous for the insurance companies because it increased their profits tremendously. It was fabulous for many policy owners because they were able to purchase much more insurance than they would otherwise have been able to afford. The 1986 Tax Act changed the rules on deducting consumer interest. It was the tax deductibility of policy interest that created the opportunity. Now that consumer interest is no longer deductible, people seldom employ the strategy of leveraging life insurance.

With the new variable insurance products, having the equivalent of a mutual fund inside the insurance contract, you can actually attain some very nice investment performance. Furthermore, there are some tax advantages that are not even available in a pension plan, like the ability to borrow money tax-free from the policy at any time for any reason. Variable insurance products may be worth a serious look as an investment option. If you do consider a variable product, be very careful to select one through a well-established investment manager who has a good investment track record. You will also want to carefully study the sales literature and prospectus for each product you consider using as an investment vehicle. Be aware that administrative charges, maintenance fees, management fees, investment expenses, and other charges vary tremendously between insurance contracts.

FINANCIAL ALERT

The life insurance industry is legendary for devising creative strategies for marketing its products. The strategies are frequently great marketing ploys but are not always in the consumers' best interest. The latest scheme I've seen for separating you from your money encourages you to use your investments—usually mutual funds—as collateral for a loan to purchase a variable life policy. The insurance company requires you to commit securities worth at least two to three times the loan amount. Should the value of your investments decline, the insurance company has the right to liquidate your assets without advance notification. The claim from the insurance company is that your investment in their variable insurance product will perform better than your other investment, which is not hampered by additional fees inherent in an insurance contract! The problem here is not the product. The problem is that the insurance company wants you to jump into debt to purchase life insurance.

Take a minute to set up the following Investment Accounts for Sam and Sally.

Account Name	Description
TaxSavers' Plan	Tax Savers' Plan
UltraFlxUniLife	UltraFlexUniverslLife
ValuableVariable	Valuable Variable

If you are not faint-hearted, you may find investing in stocks, bonds, options, and commodities interesting. We will explore those areas in the next section.

TAX TIP   It is possible to reduce the tax bite on your investments by using the money that you have already spent on a life insurance policy, as long as the policy is still in force. If you own a term or cash value life policy, it is possible to convert the money you've already spent on policy premiums into a portion of the cost basis of an investment in an annuity. When you purchase a new annuity contract, tell the insurance agent you want to do a 1035 exchange of your old life insurance policy into the new annuity contract. If the agent says you can't do it, get an agent who knows the tax laws. The tax code considers the money that you spent on the life insurance policy part of the cost of the new annuity.

For example, assume that you have paid $1,000 in premiums on your current term life insurance policy. You can exchange the term policy plus another $1,000 in cash for a new variable annuity. When you eventually cash out of the annuity, you will not need to pay taxes on $2,000 of the money you pull out. The IRS will consider it part of your investment's cost.

STOCKS, BONDS, OPTIONS, AND COMMODITIES

Stocks, bonds, options, and commodities are investments the average investor should not even consider. These investments can be highly volatile and risky. Although many people do enjoy investing in individual stocks, bonds, options, and commodities, it is not a good place to begin. You should not buy these investments until you develop a substantial portfolio. Your stockbroker will probably disagree.

The biggest problem with individual stocks and bonds is that most people don't have enough money to develop a well-diversified portfolio. Most people also are unable to buy in a large enough volume to make the commissions and transaction fees economical for an individual investor. Some investors like to purchase low-cost stocks. The industry calls stocks with share prices under five dollars "penny stocks." Penny stocks generally are riskier than higher-priced stocks. You should not invest in a penny stock unless you can afford to lose your investment capital. You should also carefully research any stock before purchasing it.

As a collegian, I invested in a stock recommended by "my broker" at a large stock brokerage company. It was a great ego trip to be the only guy in the dorm with a broker. I even made money on that first stock! After it sold at a nice profit, the broker talked me into reinvesting in another hot stock that was "going to double!" It didn't. It fell. By the time I sold, I lost all the profit from the first stock, too. The only person guaranteed to profit in a stock transaction is the broker. Your broker will make money each time you buy and sell, whether or not you profit. If you want to purchase a particular stock, shop for the least expensive "discount" broker available to place the trade on your behalf. Discount brokers advertise heavily in the major financial newspapers and magazines.

Sally heard at work that the Metropolis Water District was issuing zero-coupon tax-free bonds. In English, the water district is borrowing money. The district issues bonds, which is a fancy expression for creating loans. As a local governmental agency, the district is able to offer investors, or lenders, the interest, free from local, state, or federal income taxes, as described in the accompanying Financial Alert. Thus, we call the interest "tax-free." The bonds are called zero coupons because they pay all of the interest when the bonds mature and the debtor repays the investors.

People think of bonds as safe investments. There is a certain degree of risk associated with bonds, even bonds issued by municipalities. During the '80s, investors discovered this the hard way when some large government project bonds went into default. The government agencies didn't pay the required payments. Be aware that many government agencies and localities are facing financial hardships that could affect bond values. Orange County, California, is the most recent widely-known government entity to suffer financial setbacks. Individual and institutional investors lost millions when Orange County's bond ratings were downgraded.

The biggest risk facing most bond holders today arises from interest rates. The value of a bond relates inversely to current interest rates. When interest rates decline, the value of bonds increases. Conversely, as interest rates rise, bonds decrease in value. Many bond-holders faced a nasty little surprise when interest rates began to rise in 1994. Remember, financial markets experience cycles. Interest rates cycle up and down, also. Interest-rate cycles do not really affect investors who intend to hold their bonds until they mature, unless they must liquidate early.

FINANCIAL ALERT

Social Security recipients must include tax-free interest income in calculations for determining whether a portion of their benefits is subject to federal income tax. Beginning in 1994, if a single taxpayer's "provisional income" is $34,000 or greater, or if a couple's provisional income is $44,000 or greater, 85 percent of all or a portion of the benefits will be subject to federal income tax. Congress defines provisional income as your adjusted gross income, plus 50 percent of your Social Security benefits, plus any tax-free income you receive that year.

A full discussion of options and commodities is beyond the scope of this text. Commodities are raw materials, such as silver and gold, or financial instruments, such as currency or stock indexes. The best-known commodity is probably the infamous pork belly, which you certainly don't want to be dabbling with unless, perhaps, you are a pork farmer or you have a large amount of money and can afford to lose a bit of it.

In 1993, I wrote an article for a computer magazine on using investment analysis software to make money in the stock market. While researching this article, I spoke with an extremely successful options and commodities trader. This trader said, "ninety-five percent of traders lose money. You need at least $50,000 to get started, and you had better be able to afford to lose it all!"

If owning a few silver rounds—one ounce coins—or a couple of ounces of gold interests you, then go right ahead. You should realize that the market for gold and silver can be quite volatile. Many people bought silver and gold when the prices were very high. They are still waiting for the prices to recover so that they can sell for at least the amount they purchased the precious metals for, or more. Many people consider owning precious metals a nice hedge against inflation. Beginning investors should not concern themselves with investing in them.

Sally wants to invest some of the Dream Account into Metropolis Water District bonds. Sam's friend heard a hot tip from his broker on Risky-Frisky Pony, Inc. He wants to put some money in it. Set up the following Accounts in the Invest data file.

Account Name	Description
Metropolis H2O	Metropolis H2O 8%Zero
RiskyFriskyPony	Risky-Frisky Pony, Inc

MUTUAL FUNDS

Mutual funds are probably the most popular form of investment available today. By the middle of 1993, there were more mutual funds than stocks on the American and New York Stock Exchanges combined. There are more than 4,000 mutual funds available, and the number continues to grow. The popularity growth of mutual funds is at least partially a direct result of their fabulous investment performance in the 1980s.

Even with the current popularity of mutual funds, some of you may not know what a mutual fund is. A mutual fund is simply a large pool of professionally managed money invested to meet a certain investment objective. The money managers must follow certain criteria as they invest the money. For example, they may not have the ability to buy options in a fund with conservative objectives. Today's mutual funds are typically millions upon millions of dollars managed by a professional or a team of professionals to achieve the goal or goals set forth by the prospectus—the legal document that controls what the fund can and cannot invest in, as well as how the fund is managed. The typical mutual fund will invest in a portfolio of securities, a security being a stock, a bond, or another type of investment. This portfolio will usually have 30 or more different securities, sometimes 100 or more securities. So, mutual funds end up being very well-diversified investment portfolios in their own right. We will examine in detail how diversification works in the next chapter. A well-diversified portfolio or mutual fund, given the proper amount of time, should end up a winner, as we will see in the next section.

THE BENEFIT OF TIME

What is the probability of making a profit in a mutual fund? Managers for one large mutual-fund family, a group of funds managed by the same company, analyzed their investors' returns from 1934 to 1993. They included all of their domestic, global, international, and balanced (stocks and bonds combined) equity funds. They also assumed that the investors paid the maximum commissions and fees and held their investments for one, five, and ten-year periods. Table 6-1 summarizes the results.

As we saw in Table 6-1, there were some negative holding periods for short-term investors. Table 6-2 gives the results of those investors who held on for just one more year after such a negative period.

Showing profits in all ten-year periods is impressive, but how large were the profits? Table 6-3 records the worst, average, and best ten-year-period performance figures.

Mutual funds and investment advisors are unable to guarantee that you will never lose money on your investments. It is possible to choose an investment that has historically produced consistent profits. As long as

Length of Periods	1 Year	5 Years	10 Years
Number of Periods	278	227	173
Percent Profitable	72%	96%	100%
Percent Unprofitable	28%	4%	0%

Table 6-1. This table shows the frequency of profitable versus unprofitable holding periods for a large family of mutual funds. The longer an investment is held, the greater the probability is of producing a profit. The figures in these tables are derived from historical records and should not be considered a projection of future results.

Source: American Funds Distributors, Inc.

	Total Periods	Negative Periods	Negative Periods if Held One More Year
One-Year Periods	278	77	17
Five-Year Periods	227	9	5
Ten-Year Periods	173	0	0

Table 6-2. This table provides information on the number of holding periods with positive and negative returns. The table also includes how extending the holding period for one year would impact the number of negative returns holding periods.

Source: American Funds Distributors, Inc.

the investment is still managed by the same money managers, there is a probability that future long-term results will remain consistent with overall stock market performance.

CHOOSING A MUTUAL FUND

As we mentioned, there are over 4,000 mutual funds to choose from. There are actually more mutual funds than there are stocks listed on the New York

	Total Return	Average Annual Rate of Return
Worst Ten-Year Period	+34.06%	+2.97%
Average of 173 Ten-Year Periods	+262.52%	+13.75%
Best Ten-Year Period	+740.59%	+23.73%

Table 6-3. Rates of return varied significantly from one holding period to another. This table shows the best, worst, and average returns for ten-year holding periods.

Source: American Funds Distributors, Inc.

and American Stock Exchanges combined. If you thought it was a chore to choose a stock, you must understand that it is also a chore to choose a good mutual fund. Most of these mutual funds have been around for a very short period of time, in relation to the entire investment arena. Choose a mutual fund that has a track record, or at least choose a mutual fund family that has a long track record. Then make sure that the mutual fund in that family of funds has management with a strong track record. You can either do the research yourself or find a reliable Certified Financial Planner or other investment advisor to assist your research efforts.

This brings up the next point: you have a choice between load and no-load mutual funds. Simply put, a load fund is a fund that charges a commission. The effect is that the commission reduces the amount of money you invest. No-load funds don't charge you a commission, so all of your money goes to work for you right away. On the surface, it seems like an easy decision: buy no-loads. It isn't that simple. There are a number of no-load funds, but no-load does not mean no charges or no fees. Just because they don't charge a sales commission up front doesn't mean they don't charge a management fee along the way. All funds charge management fees—that is one area where you must be very careful. Since most no-load mutual funds don't charge a commission, stockbrokers and other financial advisors often do not offer them to their clients. No-load funds must spend millions of dollars on advertising instead of on commissions. Who pays for all that advertising? The investors do through increased management fees.

Several studies of ten-year investment results prove that load and no-load funds provide comparable net returns to their investors. My own analysis shows that assuming comparable performance short-term investments are better off in a no-load fund. Mid-term investments, six to ten years, will fare equally well in load or no-load funds. Long-term investments fare better in load funds with lower management fees. After ten years, the management fee in a no-load fund can be greater than the initial commission charged by a load fund.

Besides commissions and management fees, many funds charge for other services, too. Some fund families charge transaction fees for moving your money from one fund to another. Others charge annual account fees for smaller accounts. Others do not offer toll-free telephone numbers to contact their customer service representatives. You will especially want to watch out for fees assessed for liquidating an investment. Some funds charge you a percentage of the money you withdraw from the fund as a fee. So-called "back-end loads" can result in sizable fees if your investment grew while invested in the fund. No-load providers most frequently charge these fees.

The bottom line is that you want to invest in the fund, load or no-load, that will give you the best investment performance over time. There are good load and no-load funds, and there are horrible load and no-load funds. Whatever you do, don't choose a fund simply because it is or is not a load or no-load fund. Historically, you can look at returns on funds, but you must remember that just because a fund did well last year or for the last ten years doesn't mean it will necessarily do well next year or for the next ten years. A mutual fund cannot guarantee you a certain rate of return, nor can a financial advisor or stock broker guarantee you a rate of return. All they can do is point out the historical returns to you. They cannot even claim that those returns will reflect future results.

TAX TIP **Every time you move money from one mutual fund to another, even within a single family of funds, the IRS requires you to declare all profits or losses on your tax return. The funds must report to the IRS the amount of money you move. The IRS uses its multibillion-dollar computer system to match the amounts reported to the amounts you declare on your tax return. Significant penalties and interest can accrue on unreported transactions.**

If you do your own research, you can go to a number of places to find information on mutual funds. Articles on mutual funds fill the popular financial press. You need to be careful when reading those articles because some publications may skew their editorials and reporting based on their advertising revenues. It's very interesting to look at some publications that have certain large no-load mutual funds as advertisers. Some of these publications seem to give their advertisers a higher recommendation than non-advertisers. Remember, the load funds shouldn't need to advertise as much, or at all, because licensed security brokers offer them.

If you want to get a more independent analysis of a mutual fund, go to a library and ask for *Morningstar Mutual Funds. Morningstar Mutual Funds* is a service of Morningstar, Inc. It is a guide that lists over 1,200 of the open-end mutual funds available. It provides unbiased ratings of load and no-load mutual funds that are at least three years old. Funds receive ratings of zero to five stars, worst to best. Many investment professionals use Morningstar's reports to choose the funds they recommend to their clients. Morningstar has a software version, also. For additional information, contact Morningstar at (800) 876-5005.

When you analyze a mutual fund, you want to compare it to similar mutual funds. For example, if medical stocks interest you and you want to invest in a medical mutual fund, you would not compare it to a fund that invests in utilities or gold. You also must keep in mind that mutual funds investing in different segments of the economy have differing levels of expenses. A fund that invests only in United States companies will typically have lower operating expenses than a fund that invests only in international companies. Before investing in any mutual fund, make sure that you receive a prospectus and read it thoroughly. Understand the risks, charges, and fees before you invest a dime.

Now we'll set up an Investment Account for the **High Flyer Fund** for Sam and Sally. You can describe the Account as the **Hi Flyer Mutual Fund**, which is a single mutual fund.

The only major area we haven't covered is real estate investments. Let's do that next.

REAL ESTATE INVESTMENTS

Do you ever have a night when you just can't get to sleep? Have you ever turned on the TV only to find a late-night infomercial on investing in real estate? It sounds great on TV, especially when your mind is dull from insomnia: "Buy a million dollars of real estate without any money or credit!" "We made $17,000 on our first deal. It only took us three hours after completing our home study course. If we could do it, you can, too!" I hate to admit it, but I've gone to more than one of those seminars. Sure, I learned some good information, but not really enough to justify the cost of the materials. One in a million attendees may actually accomplish what the seminar promoters claim. Meanwhile, the promoters are raking in huge sums of cash for material that is available at your local library. As a famous comedian says, "What a country!"

The shallow claims of late-night infomercials suck people in because almost everyone dreams of owning a piece of ground someplace or a stately mansion! In this section, we will discuss some down-to-earth investment aspects of owning your home, land, rental real estate, real estate limited partnerships, and real estate investment trusts (REITs).

YOUR HOME

Many people include their home as a retirement investment. This may be fine if you have a large home and you intend to sell it and move into a smaller home when you retire. Even though many people expect to move to a smaller home after retirement, very few people do. Actually, some people sell their home and move into something larger. Entertaining and having guests over interests them more after retirement than when they were working. Your home is such an important part of your financial planning that we devote an entire chapter to it. See Chapter 8 for further information on home ownership.

Your home can be a very nice investment from the standpoint of increasing your net worth. From the standpoint of having a nest egg to use for your retirement, it is better to invest your money in other areas. The first of those areas we will discuss is land.

LAND

Someday, I would like to buy a piece of land surrounded by beautiful countryside and build my own home. Many others share this dream. If your goal is to build a home, you should not consider this an investment opportunity but a home ownership opportunity.

If purchasing land for development or for future resale sparks your fancy, you could call it an investment. The potential for gain in raw land can be tremendous. It can also be financially devastating. Keep in mind that a piece of ground often doesn't produce any money but does cost money to own—taxes, insurance, maintenance, and mortgage payments. If you do buy land, please do not mortgage it. I have seen too many people purchase a lot or other parcel of land on payments only to find the payments burdensome in the future. Some of those people lost their entire investment when they sold after the market price fell. Some investors I know even gave their property to the lender when things got tight. If you insist on mortgaging the land, buy farm land or land that can otherwise produce an income. Even this is risky.

Although land speculation is not the average investor's path to prosperity, land is a good investment if you know what you are doing and do not drown in the quagmire of government regulations. As Will Rogers commented on why land is a good investment, "They ain't makin' any more of it!" Participating in a limited partnership may provide a better balance between risk and reward.

LIMITED PARTNERSHIPS

Limited partnerships are like mutual funds for real estate. The sponsors raise a pool of money for the specific purpose of investing into a portfolio of real estate or possibly a single piece of real estate. Many different people put money into the pool. A professional or team of professionals make the investment decisions and do the work for the partnership.

Limited partnerships have two types of partners: general and limited. Typically, one or more persons act as the general partners, and manage the investment funds. The limited partners are the investors.

The general partners make all of the business and management decisions for the partners. The tax code does not allow limited partners to participate in most aspects of management. The general partners send the limited partners a copy of Schedule K-1 each year. The K-1 tells the limited partners how much money the partnership generated and the amount of their pro rata share. The limited partners use the K-1 information to complete their tax return. If someone is injured on partnership property or if the partnership can't repay an outstanding loan, the plaintiff cannot sue the limited partners. Not only does the limited partnership generate income from rent, but it also can generate income from investments. Most partnerships have some cash reserves on deposit at a bank or perhaps even invested in a mutual fund. Although some partnerships invest in raw land, most partnerships invest in houses, apartments, or commercial real estate, which means they own buildings or other structures that will someday wear out. Since buildings last only a certain length of time, Congress says they have a "useful life." The investors can deduct the cost of buying or constructing a building on their tax returns over the useful life of the structure. This is depreciation.

TAX TIP

Limited partnerships and even personally held real estate investments will sometimes generate passive losses. A passive loss results when you are not an active manager of an investment and it produces more tax losses than taxable income. The IRS will allow you to deduct your passive losses only to the extent of your passive income. You can accumulate losses that you cannot deduct concurrently. When you finally sell or liquidate an investment, you can deduct any losses that you may have accumulated over the life of the investment. This is a very complex area of tax law. You should consult a professional tax advisor for more information.

Limited partnerships were very popular in the early 1980s, until the Tax Reform Act of 1986 changed many of the tax rules relating to real estate. When the Tax Reform Act became law, it caused many real estate ventures to become unprofitable. Many of them actually went into foreclosure or bankruptcy. As a result, partnerships lost respectability in the financial community. It has taken a long time, but now partnerships are regaining some of what they lost. Just recently, I started recommending one or two limited partnerships to my clients, but very reluctantly, after having seen many of my clients suffer losses due to Congress' actions in 1986.

Limited partnership investments are not usually liquid. Most real estate investment partnerships expect to own their properties for seven to 12 years. You should not invest a large percentage of your portfolio into any single illiquid investment. You should determine when you may need access to your funds before investing in any project. On the national level, the Securities and Exchange Commission, SEC, scrutinizes limited partnerships offered to the public. Most states also review partnership offerings prior to allowing the general partner to sell them in their state. To protect the investors living in their jurisdiction, these regulatory agencies set investor requirements. These requirements measure an investor's suitability to invest in a given partnership. Investors must have income and net worth in excess of the suitability requirements for the general partner to accept the money the investor desires to invest. A typical all-cash real estate partnership may require the investors to earn at least $45,000 per year and have a minimum of $45,000 in investable assets, including their IRA and vested pension plan interest. Married investors may include their joint income and assets in these calculations.

To protect yourself in a limited partnership investment, it is very wise to make sure that you are dealing with a general partner who has a successful track history that he or she can point to. You should also invest only in partnerships that are publicly available. Privately offered partnerships typically have greater risk. You should consider one only if you are a personal acquaintance or friend of the general partners and you know you can trust them.

Personally, I rarely recommend partnerships that use leverage, that have debt. Most of the problems experienced in the 1980s with partnerships resulted from the use of leverage to purchase real estate portfolios. When the real estate market slumped, the partnerships could not meet their debt payments. This caused many partnerships difficulties. Billions of dollars worth of buildings went into foreclosure. Investors lost hundreds of millions of investment dollars. Anytime you consider investing in a limited partnership, read the prospectus thoroughly first. You can also use the following questions as a starting point to pick a good partnership:

1. What type of properties does the partnership own or plan to purchase? What criteria do they use to choose investment properties?
   How much debt can the partnership have?
2. What are the economic conditions where the properties are or will
   be located? How vulnerable are the properties to the economy?
3. What reputation and track record have the managers of the RELP
   developed?
4. What financial projections is the partnership making? How
   accurate have their prior projections been? Have their cash flow
   investor payments been increasing and on target?
5. Does the partnership plan to leverage its investments or does the
   prospectus allow long-term debt? We do not recommend investing
   in partnerships that include leverage or allow the general partners
   to take out long-term financing in the future.

If a partnership doesn't sound interesting, perhaps you would enjoy
owning rental property and managing it yourself.

RENTAL PROPERTIES

Very few people enjoy the hassle of managing their own rental properties.
Are you a person who could put up with tenants calling you in the middle
of the night? Can you handle demanding tenants who want you to unplug
their overflowing toilet, repair their water heater, light their furnace, or fix
a myriad of other items that can and will go wrong? If you said, "Yes," you
may enjoy owning rental real estate.

Besides not wanting the hassle, many people just don't have enough
money to buy rental property. Perhaps when you outgrow your current
residence, you will keep your house and rent it out when you move into a
larger place or to another part of the country. It is difficult to make money
in rental real estate unless you live near your property, so you should not
keep a rental home if you move across the country, unless you plan to
return to the area. Then it could definitely be to your advantage to rent

out the house for a short period of time, or even a couple of years, while you are on temporary assignment elsewhere. There are many advantages to rental real estate.

Rental real estate requires a great deal of financial wherewithal. Your total cash reserves, including open lines of credit, are an important consideration. Too many investors hop into a real estate transaction without due regard to the cash requirements of operating rental property. Maintaining rental units is often expensive. You should also consider the possibility of having your property sit vacant for extended periods of time. If you cannot find a tenant, you will have to pay the ongoing costs of owning the property out of cash reserves from your own pocket. How deep are your pockets?

There are other types of rental real estate besides residential. Non-residential real estate includes commercial and industrial properties. Non-residential real estate is often less of a hassle than residential rentals, although it has its share of hazards. Unfortunately, most people cannot afford the steep entry price of commercial or industrial property.

If you do seriously consider investing in rental real estate, thoroughly examine the many legal issues involved. The government is continually making real estate ownership an increasing burden. It is becoming increasingly difficult to evict tenants who shirk their rent. You must be careful of the many broadening discrimination laws. The recently enacted Americans with Disabilities Act (ADA) includes many provisions that will cost landlords tremendous amounts of money in compliance costs. Before investing, talk to investors who own properties similar to the one you find interesting. They may help you save thousands of dollars in additional expense by pointing out any potential pitfalls. The last area of real estate we will discuss here is Real Estate Investment Trusts.

REAL ESTATE INVESTMENT TRUSTS

Real Estate Investment Trusts are commonly called REITs. A REIT is basically a publicly traded limited partnership. (Publicly traded means traded on a stock exchange.) REITs offer some advantages over limited partnerships: liquidity, no K-1s, and an independent board of directors. You can sell without difficulty, as long as there are other people willing to purchase the security. The problem is that REITs often trade below their market value. You could also have a good opportunity to buy a REIT at such a point if you think the market conditions will change.

Many people invest in real estate because they view it as a stable investment. On the whole, real property is fairly predictable. REITs tend to be less predictable. When the stock market stubbed its toe in October 1987, REIT share prices followed the market in its tumble. If you study REIT prices, you will see that they tend to follow market trends. If you are investing in real estate to diversify out of the stock market, REITs may not help you meet your objectives.

Before investing in a REIT, you will want to thoroughly research it. You also should limit your REIT investments to a very small percentage of your investment dollars. Use the following questions as a guide to finding a quality REIT:

1. Does the REIT own high-quality property?
2. What are the economic conditions where the properties are located? How vulnerable are the properties to the economy?
3. What reputation and track record have the managers of the REIT developed?
4. What financial projections is the REIT's management making? How accurate have their prior projections been? Have their cash flow and dividend payments been increasing and on target?

You should include some real estate in your investment portfolio. Which type do you feel suits you best? The Richies do not desire to manage a rental property. They have no interest in purchasing land. They want real estate that does not move with the stock market, and so they ruled out REITs. They found a real estate limited partnership that does not have any debt. The general partners have a strong track record, and their reputation is sterling. Open an Investment Account for the Real Estate Investors Fund XV, a real estate limited partnership, using **RealEstateFndXV** as the Account name and **RealEstateInvstrFndXV** for the Description.

You now have a basic understanding of the investment opportunities available. Who will you turn to when you need to acquire an investment or insurance product? Who will help you determine whether a particular opportunity is best for your overall financial picture? Many people choose to educate themselves. Others choose to supplement their education by seeking the assistance of one or more professionals in the financial industry.

A portion of what you earn is yours to keep.

HOW TO CHOOSE A COMPETENT FINANCIAL ADVISOR

You may find yourself somewhat confused by the myriad of investment choices. Don't feel too bad. Most people find themselves somewhat bewildered by the dynamic state of the economy and the constant evolution occurring in the financial services industry. Many individuals rely on a financial planner to assist them on the road to riches.

Choosing someone to advise you is often difficult. Where do you look for a good advisor? Whom can you trust? Is anyone unbiased? These and a hundred other questions quickly come to mind. We will answer some of those questions and send you in the right direction to search for competent counsel.

As you look and ask around, you will find that many people call themselves financial planners. In most states, you can wake up one morning and think, "I want to be a financial planner." By noon, you are one. Kind of scary, isn't it? If you can print up business cards and find a client, you are a financial planner.

Most of these financial planners have a sales job somewhere in the financial industry—insurance agents, stockbrokers, real estate agents, bookkeepers, et cetera. I have run across part-time "financial planners" who simply peddle term insurance at night to their (former) friends. The common theme is a search for respectability. Do you even bother talking to someone if they identify themselves as a stockbroker/insurance agent/ real estate agent/et cetera? If you are like most people, you won't talk to them unless you have a pressing need they can fill.

You are not looking for a salesperson when you choose an advisor. You want someone who will spend enough time learning about your specific situation to offer you definite advice, tailored to meet your needs and goals. A quality planner is competent to advise you in a wide range of areas: income taxes, investments, and insurance (auto, disability, health, homeowners, life, and umbrella coverage). They should be able to tell you how to optimize your participation in your company's benefit programs. Competent professionals understand how the various products will affect your taxes and overall financial situation. They will advise you on how various products and services affect your financial picture, how they will interact with other products and services you already have or are considering. They will advise you on passing your earthly goods to your family when you die.

They cannot provide these services without compensation. Competent planners' fees start at $50 an hour, with some exceeding $300 an hour. If a planner offers to advise you without charge, grab your pocketbook! There still is no such thing as a free lunch. Everyone must make a living. Financial advisors are paid in one of three ways: commissions, fees, or a combination of fees and commissions. Ask planners how they are paid and how much the fees and commissions are. You will receive a straight answer from a quality planner. If they receive commissions, ask them what percentages of their income are from fees, insurance commissions, investment commissions, and other sources. If their other sources provide a significant portion of their earnings, ask them what they are.

Some people suggest that you should deal only with fee-only planners. They reason that the planner will remain unbiased and offer sound advice without personal considerations interfering. The flaw in this reasoning is that not all fee-based planners are ethical, and some can be extremely self-serving. Medical doctors are fee-oriented and do not work on a commission. Yet, I have heard many reports of doctors who run up massive amounts of fees for unnecessary tests and procedures.

Others suggest that you should deal with a commission-oriented planner since you will need to acquire investments and insurance products that usually include a commission. Why pay for the service twice? The problem is that many commission-oriented planners are simply salespeople masquerading as planners. They often must meet sales quotas for the organization with which they affiliate. Planners of this type are very biased toward their own needs and may encourage you to acquire a product simply to please the insurance or investment company they associate with.

Both arguments have ardent supporters. Highly respected and ethical planners of both types exist. One solution is to seek out a hybrid planner— one who works for fees and commissions. This is the approach we use at our financial service companies. We believe we can best serve our clients by recommending the best products available for their unique financial position. If the products pay a commission, we disclose that fact. If no or low commissions are available, we charge fees based on the time the client requires for us to help solve his or her financial question or problem. To implement this approach properly, we have two operating companies: C. E. Vogt Consulting, which is commission based, and Vogt Financial Concepts & Strategies, Inc., which is fee based. We also have a network of professionals in related fields who assist our clients when their needs extend beyond the scope of the services we offer.

The best answer is to find planners with high ethical standards. If you can trust them, it doesn't matter how they are paid. It just matters that they receive enough compensation to still be in business when you require their services in the future. Many people enter the financial service industry; few survive more than a couple of years. You will generally receive better advice from an advisor who is well-established. Look for professionals with experience in a broad base of financial issues and who have survived for at least five years as planners. Ask them about their commitment to remain in the business. Many planners are struggling and looking for other, more lucrative opportunities.

The advisor you select must also be knowledgeable and experienced. Choose a planner educated in financial matters. Begin by looking for advisors who hold the CFP®—Certified Financial Planner®—license. CFP licensees have qualified to use the mark after studying a broad range of financial curricula. They must sit through a battery of exams and meet work experience requirements. A strict code of ethics governs their professional behavior, and you have a higher authority to appeal to if you have a grievance. Even with these requirements, you should interview potential advisors to determine which one has the specific experience you desire and a personality you are comfortable with.

You can check on the status of a CFP by contacting the Institute for Certified Financial Planners, ICFP. The ICFP maintains a database of CFPs. You can check on the status of a CFP licensee by calling its toll-free number. The ICFP will also provide you with the names of three CFPs in your area (unless you are in a rural area). The names you receive are of planners who pay to be in the program. Several free pamphlets on financial planning and financial issues are also available. Contact information in Appendix B.

PRACTICAL APPLICATIONS

You now have a basic understanding of several types of available investments. You also know how to begin the process of choosing a competent financial advisor. In the next chapter, you will build on that foundation of knowledge by seeking some wisdom. You will need to acquire and employ time-tested concepts and strategies to assure your success in the realm of investing!

Everyone should have a plan to create an investment portfolio. If you don't have one already, you should consider enlisting the services of a competent financial advisor. Call a few on the phone and ask how much an initial consultation costs. You can probably visit a few without an initial fee. If you do not care to seek outside help, develop a plan to educate yourself on investment opportunities.

Whether or not you get outside help, you need a basic understanding of investments. *The Wall Street Journal Guide to Understanding Personal Finance* is an excellent reference for beginning and intermediate investors. It clearly and concisely explains how investments work. It also contains simple explanations for many financial terms, concepts, and strategies.

Most people, young and old, should begin their investment portfolio by choosing a good-quality mutual fund. Begin gathering information on mutual funds. Ask your financial advisor, family, and friends which funds they own and why they chose them.

Before you begin investing, read the next chapter. You will want to employ the concepts and strategies it contains to assure financial success.

CHAPTER 7

INVESTING FOR WEALTH

WHILE WE CONSIDER WHEN TO BEGIN, IT BECOMES
TOO LATE.

—LATIN PROVERB

In the last chapter, we explored a number of investment
opportunities the typical investor might consider. We also
established Investment Accounts for the investments we will
purchase in this chapter. After we invest our fictitious funds,
we will use those Investment Accounts as we discover the
secrets of investment success.

INVESTMENT CONCEPTS AND STRATEGIES

There are a number of key investment concepts and strategies. We will explore some of the most important ones in the
following sections. There are many different twists on
investment strategies. As you read other authors or listen to

investment shows, you will hear various ideas about how one can or should invest. We will try to limit our discussion to the basic strategies and concepts that apply to 90 percent of investors. One of the most fundamental and important concepts to grasp is the principle of diversification.

DIVERSIFICATION

"Don't keep all of your eggs in one basket." This is the concept of diversification distilled to its simplest and most basic form. This concept is especially important in creating an investment portfolio. The concept and application of diversification is one of the most important aspects of long-term investment success, and so we will spend a considerable amount of time examining it.

If you had $200,000 to invest, what would you do? If you invest it all in one place, and that particular place is the wrong one, you can lose your entire nest egg. If you diversify it among five investments, even if one of those goes south, you will still have four remaining investments that can potentially earn profits. In fact, your overall yield may be much greater with five items than it is with one.

The purpose of diversification is to reduce risk. Risk is a very important consideration in investment planning. You don't want to subject yourself to too much risk, but risk is inevitable. Without risk, there is no opportunity. The opportunity to profit arises from risk. (I'm starting to sound like Quark, the Ferengi on *Star Trek*.)

If you put your money in the bank, what is your risk? Well, the bank would like you to believe there is no risk. After all, the FDIC insures your money up to $100,000 per account, with certain restrictions. In reality, you are subjecting yourself to a tremendous amount of risk. Banks currently are willing to pay you a very, very small amount of interest on your money. Banks typically pay rates equal to or slightly less than the rate of inflation. If you have $10,000 in the bank at five percent interest while there is five percent inflation, what have you done? On the surface it looks like you are breaking even. In reality, you've lost money, because your $10,000 at five percent earns $500. Thus, you must declare that $500 as interest income on Schedule B of your federal income tax return. You will end up paying between 15 and 39.6 percent of that $500 in federal income taxes. Therefore, you've lost money because you were unable to keep up with inflation. Putting your money in a bank can be very risky to your financial well-being.

How does allocating investments into a diverse portfolio of bonds, cash, domestic stocks, foreign stocks, and real estate stack up against maintaining a less diversified portfolio? A study by Bailard, Bichl & Kaiser on results from 1970 to 1990 of various investments shows surprising results: The well-diversified portfolio produced higher rates of return and lower risk than the other investment strategies studied. Table 7-1 shows the results of their study.

A study by SEI Corporation reaffirms the importance of allocating our investments in a diverse portfolio. SEI evaluated the ten-year performance results of 91 institutional pension portfolios. The corporation concluded that 93 percent of portfolio performance is a result of properly allocating investments in a diverse portfolio. Only seven percent of performance results from specific investment selection or market timing. We will discuss timing later in this chapter.

Let's see how diversification works by investing some of the Dream Account money. Like most couples, Sam and Sally have very different ideas about how they should invest the nest egg. They want to use a reasonable time frame for studying how investment concepts work; they have determined that 25 years would work well since they want to retire in 25 years. After extensive discussion, they decided to approach the problem of making investment decisions logically—they split the pot in half. Each of them will invest $100,000 as they see fit.

Year	Stocks	Bonds	⅓ Stocks ⅓ Bonds ⅓ Cash	⅕ U.S. Stocks ⅕ Foreign Stocks ⅕ Bonds ⅕ Cash ⅕ Real Estate
Selected Years				
1972	18.98%	5.68%	9.38%	15.10%
1974	(26.47)	4.35	(5.44)	(6.60)
1978	6.56	(1.16)	4.40	13.00
1986	18.47	24.44	16.61	23.30
1990	(3.10)	6.10	3.40	(1.40)
1970 to 1990				
Compound Annual Return	10.8%	8.7%	9.6%	11.2%
Standard Deviation (Risk)	16.6%	11.8%	8.0%	7.9%

Table 7-1. Diversification increases portfolio return and decreases risk. The investment study results in this table show how various investment portfolio mixes performed in selected years. The lower part of the table shows cumulative results for the twenty-year period.

Source: Bailard, Bichl & Kaiser

You may remember that the Metropolis Water District zero-coupon bonds enticed Sally in the last chapter. She feels that there will always be a need for water and that the water district will maintain a monopoly position in the market. She is confident in the water district's management. The eight percent tax-free yield is also extremely attractive.

Sam can't settle on one thing to invest in and wants to follow Grandpa Richie's sage advice. Grandpa always said, "Money is like fertilizer, it works best if you spread it around." He has decided to split his $100,000 into five equal shares.

Sam wants to make sure that some of his money is really safe, so he is investing his first $20,000 into the Tax Saver's Plan that his bank promotes. He figures that bank-offered products must be FDIC insured. What Sam doesn't realize is that many banks are diversifying out of the banking business and into the insurance and investment fields. The "investment counselor" at the bank is just a salesperson who sells insurance and common investments like mutual funds. Some banks are now establishing subsidiary insurance and investment companies to create the products they sell. The insurance and investments offered in the bank lobby aren't eligible for FDIC insurance coverage. They are often inferior products or the same products offered by many other insurance agents and investment salespeople.

The bank's investment counselor told Sam about the safety the Tax Saver's Plan offers, along with the generous tax benefits. The money is not taxed until withdrawn. The counselor said the plan is "insured" and guaranteed to pay at least four percent interest. The small print in the sales literature mentions that the plan is actually an annuity issued by a B-rated (A is better) insurance company that pays simple interest compounded annually. If Sam were investing real money, he would receive the annuity contract (policy) about three or four weeks after investing his money. At that point, he may notice that the Tax Saver's Plan is an insurance product, not a bank product.

The second "investment" Sam will make with his play money is in a universal life insurance policy. A few months ago, his agent from Monolith Life called to say hello. The agent is an old fraternity brother, and so Sam feels an obligation to buy insurance from him. The agent showed Sam how he could purchase a life insurance policy that wouldn't cost him anything! All Sam has to do is deposit money into a policy. The money earns interest that is not subject to income taxes. The interest pays for Sam's life insurance. When Sam no longer needs the insurance, the insurance company will refund all of his initial money. If Sam deposits

$20,000 into the policy, it will earn more than enough interest to pay for all of the life insurance that he and Sally need to protect their family. Sam needs to realize that, under current tax law, the IRS will classify his contract as a Modified Endowment Contract. He can easily escape this potential tax trap by depositing the premium into the policy over a few years. If he does deposit his money as a single premium, under current tax laws he can exchange the life policy for an annuity contract without penalty when he no longer needs the insurance coverage.

Sam's third investment is in the Valuable Variable Annuity, a variable annuity offered by his fraternity brother. He is investing the money into several of the equity funds available as investment options in the contract. On the basis of historical yields, Sam hopes to achieve a 15 percent annual return over the next 25 years.

On the advice of his mother, Sam feels that he should invest some money in real estate. After reviewing several real estate investments, Sam has chosen a limited partnership that purchases properties for cash. He knows that cash buyers often receive better prices than buyers who must finance their purchases. He also appreciates the additional safety that the avoidance of leverage, debt, offers. Sam realistically expects his real estate investment to grow at a ten percent annual rate of return.

With the final $20,000, Sam plans to satisfy his gambler's urge. His friend, Ben, just bought a hot stock recommended by his broker, Willie, at the Sure-Fire Investors' Group. Sally thinks Mark Twain had it right when he said, "There are two times in a man's life when he should not speculate: when he can't afford it, and when he can." She thinks Sam is crazy to even consider investing in a company with a name like Risky-Frisky Pony, Inc. Sam considers it the long shot that could make them rich (in their phantom portfolio). On Monday, February 5, Sam and Sally go on their make-believe rounds to invest their fantasy inheritance in fictitious investments.

Now, please take time to confirm that you've set your computer's internal clock to 2/5/96. Also, confirm that you are in the Invest data file, not the Richie file.

We will now review how to transfer money between Quicken Accounts. Open the Dream Account Register. The Category field in your Dream Account Register has a list of categories and includes all of your other Quicken Accounts in the Investments data file, too. The Accounts appear at the bottom of the list. We do not recommend the Transfer Money option in the category drop-down list because it does not allow you to enter complete information in the Register. Entering all of the information pertaining to a transaction is important to creating a proper paper trail.

Figure 7-1 shows the transactions required to transfer the Richies' money into each of the Investment Accounts. The Payee is the party to

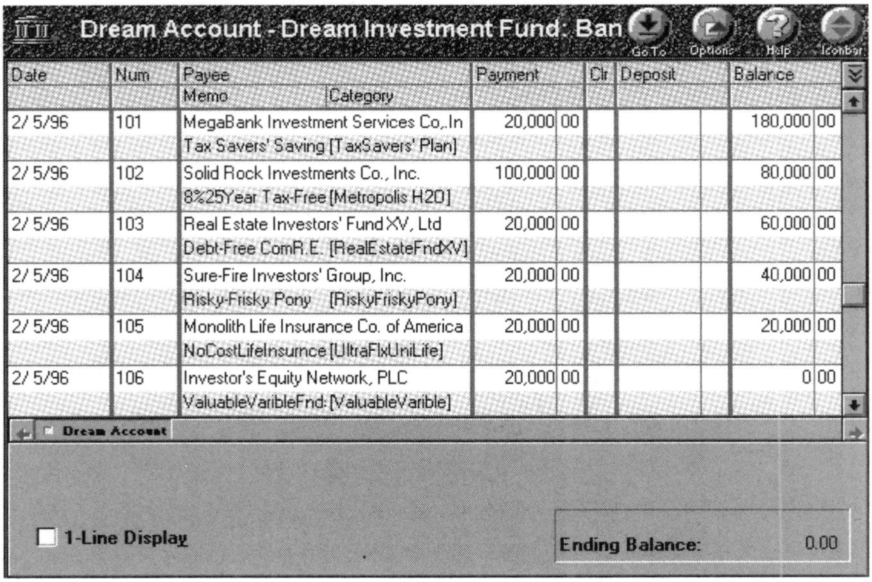

Date	Num	Payee		Payment	Clr	Deposit	Balance	
		Memo	Category					
2/ 5/96	101	MegaBank Investment Services Co,.In		20,000 00			180,000 00	
		Tax Savers' Saving	[TaxSavers' Plan]					
2/ 5/96	102	Solid Rock Investments Co., Inc.		100,000 00			80,000 00	
		8%25Year Tax-Free	[Metropolis H2O]					
2/ 5/96	103	Real Estate Investors' Fund XV, Ltd		20,000 00			60,000 00	
		Debt-Free ComR.E.	[RealEstateFndXV]					
2/ 5/96	104	Sure-Fire Investors' Group, Inc.		20,000 00			40,000 00	
		Risky-Frisky Pony	[RiskyFriskyPony]					
2/ 5/96	105	Monolith Life Insurance Co. of America		20,000 00			20,000 00	
		NoCostLifeInsurnce	[UltraFlxUniLife]					
2/ 5/96	106	Investor's Equity Network, PLC		20,000 00			0 00	
		ValuableVaribleFnd:	[ValuableVarible]					

Dream Account

□ 1-Line Display

Ending Balance: 0.00

Figure 7-1. Transfer money to the Richies' Investment Accounts by completing the above transactions in the Dream Account.

whom each check is payable. The Category field transfers the funds from the Checking Account to the proper Investment Account. Use Figure 7-1 to complete the transactions in your Quicken file.

 Enter the checks listed in Figure 7-1 in your Dream Account. All of your checks' Category fields will use the Investments Portfolio Account.

Now each Investment Account (Investments Portfolio in DOS), except the High Flyer Fund that we will use later, has money in it. Our next project is to discover how the investments might perform and how diversification affects the portfolio's overall performance. In the following paragraphs, we will invest each Account's funds and enter projected price histories for each investment. Begin by returning to the Account List and double-clicking on Metropolis H2O. This will open the Metropolis H2O Account window. The present balance is $100,000, which you transferred from the Dream Account. Purchase the Metropolis zero-coupon bonds using the information in Figure 7-2.

 Go to the Investments Account. There are two views available: Register and Portfolio. Use Ctrl-R to switch between them. The cash balance should equal $200,000. In the Register, you can buy the Metropolis Water District bonds using Figure 7-2. You can also buy the shares from the Portfolio view. Press Ctrl-B to bring up the Buy window and provide the information requested using the figure. Purchase the remaining securities listed in Table 7-2 to complete the Richies' portfolio.

Repeat the steps you followed to purchase the Metropolis Water District zero-coupon bonds with the investments in Table 7-2. Enter each transaction into its respective Investment Account.

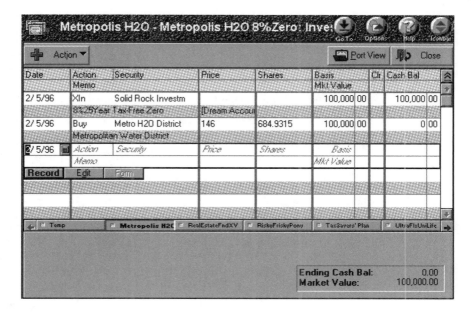

Figure 7-2. Sally purchased Metropolis Water District zero-coupon bonds. This is how she recorded the transaction in her Quicken Register.

Action	Security	Share Price	Shares In	Commission
Buy	MegaBank TaxSavers	20,000	1	
Buy	RealEstateFndXVLtd	500	40	
Buy	Risky–Frisky Pony	0 ¼	75,000	1,250.00
Buy	UltraFlexible Life	20,000	1	
Buy	Valuable Variable	10	2,000	

Table 7-2. Create the transactions to buy these investments in their respective Accounts using this information. Note: Enter Risky-Frisky Pony's price as ⊡ ⟋ ④. Quicken will convert it to a decimal while you are entering the remainder of the transaction, but record the price as a fraction.

After you enter the purchase of each investment in its Account, go to the Portfolio View. DOS Instructions follow, but DOS users should read through this section. To go to the Portfolio View from a Register, click on the Portfolio button at the top of the Register. This opens the Portfolio View window. Check the Account selector option in the Portfolio window, shown in Figure 7-3—we want to include **All Accounts**. Use the drop-down list to the left of the View selector to make your choice.

When All Accounts is chosen, the Register button is grayed out. If you want to use the Register button in the Portfolio View window, you must choose a single Account instead of All Accounts. The Account you select is the Register that is available using the Register button. When a single Account or Selected Accounts are selected, only those Accounts' values are visible.

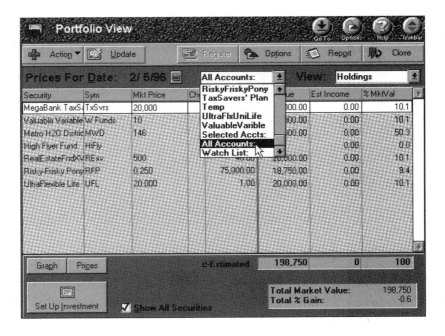

Figure 7-3. The Richies' Portfolio View window will look like this with All Accounts selected.

Normally, you will set up historical prices. We are projecting future ficti-tious prices for our phantom portfolio. Our first price is on February 5, 1996. The final price is on February 5, 2021. To enter dates after the year 1999, use an apostrophe instead of a slash to separate the month and year, as shown in Figure 7-4.

Prices

To enter a price history, click on the Prices button on the bottom of the Portfolio View window. Begin by entering the price history for Metropolis Water District's zero-coupon bonds. Highlight **Metro H2O Dist** in the portfolio. Click on the Prices button at the bottom of the Portfolio View window. You can enter prices for past or future dates. Enter the prices in Figure 7-4, which shows the projected price history for Sally's Metropolis Water District zero-coupon bonds. The initial price is for February 5, 1996, which appears at the bottom of the list. The last price for February 5, 2021, is in the New Price for:MWS window. Keyboard users can press

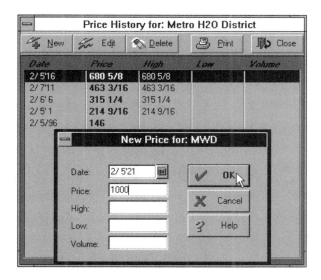

Figure 7-4. Use the above Price History for: window and New Price for: window to create a future price history for Sally's Metropolis Water District bonds.

Alt-N instead of clicking on the New button. If you edit fractional prices, the Edit Price for: window will give you a decimal value to edit. Simply enter the new fractional value.

> **Q-TIP**
>
> **If the values in the Price History window display as fractions when they should be decimals or vise-a-versa, go to List on the main menu. Select Security Type to open the Security Type List window. Select the Security Type of the investment that is displaying improperly, i.e., Metro H20 Dist is a bond so highlight Bond on the list. Click the Edit button to open the Edit Security Type window. Change the Price Display to reflect your preference—Decimal or Fraction. Click OK to save your change.**

Repeat the steps to set up price histories for the Metropolis Water District zero-coupon bonds with the price histories in Table 7-3 then enter the

Date	MegaBank TaxSavers	RealEstateFndXVLtd	Valuable Variable
02/05/96	20,000.00	500.00	10.00
02/05'01	25,525.63	643.00	19.87
02/06'06	32,577.89	1569.00	42.31
02/07'11	41,578.49	1427.00	80.64
02/05'16	53,065.95	3821.00	161.43
02/05'21	67,727.10	5417.35	329.19

Table 7-3. Enter these projected price histories into the appropriate investments' portfolios. Quicken uses an apostrophe instead of a slash to precede the years in the 21st century. Notice that the Tax Savers value grows at an even rate as an interest-earning investment, while the real estate partnership and variable annuity grow at uneven rates as their simulated market values spurt and lag with the stock and real estate markets.

prices for Risky-Frisky Pony, whose price history is in Figure 7-5. If the Portfolio View window does not show a cash balance after you finish entering the price history, confirm that the Prices For Date is 2/5/96 or later.

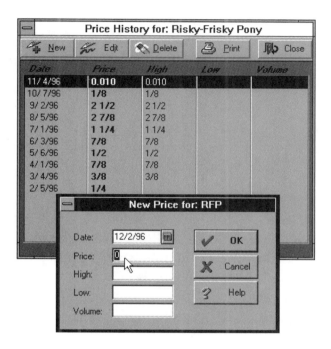

Figure 7-5. Use the above Price History for: window to create a future price history for Sam's speculative Risky-Frisky Pony penny stock. Since stock prices are quoted in fractions, the above prices are entered as fractions. Prices less than a dollar have a zero before the fraction. The only exceptions is the entry for 11/4/96, which is one penny as a decimal (very low value penny stocks are sometimes quoted in single penny increments). In some months, the 5th falls on a weekend. Because the stock market is not open on weekends, we use the following weekday when this occurs. The value on 12/2/96 is $0.00. When Quicken records a zero value, it displays as a blank field in the Price History for: window but does display 0.00 in the Portfolio View window.

Go to the Portfolio View from the Register. To move between the Register and Portfolio Views, press Ctrl-R. From the Portfolio View, complete the following steps to enter price histories:

1. Select the security whose prices you want to enter or edit.
2. Press Ctrl-H to open the Price History window.
3. Select <New Price> and press Enter.
4. Enter the date and price. Press Enter to record the price.
5. Repeat steps 3 and 4 until you finish entering the selected security's price data.
6. Press Enter to return to the Portfolio View.
7. Repeat steps 1 through 5 for each investment.

One of the powerful features of Quicken's investment portfolio is the ability to graph investment results. Go to the Portfolio View window. Change the Prices For Date to 12/2/96, highlight Risky-Frisky Pony by clicking on it, as shown in Figure 7-6. This date is the final entry in Risky-Frisky's brief but volatile history. The authorities will arrest Risky-Frisky's promoters for securities fraud, embezzlement, and a host of other charges on that day in Richie history, too.

Click on the Graph button at the bottom of the Portfolio View window. The Graph Price History window opens with a graph showing the history of Risky-Frisky Pony's share prices, as shown in Figure 7-7. Notice that you can adjust the beginning and ending dates to graph using the date selectors in the upper right and left corners of the graph. The left side of the graph provides a reference for the share values. If you want to see how the total value of the investment fared, click the Show Mrkt Value check-box to redraw the graph like Figure 7-8. The new graph provides a reference for the investment's value along the right side of the graph. If you have a color monitor, the blue (upper) line shows the share price, while the green (lower) line provides information on the investment's market value.

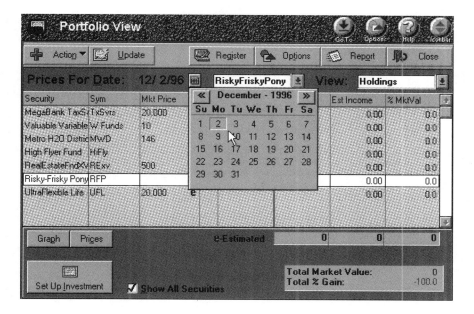

Figure 7-6. Since we are going to graph the prices for Risky-Frisky Pony, we choose to display price information exclusively for that Account.

You can see that Risky-Frisky Pony was a thrilling ride and can teach investors a valuable investment lesson.

If you have turned QuickTabs off (in the Options, General window) you can adjust the Price History Graph window's size and scale by dragging the window's borders. If you move your cursor to the various elements on the graph, you will notice that the cursor changes from an arrow to a magnifying glass. When the magnifying glass appears, hold down your left or secondary mouse button. Quicken shows the value or price of the graph element under the cursor. Move your cursor to the highest point along the green (lower) line in the chart. Click and hold the secondary mouse button when the magnifying glass appears. The highest value of Risky-Frisky was $215,625. That is a pretty phenomenal amount of return considering that Sam invested only $20,000!

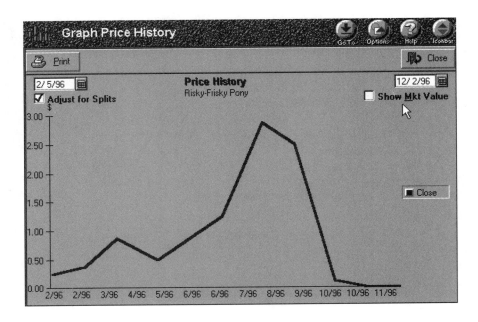

Figure 7-7. This graph shows the share prices for Risky-Frisky Pony. That horse started with a lot of kick but ended up in the glue factory! This figure shows the Graph Price History window in Full-Window mode (selectable by clicking the Options icon then the General button). Please notice the graph is not to scale. Even though we only entered one share price per month, some months appear multiple times on the graph.

 To view a Price History graph, select the investment you want to graph while in the Portfolio View and press ⎡Ctrl⎤-⎡F⎤. Press ⎡Enter⎤ to create the graph. Try this with Risky-Frisky.

For investors who purchase individual stocks, the biggest problem is determining when to sell their investments. If you ever "gamble" on a "hot" stock or penny stock, consider selling portions of your holdings as the price rises. If the price drops again, you will at least recover a portion

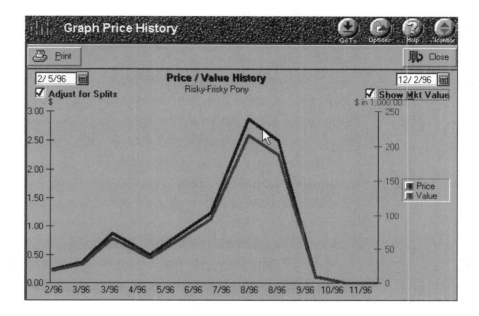

Figure 7-8. You can also graph the total investment value along with the share prices. This graph is more valuable when you are adding to your investment over time, as we will see later in this chapter.

of your original investment. If you buy at $1 per share and the price doubles, sell half your shares to recoup your initial investment capital, less taxes on the profit. If the price continues to soar, you will have lowered your profits but reduced your risk substantially. If the stock "tanks," (this is a technical term used by some financial professionals to indicate that you have just "lost your shirt") you have most of your money back. You don't really get all of your money back because Uncle Sam claims a portion of your profits as taxes, but you can claim the loss on the shares that drop in price when you sell them or when they become worthless.

TAX TIP

Most investors have investments that are losers. If you choose to hang on to the investment, you have a large paper loss. A paper loss means that you own an investment that is worth less than you paid for it. If you believe the investment has good long-term prospects, but you need a tax deduction today, sell the investment to a close friend at the fair market value. If the investment is worthless, e.g., the company is in bankruptcy and you do not expect it to recover, sell your investment for $1. Repurchase the investment from your friend after 31 days. If you repurchase the investment within 30 days of selling it (before or after the sale), you are subject to the "Wash Sale Rule." Under the Wash Sale Rule, you cannot deduct your losses. If you employ this tax strategy, document your actions. You must legally re-register the investment. Do not sell your investment to a "related party." Under the tax law, related parties include spouses, siblings, parents, grandparents, children, grandchildren, trusts, pension plans, IRAs, and fiduciaries. Your in-laws (parents or children) are not related parties. If you sell the investment to in-laws, it must be their separate property. If they do not legally hold the investment as separate property, you could void the tax benefits of the sale.

Not only will Quicken graph individual investments, it will also produce composites of any combination of investments you desire. We will create graphs to show the Richies' investments' annual returns and a graph that shows how the portfolio grows over time.

You can use the Graphs icon on the icon-bar to directly access the Create Graph window (DOS instructions follow). Don't use the Graph button in the Portfolio View window; it cannot be customized to meet our needs. We provide DOS instructions later in this section. We want to graph from February 1996 through February 2021, as shown in Figure 7-9. Remember to use an apostrophe instead of a slash to separate the month

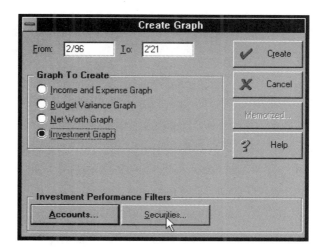

Figure 7-9. Use the Create Graph window to select the date range you want to graph and the graph type. Before creating the graph, it is important to choose which Accounts or Securities you want to include in the graph.

and year for dates after the year 1999. Choose Investment Graph as the Graph to Create.

We can limit the selection of the Accounts and Securities that appear in our graphs by using the Investment Performance Filters at the bottom of the Create Graph window. Initially, we only want to examine Sam's investments. Click the Securities button at the bottom of the Create Graph window to open the Select Securities to Include window. Mark Sam's investments, shown in Figure 7-10, and then click OK to return to the Create Graph window. Now click the Accounts button and mark the Accounts that contain Sam's investments, shown in Figure 7-10. When you finish, click OK to return to the Create Graph window. Click Create to view the Investment Performance Graph, which is really two graphs in one window.

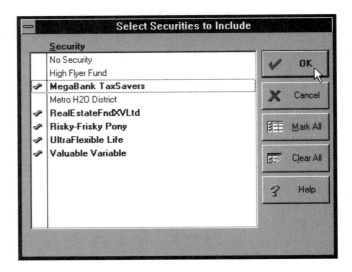

Figure 7-10. Use the Select Securities to Include window to mark Sam's investments to graph.

Quicken sometimes defaults to creating multiple graphs in a single graph window. If you want larger graphs, you can choose for them to appear in separate windows. For example, in our current situation use the Options button in the Investment Performance Graph window. Select Create All Graphs in Separate Windows. Click OK to save your change. Now close the Investment Performance Graph window and repeat the graph creation process to create two new Investment Performance Graphs in separate windows. When you repeat the process, Quicken remembers the date selections you made the last time you created the graphs.

To move between the graphs when QuickTabs are turned on, click the gray Zoom Graph tab to the left of the graph window. If you want to change the graph size or scale, you need to be in Full-Window Mode. To switch between using QuickTabs and

Full-Window Mode, choose the Options icon from the main menu bar then click the General button. Make your selection in the QuickTabs section of the General Options window. Once you are in Full-Windows Mode, use standard Windows click-and-dragging to resize your graph windows.

Quicken creates two Investment Performance Graphs: Average Annual Total Return and Monthly Portfolio Value. The DOS version creates only the Monthly Portfolio Value graph. The graphs appear in the same window unless you change the default setting, which creates separate graphs in two windows, as described in the preceding Q-Tip.

The Monthly Portfolio Value graph, Figure 7-11, shows annual investment performance because we used an extended time frame. If you graph a short enough time-frame, the graph actually does give monthly performance results. Experiment with the Type, Goal, Sec (Security), and Account buttons at the top of the graph window to see how the graph changes.

The Average Annual Total Return Graph, Figure 7-12, is useful for judging which investments perform best. When you invest different amounts of money in different investments at different times, it is much more difficult to determine which investments are performing best. The investment's rate of return is a good performance yardstick.

The graph is color-coded, making it easier to decipher. The horizontal line running through the bars on the graph tells you the total performance of the selected investments. Quicken assumes that you reinvest your profits into one of the Accounts appearing on the graph. The total investment performance of one or more securities along with the reinvested profits from those investments is the Internal Rate of Return. The horizontal line shows the internal rate of return for the selected investments. When you click the solid box at either end of the line or Total IRR in the graph legend, Quicken shows that it calculates this portfolio's internal rate of return at 9.40 percent.

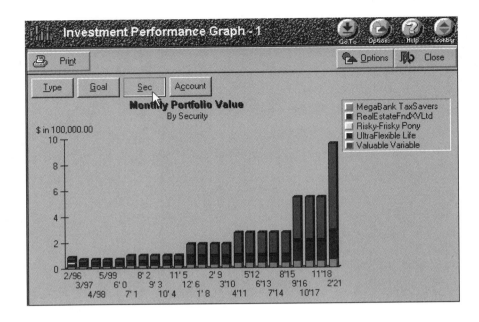

Figure 7-11. This Monthly Portfolio Value graph shows a 25-year projection of Sam's investment portfolio. His initial $100,000 investment fund grew to $962,801.10 even though one investment was a total loss and another didn't make any money! This is known as the Portfolio Value Trend graph in DOS.

Create the Monthly Portfolio Value graph, known as the Portfolio Value Trend graph in DOS, using the steps that follow. This version of Quicken does not create the Average Annual Return graph.

1. While in Portfolio view choose Graph from the menu bar.
2. Select Investment and then select Portfolio Value Trend to open the Portfolio Value Trend window.

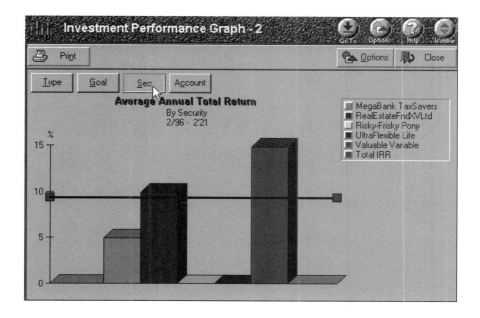

Figure 7-12. This Average Annual Total Return graph shows how well each of Sam's investments will have performed over the 25-year projection period. The horizontal line running through the bars on the bar chart shows that Quicken calculates the portfolio's Internal Rate of Return at 9.40 percent! This graph is not available in DOS.

3. Graph ending balances for months: 2/96 through 2'21. Leave Display the Balances at the default setting, By Security.

4. Filter what will appear on the graph by pressing F9 to go to the Investment Filters window.

5. In the Investment Filters window, type Y to Select securities to graph.

6. Press Enter to open the Select Securities to Include window.

7. Select the appropriate investments, shown in Figure 7-10, and then press Enter to return to the Portfolio Value Trend

window. Press ⟨Enter⟩ again to create the graph. The next step the Windows users will take is to create a report of the graph's results. In DOS, simply click the Report button.

We projected that Sam's investments will yield various amounts of return, from a total loss to a 15 percent annual rate of return. You can create a report showing your portfolio's investment performance using the following steps:

1. Click the Reports icon on the main icon bar to open the Create Report window.

2. Click the Investment tab, then choose Investment Performance. Set the report dates to **2/5/96** to **2/8'21** as shown in Figure 7-13.

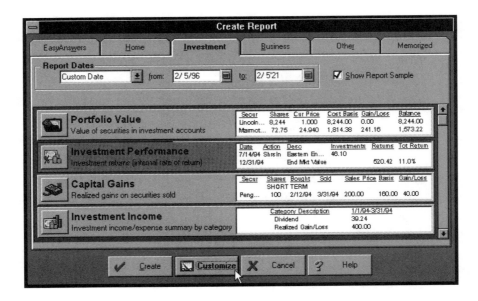

Figure 7-13. Complete your Create Report window to match this example then click the Customize button to open the Customize Investment Performance Report window.

3. Click on Customize to open the Customize Investment Performance Report window. When this window opens, the default tab setting is Display. In the Headings section, select Don't Subtotal from the drop-down list, then select the Accounts tab. Use the Clear All button, then set up your window to match Figure 7-14. Confirm that your report dates are 2/5/96 to 2/5'21.

4. Now choose the Include tab in the Customize Investment Performance Report window. Confirm that all of Sam's securities are selected. You can click the Mark All button and select all of the securities since only those securities in a selected Account will

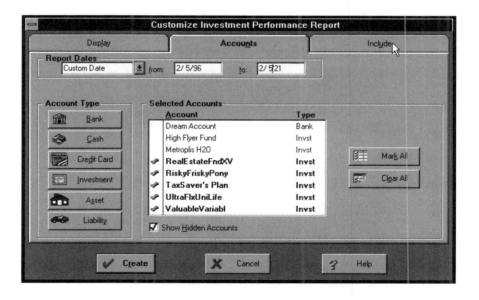

Figure 7-14. The appearance of this window changed substantially when you chose Accounts tab. Enter the information in this figure to create an Investment Performance Report for Sam's Portfolio. Notice that you must choose which Investment Accounts to include in your report. You only want to mark the five Accounts shown above. The other Accounts, not shown, should not be marked.

appear on the Investment Performance Report. When you finish, click Create to create the report. Your report should resemble the one shown in Figure 7-15. If your screen looks different, return to the customize display section and confirm that Subtotal By is set to Don't Subtotal.

Go to the Investments' Portfolio View. Follow these steps to create an Investment Performance Report.

1. From the Menu bar, select Report, then Investment Reports, and finally Investment Performance.

2. Change the Report Performance date to: 2/5/96 through 2/5'21.

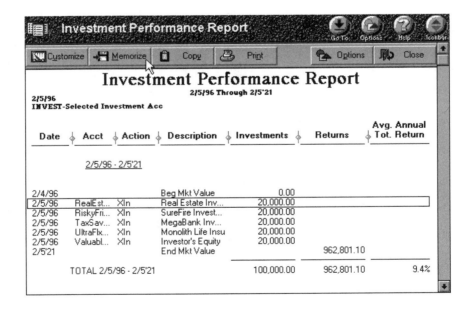

Figure 7-15. Although reports don't look as nice as graphs, they contain valuable information for your reference. If you plan to use a report multiple times, click the Memorize button to save it for future use.

3. Type 6 for Security in Subtotal by:.

4. Enter Y to Show Cash flow Detail.

5. Input C to show Current Investment Accounts.

6. Press [F9] to open the Filter Investment Transactions window. Change Select Securities to Include to Y. Press [Enter] to open the Select Securities to Include window. Select the five securities in Sam's portfolio, shown in Figure 7-14. To select or deselect securities, highlight one and press the spacebar to toggle the Include in Reports column between Include and blank to exclude. Press [Enter] to return to the Investment Performance Report window.

7. Change Subtotal by: to 5 (Account). Press [Enter] to create the report, which should resemble the one shown in Figure 7-15. Note: Making a choice other than 5, you can create an alternate report that lists performance by Security.

INVESTMENT MARKET CYCLES

All investments experience market cycles. A market cycle includes a time of increasing values or prices, a peak, then a period of declining values or prices resulting in a low point followed by the next cycle. Typically, market cycles last approximately seven years. Occasionally, abnormalities occur, with longer or shorter cycles resulting. With stocks experiencing an up-trend for 14 years—except for a little hiccup in October 1987 that people thought was a crash at the time. It may be time for the market to peak and begin a period of decline.

Many people believe that it is possible to time the market. A number of companies even offer timing services, which use complex computer models to attempt to predict when an investor should buy and sell investments, typically mutual funds. They charge their clients on the basis of a percentage of the assets managed. These fees are usually between .5 percent and three percent of the assets managed. Every time I have met a client using a timing service, the timing service's performance results have been disappointing. One client lost a substantial amount of money when he could have earned a healthy return on that particular investment without the timing service. The fees and additional taxes often exceed the profits generated from the attempt at timing.

A couple of summers ago, I attended an investment conference in San Francisco. One of the speakers included a study of the Standard and Poor's 500 annual performance in his presentation. The study found that the S&P 500 had an annual return of 17.6 percent during the 1980s. If you take out the 10 best days during that decade, the return drops to 12.6 percent per year, as shown in Table 7-4. The same presentation included another study that considered 1970 to 1990. The S&P grew at a 10.8 percent annual rate during those two decades. If you remove the four best quarters, the return drops to 7.4 percent.

It is difficult to know when the best investment days will occur. It is better to find a quality money manager and remain invested than to jump in and out of the market. The situation most investors worry about is buying when prices are high just before they fall.

1980-1989	S&P 500 Index Annualized Return
All 2528 Trading Days	17.5%
Less the 10 Best Days	12.6
Less the 20 Best Days	9.3
Less the 30 Best Days	6.5
Less the 40 Best Days	3.9

Table 7-4. Time or Timing: The Penalty for Missing the Market. Funds not invested in the S&P 500 are invested in U.S. Treasury Bills.

Sources: Datastream, Ibbotson Associates, Inc. and Sanford C. Bernstein & Company

Although it is difficult or impossible to accurately time the stock market in the short term, it is possible to spot trends. If you can stop and exploit an investment's market trend, you can reduce your risk while increasing your probability of producing profits.

Some successful investors employ a contrarian theory in spotting investment trends. Contrarians believe that when a majority of investors decide to buy a particular investment, the time to sell is near. When few people find an investment interesting, it is a good time to consider buying. The basis for contrarian investing is supply and demand. When something is popular, supply is limited so prices rise. When the same investment falls from favor, the supply is ample so prices fall. Contrarians try to buy out of favor and hold until demand and prices rise. The trick is determining when to sell the investment. The preferred time to sell is when the demand and prices peak, before they begin falling.

Consistently discovering the optimal times to buy and sell is impossible. One must be willing to settle for less than optimal results. One way to reduce your risk is dollar-cost averaging, which we will discuss in a minute. First, we want to discuss the difference between owning and loaning.

OWNING VERSUS LOANING

Most people create wealth by owning assets, not by loaning their money to others to use. The logic seems fairly straightforward. Why would anyone want to borrow your money unless he can pay you back with interest and still produce a profit for himself? Instead of loaning money to others to produce profits, why not invest in the item that will create the profits for yourself?

The most popular form of loaning is placing money on deposit in a bank or another savings institution. However, over long periods of time, equity investments always outperform deposit accounts. Ibbotson Associates in Chicago, Illinois, has a reputation in the financial community for providing excellent historical data. The graph in Figure 7-16 shows how a dollar performed from 1925 through 1993 when invested in small company stocks, common stocks, long-term government bonds, and Treasury Bills. The chart also shows how these investments performed relative to inflation. One dollar invested in small company stocks in 1925 was worth $2,757.15 by the end of 1993! The same dollar invested in long-term government bonds was only worth $28.03. Where do you think your money will grow the most over the next 50 years?

Now let's compare how an actual $10,000 investment in one conserva- tively managed mutual fund—the Investment Company of America (ICA)—fared versus how a $10,000 investment in U.S. Treasury Bills fared over the same 25-year time frame, as shown in Figure 7-17.

One reason people lend their money is that they believe it is safer than investing in equities. Equities are investments in which you have an own- ership position in the underlying asset, for example, a share of stock in a corporation. Bonds are popular debt instruments. A debt instrument is an investment in a loan, bond, or other form of debt. You only own the loan, someone else owns the asset.

In 1983, interest rates were very high in comparison to today's rates. However, they were much lower than in 1979 and 1980, when Americans had come to accept inflation as inevitable and expected rates to increase again. Rates continued to decline to today's relatively low levels.

As we discussed earlier, the '80s were unusual. Do not expect the '90s to have the same results. How did the decline in interest rates affect bond prices? Investors in the Bond Fund of America saw the value of their investment increase 228 percent—12.6 percent per year—from June 1983 through July 1993. Bond prices increase as interest rates decline. Bond prices decrease as interest rates rise. It is like a teeter-totter. One end goes up as the other goes down. In 1993, the question bond investors needed to ask was, "How much lower can interest rates go?" In 1993, fixed-rate home mortgages were as low as they were 30 years ago! In early 1994,

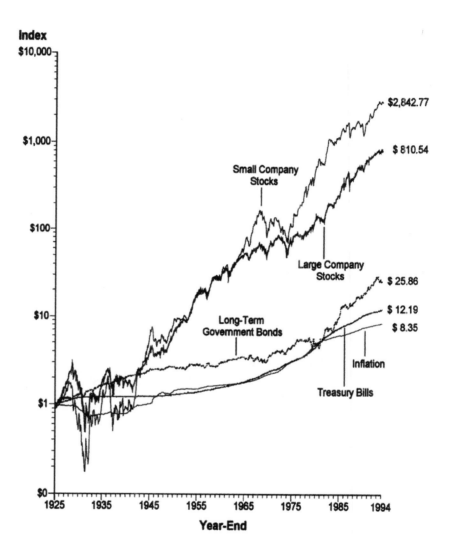

Figure 7-16. This graph shows how a dollar invested in small company stocks, common stocks, long-term government bonds, and Treasury Bills grew from 1925 through 1993. The amount of inflation is also shown. If history is a teacher, what can you learn from this graph?

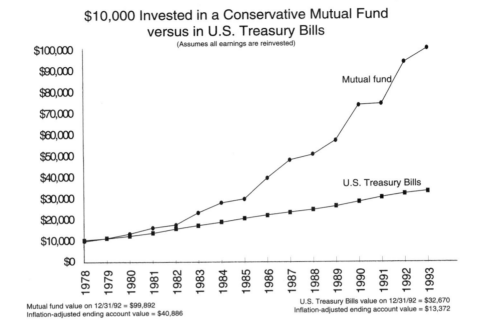

$10,000 Invested in a Conservative Mutual Fund
versus in U.S. Treasury Bills
(Assumes all earnings are reinvested)

Mutual fund value on 12/31/92 = $99,892
Inflation-adjusted ending account value = $40,886

U.S. Treasury Bills value on 12/31/92 = $32,670
Inflation-adjusted ending account value = $13,372

Figure 7-17. A $10,000 investment fared much better in the conservatively managed mutual fund than in U.S. Treasury Bills from 1977 through 1992.

Used with permission, Vogt Financial Concepts & Strategies, Inc.

interest rates began moving upward. As interest rates rose, bond investors lost billions of dollars in profits as their portfolios declined in value. Rates peaked in early 1995, then began dropping. By October 1995, rates had stabilized. One rate index most people can identify with is for 30-year fixed rate mortgages. Mortgage rates were hovering around 9.5 percent in January 1995 and were steady at 7.5 percent in October. Investors with clear crystal balls would have sold their bonds before interest rates began climbing in early 1994. They would have bought bonds in early 1995 and rode the rates down, raking in profits as bond values rose due to rates falling. The really questions are: "Will rates fall further," "How much further will rates fall before they bottom out," and "When should I sell to cash in on those profits?"

Even though bonds were a great investment from 1983 to 1992, stocks were an even better investment! The same money managers who manage the Bond Fund of America also manage a number of stock funds.

Three of the conservative, as opposed to aggressive, stock funds increased over 300 percent—about 15 percent per year, compounded— during the same time frame.

Another problem with debt-oriented investments is the possibility of future inflation wiping out your purchasing power. Have you ever considered the impact of inflation on your purchasing power? From the beginning of 1978 to the end of 1992, a 15-year period, the purchasing power of a dollar fell to only 41 cents. That is a 59 percent loss in purchasing power, illustrated in Figure 7-18. I will try to explain in simple language the concern some people have about the probability of future inflation.

Many people worry about the future effect of the national debt on our financial system. When a country accumulates more debt than it can repay, it must do something. Some countries simply declare that they will not pay their debts. It is unacceptable in the world economy to simply refuse to repay what you owe. Other countries print more money to pay off their debt. (Have you ever wondered how the government knows how much money it can print?) As more money enters the economy, it becomes less valuable, causing prices to rise. Thus the government repays their debt with dollars that are worth less than the dollars borrowed. Printing too much money causes a substantial amount of economic harm. When a country prints currency without assets to back it, inflation results. During a period of rising inflation, you do not want your money invested in debt instruments.

In 1993, the Russian people and others in Eastern Europe experienced a version of this problem first-hand. The government switched cur-

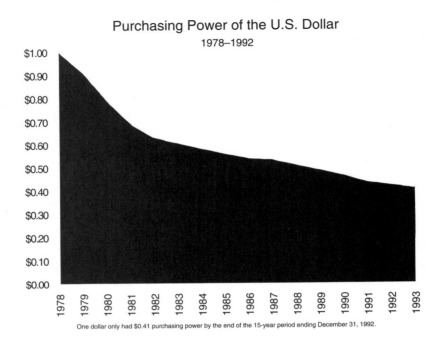

Purchasing Power of the U.S. Dollar
1978–1992

One dollar only had $0.41 purchasing power by the end of the 15-year period ending December 31, 1992.

Figure 7-18. The U.S. Dollar lost 59 percent of its purchasing power from 1978 to 1992.

Used with permission, Vogt Financial Concepts & Strategies, Inc.

rencies. Everyone had to turn in their old money for new money. The authorities also allowed prices to move freely. (Remember that the Soviet government fixed prices at artificial levels for decades.) The government did not adjust wages and pensions for the resulting inflation. In a short period, the government reduced its real cost of paying salaries and pensions. Meanwhile, the prices that government-owned industries charged for food, clothing, and other products rose tremendously. Some reports from Russia told of retirees' monthly pensions being less than the cost of meat for a day's meals.

Variations on what happened in Russia occur frequently in economic history. Many South American countries have experienced ravaging inflation. At times, inflation exceeded 1,000 percent per month! In pre–World War II Germany, inflation was so rapid that prices rose while customers stood in checkout lines.

Rapid inflation decimates saving accounts, non-variable annuities, cash value life insurance, and debt instrument investments. Pension income is not usually indexed for inflation, either. Investments in real estate and equities tend to hold their value during inflationary times.

Some financial experts have been warning that the government will collect less money in personal income taxes than it will pay in interest on the national debt. This will occur sooner than most experts predicted because rising interest rates add to the government's annual expenses. When Congress passed the Revenue Reconciliation Act of 1993, members promised to cut spending and reduce the national debt. If you look past the smoke and mirrors, the actual number of dollars the government spent in 1994 was greater than it spent in 1993. The annual budget deficit actually increases instead of decreases. Over the five years in the final budget plan passed by the Democratic controlled Congress, the Congressional Budget Office projected the national debt to continue its increase, not decrease! (The difference between the deficit and the national debt can be confusing. The deficit is the amount of money the government spends in excess of what it collects in taxes and other revenue. The national debt is the total debt Congress' deficit spending has accumulated.) Something drastic will occur within 10 to 15 years if our senseless leaders continue to spend money they don't have. J. Peter Grace, Chairman and CEO of W.R. Grace & Co. and former head of the Grace Commission, says, "We're on a disaster course and the time for action is right now.... By the year 2000, interest payments [on the federal debt] will take 102 percent of all personal income taxes.... What do you think will happen next?"

Fortunately, the Republicans took control of Congress in the 1994 elections, they are not perfect but they are making real progress in Congress for the first time in years. They actually debated and voted on all ten points of the Republican *Contract with America*. They have a realistic plan to stop wasting billions of dollars of our hard-earned dollars and balance the federal budget in seven years!

As this book went to press, the budget battle was just beginning between the Republican-controlled Congress, entrenched bureaucrats, liberal left-wing special interests, and our President—William Jefferson Clinton.

If the Republicans fail to stop the ballooning budget deficit, inflation will probably increase and taxes will definitely rise. How will you fare?

If you are not already concerned about the national debt and the government's out-of-control spending, you should be. As 1995 drew to a close, the national debt was approaching $4.725 trillion. Divide that staggering amount by 263 million Americans, and you will discover that those irresponsible politicians in Washington, D.C., have spent about $18,000 of your money and signed your name on the loan. When you think about this for awhile, it is evident that your elected representatives have spent every last dollar you have ever paid in taxes. Furthermore, they have already spent $18,000 for every American man, woman, and child. Our children and grandchildren will pay interest on this debt and more for decades to come.

Most people fail to see how the value of debt investments decreases over time as inflation erodes their purchasing power. They only consider the amount of interest they can earn. Sharp investors consider an investment's total return potential—earnings plus growth.

Let's compare the historical results of a debt instrument to those of an actual investment in a conservatively managed mutual fund. We will compare them over the same 15-year period—January 1, 1978, through December 31, 1992—as is shown in our inflation chart, Figure 7-19. Let's invest $200,000 in each. Assume the debt instrument is a fixed-income investment earning six percent. All interest is removed from the account as it is earned. Also assume that six percent of the fund's value is removed each year.

At the end of the 15-year period, the fixed-income account still has the original $200,000 investment in it. Over the account's life, it has earned $180,000 in interest. Our inflation chart, provided in Figure 7-19, shows

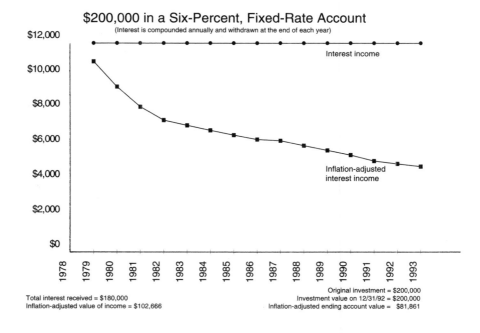

$200,000 in a Six-Percent, Fixed-Rate Account
(Interest is compounded annually and withdrawn at the end of each year)

Interest income

Inflation-adjusted interest income

Total interest received = $180,000
Inflation-adjusted value of income = $102,666

Original investment = $200,000
Investment value on 12/31/92 = $200,000
Inflation-adjusted ending account value = $81,861

Figure 7-19. This figure shows how a fixed investment account earning six percent would fare over a 15-year period. The top line represents the $12,000 annual earnings in the account. The lower line shows how the purchasing power of the $12,000 declines over time.

Used with permission, Vogt Financial Concepts & Strategies, Inc.

that the $200,000 has lost almost 60 percent of its original purchasing power. Forty-one percent of $200,000 is only $82,000.

The investors also receive six percent of the mutual fund's value as income. The difference is that the investment can grow in value. From the beginning of 1978 through 1992, the investors receive $343,872 in income while the account value of the fund grows to $840,137! When you adjust the ending values for inflation, the 1992 income of $50,408 has $20,632 of purchasing power, and the account value has $343,872 of purchasing power. Figures 7-19 and 7-20 graphically represents the results. Compare Figures 7-19 and 7-20. Which investment would you have liked to own? Please remember historical returns should not be used as a basis of expectation of future result.

Many people feel trapped. The stock market has attained record highs in 1995, and so they are afraid of a market decline or even a crash. Interest rates are low. Banks offer interest rates that are less than the inflation rate. Bonds pay higher rates, but their values will drop if interest rates rise. What should an investor do? They should reduce their risk by creating a diversified portfolio of equity investments, not debt investments. They should build their portfolio over time using dollar-cost averaging.

To learn more about the potential financial crisis that looms on the horizon, read *The Coming Economic Earthquake* by Larry Burkett.

DOLLAR-COST AVERAGING

The concept of dollar-cost averaging is one of the most fundamental principles you need to understand for long-term investing. The basic concept is to invest a set amount of money on a consistent basis over a long period of time. Your average cost per share is less than the average price per share over that same period of time. This principle works with all types of investments. We will demonstrate this concept using the High Flyer Fund.

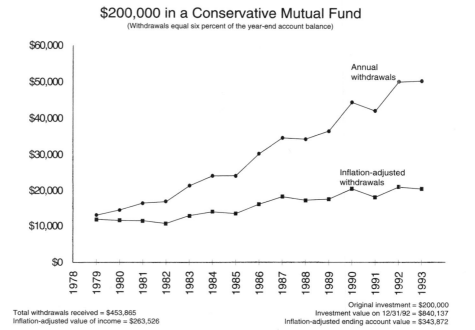

$200,000 in a Conservative Mutual Fund
(Withdrawals equal six percent of the year-end account balance)

Annual withdrawals

Inflation-adjusted withdrawals

Total withdrawals received = $453,865
Inflation-adjusted value of income = $263,526

Original investment = $200,000
Investment value on 12/31/92 = $840,137
Inflation-adjusted ending account value = $343,872

Figure 7-20. This figure shows the historical performance of a conservatively managed mutual fund over the same period shown in Figure 7-19. The upper line shows the amount an investor would have withdrawn by taking six percent of the account value at the conclusion of each year. The lower line represents the inflation-adjusted purchasing power of those withdrawals.

Used with permission, Vogt Financial Concepts & Strategies, Inc.

Consider the following scenario. The Richies begin investing in the High Flyer Fund on March 1, 1996. They invest $200 on the first business day of each month. The price begins to fall after they start, but it later rises to the price it was at when they began investing. Did they make any money?

Enter the transactions from Table 7-5 into your High Flyer Fund Register. (The easiest method of opening the Register is to use the Accounts icon.) Use the same procedures given earlier in this chapter to complete these transactions. Refer to the instructions that accompany Table 7-2. Your Register should look like Figure 7-21 after you finish.

When you complete the entries, go to the Portfolio view. Change the Set Prices For: date to August 1, 1996, per Figure 7-22. Both DOS and Windows users can use the [Ctrl]-[G] Quick Key to change the date. Highlight the High Flyer Fund by clicking on it. You are ready to graph the fund's results.

Click the Graph button in the lower-left corner of the Portfolio View window. Quicken will graph your High Flyer Fund investments from March 1 to August 1. Check Show Mkt Value in the upper-right corner of the Graph Price History window. Your graph should look like Figure 7-23.

Date	Action Memo	Security	Price	Shares	Basis Mkt Value	Clr	Share Bal
3/ 1/96	BuyX	High Flyer Fund	10	20	200 00		20 00
			[Dream Accou	200.00			
4/ 1/96	BuyX	High Flyer Fund	8.500	23.529	200 00		43 52
			[Dream Accou	200.00			
5/ 1/96	BuyX	High Flyer Fund	7	28.571	200 00		72 10
			[Dream Accou	200.00			
6/ 3/96	BuyX	High Flyer Fund	8	25	200 00		97 10
			[Dream Accou	200.00			
7/ 1/96	BuyX	High Flyer Fund	9	22.222	200 00		119 32
			[Dream Accou	200.00			
8/ 1/96	BuyX	High Flyer Fund	10	20	200 00		139 32
			[Dream Accou	200.00			
3/ 1/96	Action Memo	Security	Price	Shares	Basis Mkt Value		

High Flyer Fund - High Flyer MutualFund: Inv...   Go To   Options   Help   Iconbar

Action ▼   Port View   Close

Temp   Metropolis H2O   RealEstateFndXV   RiskyFrickyPony   TaxSavers' Plan   UltrsFlxUniLife

Record   Edit   Form

Ending Share Bal: 139.32
Market Value: 1,393.22

Figure 7-21. Your High Flyer Fund Register should look like this after entering the transactions in Table 7-5.

Date	Amount Invested	Number of Shares Bought	Price per Share
3/1/96	$200.00	20.000	$10.00
4/3	200.00	23.529	8.50
5/2	200.00	28.571	7.00
6/3	200.00	25.000	8.00
7/1	200.00	22.222	9.00
8/1	200.00	20.000	10.00
Totals	$1,200.00	139.322	Average Price per Share $8.75

Table 7-5. Enter these transactions into your High Flyer Fund Investment Account. To keep the example simple, we do not include any transaction costs. Use Buy as the Action and transfer the funds from the Dream Account.

DOS users should refer to the instructions that correspond to Figure 7-7. The lower line (green) represents the total value of the High Flyer Fund shares. The upper line (blue) represents the prices paid for the shares in each transaction. The graph tick marks on the right indicate the Account value, while the marks on the left show the price paid per share.

When you graph a mutual fund that you actually own, you will probably want to update the share prices once a week. Mutual funds are typically long-term investments. To graph an investment's daily prices, you should consider purchasing investment analysis software. I recommend *MetaStock-Professional* from Equis International. For additional information, contact Equis at (800) 882-3040.

You probably want to know a little more about your investment's performance. Move your cursor over the various graph components. When it becomes a magnifying glass, click your left mouse button to see that component's value.

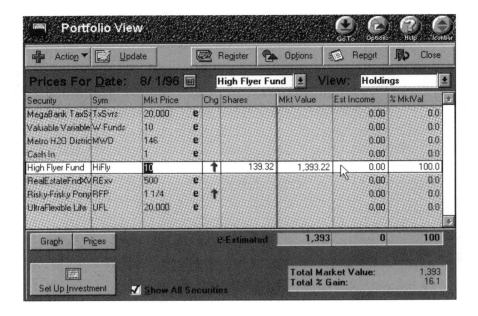

Figure 7-22. The lower right region of the Portfolio View window contains valuable investment information. The High Flyer Fund has a total value of $1,393 (rounded to the nearest dollar) and is worth 16.1 percent more than the shares cost.

You can easily create a Security Report by returning to the Portfolio View and clicking the Report button. The report includes transaction information on the security. Your report should resemble Figure 7-24. You can also create a Price and Value History report using the instructions given earlier in this chapter.

If making an entry on the report seems strange, you can access the Buy Shares window for that transaction. Just double-click on a transaction you want to examine. If there is a mistake, correct it in the Buy Shares window before returning to the Price and Value History report window. When you leave the Buy Shares window after making a correction, the report, graph, and Register entries all adjust.

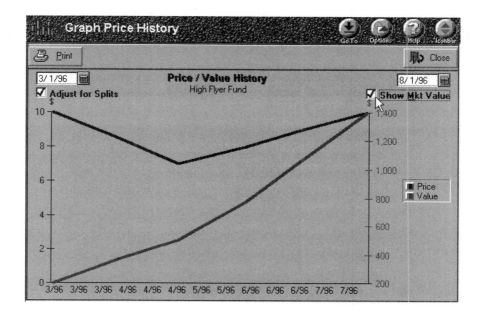

Figure 7-23. The Graph Price History window graphs historical share prices and the total value of your investment for the dates graphed. The tick marks to the left correspond to share prices, graphed on the upper line. The tick marks to the right of the graph provide a reference to the portfolio's value, shown by the lower line. The DOS version does not include share price information.

Go to Sam's Portfolio View. Follow these steps to create an Investment Transactions Report.

1. From the menu bar, select Report, then Investment Reports, and finally Investment Transactions.
2. Change the Report Performance date to 3/1/96 through 8/1/96.
3. Choose 6 for Security in the Subtotal By field.

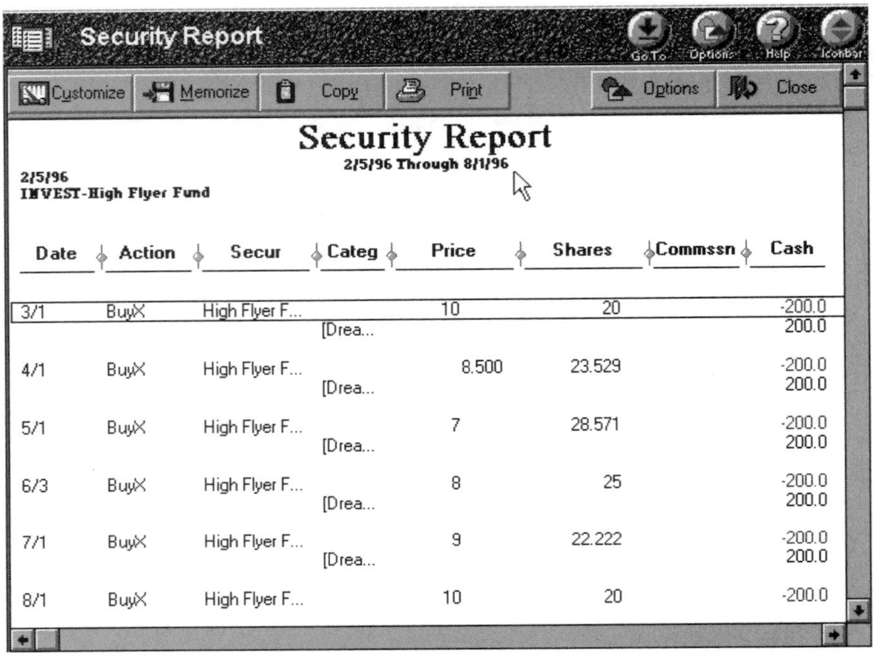

Figure 7-24. The Security Report window shows a history of the security you selected. To view the entire report, click the Reports button.

4. Press F9 to filter your transactions. Select Y for Securities To Include, and then press Ctrl-Enter to open the Select Securities to Include window.

5. Select High Flyer Fund and then press Ctrl-Enter twice to create the report.

You have just experienced the power of dollar-cost averaging. You invested a total of $1,200 over six months. The average purchase price of the shares was $8.75 each. The average cost per share was $8.61. The difference between the cost and price per share in this example is more than 1.5 percent. It may not seem like much, but every little bit helps. Find the average cost per share by dividing the total amount invested by the number of shares purchased—$1,200.00/139.322 shares = $8.61. The value of your investment increased from $1,200 to $1,393.22. That is a 16.1 percent gain in only six months, or 32.2 percent, annualized.

Quicken's value in this exercise lies in its ability to help us visualize an investment's steady growth even as share prices fluctuate. Graphs help us see an investment's consistent increase in value. It would have been easy to calculate the benefits of dollar-cost averaging from the table at the beginning of this section. How many people take time to create tables of their investment transactions? Not very many do. From Quicken's investment reports, you can easily glean the information you need to calculate your average cost per share. Maybe the next Quicken release will contain dollar-cost averaging formulas and reports. If this capability interests you, let Intuit know!

Dollar-cost averaging reduces the uncertainty often involved in making decisions. You know you will invest a certain number of dollars each month on a certain day. You have already made the decision. You know you will not buy all of your shares on the absolute best day to buy, but you won't buy them all on the worst day, either. Mathematically, you know you will buy your shares for a lower per-share cost than the average price you pay for the shares. The most important aspect of investing is to take action. In the long run, it is not as important when you invest as it is that you do invest!

Dollar-cost averaging is well suited for long-term investors who are uncertain about the market's direction. If shares begin to decline, you have the satisfaction of knowing you are buying more shares for the same amount of money. If prices rise, you know that the market experiences cycles, so you will buy shares at off-peak prices again in the future. You can sleep soundly at night knowing that the long-term trend in the market is up and that you are moving with the trend as prices fluctuate.

Although dollar-cost averaging is an important investment concept, maintaining proper reserve funds is critical to your long-term financial success.

OPPORTUNITY AND CRISIS FUNDS

Before you consider a serious investment program, calculate the amount of accessible cash reserves you have. Include the cash you keep in savings, the minimum balance you maintain in a checking account, your money market fund balance (if you have check-writing privileges), and the value of U.S. Savings Bonds in your computations. Do not include your vacation fund, Christmas fund, or other money you expect to spend within a year as cash reserves. You should have at least one month's expenses in your reserves that consist of cash and cash equivalents.

The balance of your reserves can be an assortment of items. The basic principle is that you are able to get your hands on the cash within one or two weeks. You want to consider how much it costs to use these other assets as reserves.

The cash value of your life insurance is an important item to include in your long-term reserves. Most companies can cut you a check within a couple of days. If you think you may need money from your insurance company, call them in advance. Ask how soon you can get money from them and how to request it. Ask if the local office can issue checks and if there is a dollar limit to locally written checks. One of my clients in California recently needed a substantial sum from his life insurance policy. His insurance company required him to submit original signatures to their East Coast office before they would write his check. You will usually find it more advantageous to borrow money from a life insurance policy than to withdraw it.

In a pinch, you may consider cashing in some mutual fund shares. Again, call the company well in advance. Some companies issue checks promptly, while others let mold grow on redemption requests.

It is also possible to get money out of an IRA or other pension fund in emergencies. If you are under age 59½, the government requires your IRA or pension custodian to withhold 20 percent of the distribution for federal income taxes. Some states also impose withholding requirements. Tax withholding is in addition to any early withdrawal penalties you may face on your account. You do not lose the taxes that are withheld, but you can't get them back until you file a tax return for your refund. You have 60 days from the date your custodian writes the check to replace the funds into an IRA to avoid paying the taxes and penalty on the withdrawal. You must also put enough money back in to replace any taxes withheld. Remember that the government taxes you on the gross, not net, amount you withdraw from a pension plan, so your income taxes will rise if you keep a distribution.

You can use a line of credit to supplement your reserves, too. This is sometimes helpful while waiting for an insurance company or mutual fund check to arrive.

Many investors have unrealistic expectations for their investments. In the next section, we share some thoughts on what is realistic in the investment realm.

TAX TIP   **Make a photocopy of any checks you receive from an IRA or other pension plan if you think you may put the money back into the plan or another plan. Send any checks to an IRA or other pension plan by Certified Mail—Return Receipt Requested. The IRS will accept the post office's receipt as proof substantiating your claim should your check get lost in the mail.**

REALISTIC EXPECTATIONS

If you watch investor behavior for a while, you will observe that people expect history to repeat itself—immediately! It is amazing how quickly people forget to consider a long-term historical perspective, amid the clamor of current events. It is important to remember that markets go through cycles and to consider long-term average rates of return.

Stock and bond investors in the 1980s entered the 1990s with smiles on their faces. Both stock and bond markets yielded double-digit rates of return. As a result of the markets' performance, most mutual funds, variable annuities, and variable life products also did very well.

It is useful to compare Ibbotson Associates' data from 1926 to 1991 with the 1980s, as shown in Table 7-6.

Overall, the 1980s were the second-best decade, after the 1950s, for stocks between 1926 and 1991. By examining the table, you can see clearly that the 17.5 percent return for common stocks in the 1980s is substantially higher than the 10.4 percent return for the entire 50-year time frame. If we base future performance expectations on the great returns of the 1980s, we are likely to be disappointed.

The performance gap between the 1980s and the last half century is even more pronounced than for stock yields. Although bond yields have risen steadily since the 1940s, the 1980s bond market yields are unparalleled in U.S. post-Revolutionary War history.

Annual Compound Returns	1925-1991	1980s
Common Stocks/S&P 500	10.4%	17.5%
Small Company Stocks	12.1	15.8
Long-Term Corporate Bonds	5.4	13.0
Long-Term Government Bonds	4.8	12.6
Intermediate-Term Government Bonds	5.1	11.9
U.S. Treasury Bills	3.7	8.9
Inflation	3.1	5.1

Table 7-6. Comparing annual compound returns long-term results versus the '80s shows that the '80s had unusually high investment returns.

Source: Ibbotson Associates, Inc., Chicago, Illinois.

The point is that although no one can predict the future, we can use the past to help us set realistic projections for the future. In setting our expectations, we need to use a long enough historical time frame to encompass multiple market cycles. The 1980s are part of the longest-running bull market in modern U.S. history, but they do not include a full market cycle—including a down market. We can expect the market to continue to cycle in the future, and we must adjust our investment strategies accordingly.

It is safe to say that a prudent investment in the market will grow and compound over an extended time frame at rates that can reasonably be expected to approximate historical norms.

RISK VERSUS REWARD

Whenever you consider investing your money, you have to understand that there is always risk involved. As we pointed out earlier, you are subject to risk when you put your money into a bank. Typically, the greater the risk, the greater is the potential for reward.

Items that have very low risk also tend to have very low rates of return, such as your bank account, CDs, and cash value life insurance policies. At the other end of the investment spectrum are exotic investments such as options and commodities, in which you have a tremendous amount of risk of losing all or part of your money, but also, if you're lucky or have a fabulous understanding of what you're doing, you can make tremendous amounts of profit. In between are various levels of investments with risk versus reward ratios.

TAXABLE, TAX-DEFERRED, AND TAX-FREE INCOME

There are three basic types of investment income: taxable, tax-deferred, and tax-free. We will discuss them in Chapter 8.

THE TEN PERCENT SOLUTION

Cash flow, as we've mentioned many times, is the key to creating wealth. If you take a large enough percentage of your income and invest it on a regular basis, unless there are some major calamities, you will not have any choice but to become wealthy. Take just ten percent of your net income—of course, it would be better if you took ten percent of your gross income—and invest it on a regular basis into a well-diversified portfolio of investments. You will become a very wealthy individual by the time you retire. It is unlikely that you will be able to begin to invest 10 percent of your income immediately. So start small. Don't try to invest more than you can successfully do on a short-term basis. If you have not been investing at all, or you have not been setting aside money to invest, you need to start out with $50 or $100 per month. Begin with a figure proportionate to your income. If you're making $100,000 per year, you obviously shouldn't start out with $50 per month, unless you're spending 101 percent of what you make. As time goes by, slowly increase the amount you're investing. Every three to four months, you should be able to increase the amount you invest by a little bit. Work your way up to the point that you're able to invest ten percent of your net income. It may take a couple of years to reach the ten percent goal.

One strategy that many people like to use is to invest 100 percent of their pay raises. If you could live on 100 percent of your pay two weeks ago, why can't you live on the same amount of money today? You will also find that as you pay off your consumer debt, you will free up a tremendous amount of cash flow. Use the money you free up as you pay off one debt to accelerate the payments on your remaining debts. Then, when you pay all of your debts in full, invest all of the money you used to pay your debts to build your investment portfolio.

Don't forget that you will also have some major items in your life that you will want to replace. If you had an automobile loan that you've paid off, you will want to earmark part of those funds for your next car. When you are ready to buy your next car, you can pay cash for it. You will probably get a better buy if you walk into the showroom with a fist full of cash, too!

 **A portion of what you earn is yours to keep.**

PRACTICAL APPLICATIONS

Everyone should have a plan to create an investment portfolio.

Begin by accumulating one month's cash reserves in a deposit account at your credit union or in a money market fund. Then begin investing a small portion of your monthly savings while you use the balance to finish building your cash reserves. You can meet some, but not all, of your cash reserve requirements through the credit available on your credit cards, home equity line, or personal line of credit. If you own a cash value life insurance policy, don't forget to include your net loan value in your cash reserve computations.

Once you are well on your way to building a cash reserve of three to six months' expenses, you are ready to begin investing. How is your debt repayment program coming? If you are making good progress toward eliminating your debt, then plow all of your investment funds toward debt reduction. Some people continually struggle with reducing their debts. It doesn't matter how long and hard they try, something defeats their plans. If you are one of those strugglers, start investing now instead of paying your debts off first.

Most people, young and old, should begin their investment portfolio by choosing a high-quality equity fund. Set up an automatic draft on your checking account. The draft should occur within a day or two of payday. Remember, a portion of what you earn is yours to keep! Pay yourself, then everyone else.

After you have built a decent mutual fund balance, you can consider branching out into other types of investments. Some people never invest in anything more adventurous than a handful of solid-performing mutual funds. Don't be ashamed if more exotic investment opportunities do not interest you.

If your appetite to learn about investments is not satisfied, get *The First Book of Investing* by Sam Case/Prima. It is for beginners, but even those with investment experience will appreciate Case's insights.

CHAPTER 8

HOME SWEET HOME

SOME DEBTS ARE FUN WHEN YOU ARE ACQUIRING
THEM, BUT NONE ARE FUN WHEN YOU SET ABOUT
RETIRING THEM.

—OGDEN NASH

The largest purchase the average American will ever make is a home. Home ownership plays a key role in financial and income tax planning, so we will spend an entire chapter dealing specifically with this important subject. If you don't have a home, you probably aspire to become a homeowner someday. Therefore, this chapter will be important to almost everyone reading this book.

In this chapter, we will discuss financing, purchasing, owning, and selling an American dream—a home. Most people have no idea how much record-keeping the IRS requires for homeowners. The government wants you to keep records from the purchase of your first home through the sale of your final home when you retire or die. Those records may be 50 years old or more before the IRS wants to see them. Furthermore, you must keep records along the way for your annual tax planning. Every year, you want to deduct interest and real estate taxes.

If owning a home is a record-keeping quagmire, why does everyone want one? There are many reasons, but an almost universal belief is that home ownership is the last great American tax shelter.

THE GREAT AMERICAN TAX SHELTER

In the course of interviewing home-owning clients, I'm usually drawn into a discussion of why the clients own or want to own a home. Almost every time, the answer includes the tax deductions that home ownership offers. Yet, when asked how much the tax savings are, no one knows.

Someone created a myth, and the American public bought it hook, line, and sinker: *Home ownership is the best way for average Americans to reduce their taxes.* There is enough truth in this statement to make it believable. But how true is it, really?

One summer, my wife and I went on a business trip. We stopped in to see some friends during the course of our travels. While catching up on the events of the past few years, the friends asked if they should pay off their mortgage. They had enough money in the bank and were planning to invest it at the recommendation of a financial planner. The financial planner said they needed the tax deductions, but they were still curious if paying off the mortgage might be better.

They pulled out their latest tax return, and I pulled out my trusty calculator. In five minutes, we determined that they saved less than $300 per year in federal income taxes. They received this measly return by spending over $2,500 in interest on a $30,000 mortgage—to save less than $300! The next morning, our friends were at the bank when the doors opened. A short time later, they walked out of the bank without a mortgage. They also knew they would have more money to spend on themselves in the coming year. Although they didn't make the large investment recommended by a salesperson masquerading as a financial planner, they now have a few hundred extra dollars a month to invest, and they are saving $2,500 a year in interest expense—a very nice investment in my humble opinion!

Let's work through a typical mortgage tax-savings example together. My average tax clients have a recently refinanced mortgage with about a $100,000 balance at eight percent interest, fixed. So, they will have just under $8,000 in mortgage interest to deduct on their tax return. In our area, most married clients claim the following Schedule A deductions: no medical expenses, about $1,300 in real estate and personal property taxes, around $2,000 in state and local taxes, and about $300 in charitable contributions, for a total of $3,600 in non-mortgage interest itemized deductions. Total itemized deductions, including $8,000 in mortgage interest, equal $11,600. Most clients are in the 28 percent marginal federal income tax bracket and three percent state income tax bracket, which gives them a combined income tax bracket of approximately 31 percent. (It is slightly less than 31 percent because state taxes are deductible on the federal return.)

On the surface, most people think that, with a 31 percent combined tax bracket, they save about $2,480 ($8,000×.31) in income taxes! That sounds pretty good, but not all of the mortgage interest is really deductible. Yes, you read it right. The 1995 standard deduction for married couples was $6,550, but without the mortgage interest, they would claim the standard deduction. If you subtract the non-mortgage interest itemized deductions of $3,600 from the $6,550 standard deduction, that leaves $2,950. Therefore, the tax deduction value of the $8,000 of mortgage interest reduces by $2,950. Thus, the true tax deduction value of their mortgage interest is only $5,050. Multiply that by 31 percent to see that they only save $1,565.50 in combined state and federal taxes. (Remember, they actually save a little less than that because their state income taxes also reduce their federal income taxes.)

The bottom line is that the average taxpayer in my area will save slightly more than $1,550 in taxes and spend $8,000 in interest to do it! When I speak to groups about debt, I always present a similar scenario. Then, I ask home owners with mortgages to pull out their checkbooks and form a line in front of me, because they can write a check to me for the amount of interest they pay the bank each year, and I will mail them a "refund" check equal to their tax savings as soon as their check clears— just like the IRS, but faster!

It's ironic that each year mortgage-holders pay less mortgage interest, **and** the standard deduction increases every year, too. If we assume that the economy stays steady and that the average person pays his or her mortgage on schedule without refinancing to a lower rate, in about eight years that person will not have enough itemized deductions to exceed the standard deduction. What value will the American home have as a tax shelter then? How will tax preparers replace the fees charged for preparing Schedule A?

If you are buying a home as a tax shelter, think again. The value of home ownership is not in tax savings. The value of home ownership lies in other areas, which we will discuss in the next section.

TAX TIP

Most new home buyers hear that owning a home will make a significant difference on their tax bill. They are not told that the time of year they buy the home is also very significant. If you purchase your home in December, you may have little, if any, tax deductions available because of the standard deduction. If you purchase your home in January, all of the interest you pay during the year will build and accumulate to help reduce your taxes. Remember, you must exceed the standard deduction before any of your itemized deductions save you one penny in income tax. If you are looking at purchasing a home toward the end of a year, it may be in your best interest to delay the purchase until January of the next year. Another consideration, when timing

the purchase of your home, is whether you about to get married. If so, it may be more advantageous to purchase the home in the tax year prior to marriage. This strategy could delay your marriage until the next tax year, because the 1995 Standard Deduction for singles was $3,900 versus $6,550 for a married couple.

BUYING INTO THE DREAM

Since tax savings really are less meaningful than the average home owner thinks, should you buy a home? The answer is a qualified "Maybe!"

Buying a home may not make you rich. In many areas of the country, you could have picked any home and paid the list price in 1970. By 1990, you had a solid return on your investment. If you didn't refinance, your house payment was a fraction of the cost to rent a small apartment. This was not a bad deal by anyone's standards. Will the same be true for a house bought in the mid-'90s?

Most real estate people think so, but many economists think real estate will be more sluggish in the next twenty years than it was in the last twenty. To make money in real estate in the '90s, you need to be a selective buyer. Real estate investors say that you don't make your profits when you sell—you lock in the profit when you buy. If you pay too much for a home, you are chopping off your profit potential at the knees.

Don't be too hasty to buy. It is a good idea to rent a home similar to the one you want before purchasing your first home. If you have your heart set on a certain home, see if you can lease it with an option to buy. As a kid, I always dreamed of living in a two-story house. My first home was probably the last two-story I will ever buy. We moved exactly one week after our first child was born. My wife decided, within hours of moving in, that two-story homes and small children don't mesh with her idea of happy living. Can you guess what our dream home is now? (Wrong! We just bought a tri-level—breaking up the stairs really helps a lot!)

Owning a home is more expensive than renting. When you rent, the landlord pays for all of the repairs and maintenance. When its your own home, lawn mowing, weed pulling, and tree trimming replace the care-free weekends of a renter's life. Fortunately, some of us enjoy those tasks, even if we don't always have time to do them.

As time progresses, the cost of owning will be less than the cost of renting a similar abode, assuming you keep the place well maintained and don't refinance to pay off consumer debts every couple years. You can quickly produce a table or chart in a spreadsheet program to compare the cost of renting a home to the cost of owning one.

The graph shown in Figure 8-1 only took about five minutes to create (and another five to make it look nice) in Microsoft Excel. It shows a projection of how the cost of owning my first home compares to what

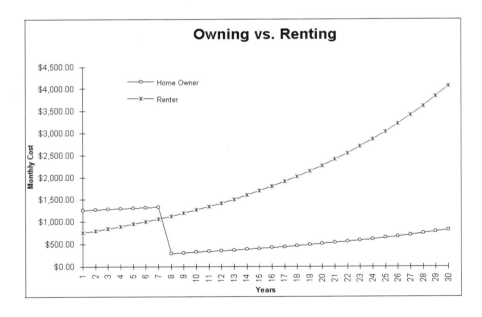

Figure 8-1. It is easy to compare the cost of owning a home to renting.

Used with permission, Vogt Financial Concepts and Strategies, Inc.

landlords in my neighborhood charge to rent houses with our floor-plan. I adjusted the rental rate upward by six percent each year. The costs of owning my home are also adjusted upward. I used the minimum payment that my mortgage company requires, which extends the length of the loan. I calculated the property taxes to increase by the maximum the law allows and increased maintenance expenses by six percent each year.

Before you buy, thoroughly check out the areas of town that interest you. Visit the local schools or at least talk to people familiar with schools around the area. How do the schools compare? Which schools have the most potential? Even if you don't have children or won't raise children in the home, find out about the schools, because the people you eventually sell to will think it is important. Go to the local police or sheriff's office and look at the crime logs. What types of crimes are happening in the areas you like? What do the authorities expect for that area in the future?

When you purchase a home, always consider who will want to purchase it from you when you are ready to move. If you are handy with tools, find the worst-looking home for sale in the neighborhood. It will cost less but be worth as much as the other homes when you finish sprucing it up.

Another option is to find a buyer anxious to sell. Our new home was sitting vacant—empty homes usually mean that the owner is making monthly mortgage payments, paying for a gardener, and doling out for a number of other miscellaneous expenses. Most people can not pay out without rental income to cover the expenses for very long. The prior owners also had previously sold our house twice to buyers that were unable to complete the deal. By the time we came along, they were ready to make some serious concessions!

It is also wise to talk to real estate agents and friends who are home owners about the things you should know before you buy. I tend to be a skeptic, so I recommend that you weigh the Realtor's advice against his desire to earn a commission. It is also important to realize that the law does not set the commission rate a real estate agent quotes. You are free to negotiate the best deal you can get.

If you think you want to buy a new home, you need to consider the additional expenses involved. In our area, most new homes require a substantial investment in landscaping, window treatments, and an assortment of other items. These costs mount rapidly. Please consider them in your budget before signing a purchase contract. When obtaining a new home from a developer, you may find that the developer will cooperate with your Realtor. The real estate agent can greatly assist you as you pore over the purchase contracts, saving you some headaches. Furthermore, the developer may pay your Realtor a commission without it affecting your price. Knowing that the developer will pay a commission to a "cooperating broker" is something you can also factor into your offer if you deal direct with the builder. After all, if the developer is willing to pay a real estate agent three percent, why shouldn't he be willing to accept an offer that is at least three percent less than he is asking?

One of your major concerns as rulers of the kingdom is paying for the castle. So let's discuss financing the dream.

FINANCING THE DREAM

Few people pay cash for their homes. Most people are swimming in mortgage payments when they buy their first home. Homeowners typically refinance their homes at least once or twice. Few understand how the costs of purchasing or refinancing their home affect their income taxes.

If you already have a home, read this section anyway—you may find some tax–saving ideas you had not considered. We will discuss purchase and refinance records first.

TAX TIP **Whether you are purchasing a home or refinancing an existing home, your lender should give you a HUD-1 statement. Closing Statements and Settlement Statements are other names for the**

HUD-1. The HUD-1 is a detailed listing of all the expenses that relate to your transaction. Your lender or escrow company should certify your copy with an original signature. Most lenders either have a statement pre-printed on the form or use a stamp that states it is a certified copy. Your escrow officer or another official connected with the transaction will sign a properly certified copy. This is an extremely important document, and you want to keep it in a very safe place. You must maintain these documents until you eventually sell your final home.

PURCHASE AND REFINANCE TRANSACTIONS

Most people have no idea how much it costs to purchase a home until they complete a purchase transaction. Even someone who bought a home several years ago may not realize how much the prices for title insurance and other closing costs have escalated in the last few years. Even if a purchase transaction doesn't interest you, you may have refinanced or wanted to refinance to a lower interest rate. Whether you are purchasing or refinancing a home, many of the expenses you incur are tax-deductible. You can add some of the non-deductible expenses to the cost of your home. When you eventually sell, they will reduce the taxable profit.

The Internal Revenue Code places home loans in two categories: acquisition debt and home equity debt. This distinction went into effect on October 14, 1987. We will discuss the current law. If your mortgage is older, you may have higher deductibility limits.

Acquisition debt is debt you incur to acquire, construct, or substantially improve your primary or second residence. You must use your home as collateral for the loan. Interest is deductible on up to $1,000,000 ($500,000 married filing separately) of acquisition debt. As you repay the acquisition debt principal, the amount that qualifies decreases. When you refinance, the amount of acquisition debt equals the previous acquisition debt's principal balance immediately prior to refinancing. Any additional debt is considered home equity debt, unless you use the loan proceeds to improve your home. You may borrow additional money to improve your home. That amount increases your acquisition debt. If you borrow more than you use to make improvements, it is considered either home equity debt or non-qualified debt. The law limits home equity debt to the fair market value of the home, less the principal balance of any acquisition debt. Home equity debt is deductible to a limit of $100,000 ($50,000 married filing separately) principal balance.

That was the simple explanation. Now you know why all of the mortgage refinance advertisements say, "Consult your tax advisor!" There are many additional caveats and details that apply to pre-October 14, 1987 mortgages, but they are beyond the scope of our discussion. The tax law frequently changes, and the home mortgage interest deduction is a target for change.

Now that we have a clear understanding of acquisition, home equity, and non-qualified debt, we can discuss acquisition points.

TAX TIP   **It is critical for you to keep detailed records on all mortgage transactions. The IRS is targeting refinances in some audits. You must show that the money received from the refinance paid for improvements, if you exceed the home equity debt limits. The safest method of creating a paper trail is opening a separate checking account to pay home improvement expenses. Place the loan proceeds directly into the separate checking account. Also, get an account that returns your canceled checks to substantiate your expenses.**

DEDUCTING "POINTS"

It is important to understand up front that your lender and the IRS define the term "points" differently. The IRS definition is the important one when you do your taxes. It doesn't matter what the lender calls the fee; if the IRS considers it a point, you can usually deduct or capitalize it. To capitalize an expense means to add it to your home's cost for tax purposes.

There are two types of deductible mortgage expenses in the eyes of the IRS: **points** (charges you pay to secure your mortgage; the industry usually calls them loan origination fees and other fees) and **prepaid interest expense** (which your lender probably calls "points").

The IRS says that when you pay fees "**only** for the use of the money, it is interest. [IRS' emphasis]. These points are interest paid in advance and you cannot deduct the full amount for points in the year paid." (IRS *Publication 17*) The instructions then describe how you must deduct the prepaid interest over the term of the mortgage. (For additional information on points as defined by the IRS, see *Publication 17*, January 1994.) We clarify deducting expenses over the life of the loan in the next section on refinancing.

Points are fully deductible in the year that acquisition financing on your main home occurs. You must always deduct points relating to a second home over the life of the loan. For the purposes of our discussion, a second home is a home in addition to your main residence, for example, a vacation home. The IRS definition of points includes non-recurring charges you pay in the process of securing your mortgage. These expenses include: fees charged based on a percentage of the principal amount of the mortgage (including FHA or VA funding fees) and fees paid for specific services: appraisal fees, credit report fees, document preparation fees, notary fees, and settlement fees. If you qualify for a Veterans Affairs or a Federal Housing Administration loan, any points not considered interest are also deductible as points.

When you purchase a home, you can pay the points out of your loan proceeds, *but* the IRS requires you to pay with your own funds, as a down payment on the house, an amount at least equal to the amount you intend to deduct as points on your tax return. (You may need to read that sentence two or three times to comprehend it. Tax laws require precise application, or you may lose if challenged in an audit.)

Some of the items that are not deductible as points you may add to the cost basis of the home. These are capital expenses, including commissions, abstract fees, and recording fees. Eventually, when you sell the house, these expenses will reduce the amount of taxable profit.

In addition to prepaid interest, deductible points, and capital expenses, certain items are not deductible for home owners. These non-deductible expenses include fire insurance premiums, mortgage insurance premiums, utility or other services related to occupying the house, prepaid rent (if you rent from the owner before you close escrow), the cost of any repairs you make on the home, and any items that you deduct as moving expenses on Form 3903: Moving Expenses (for tax years ending prior to 1995).

If you obtain a loan specifically to improve your main home, you may also deduct the cost of points on that loan on your tax return as points in the year the loan funds. There is an important distinction made by the IRS between purchase financing and improvement financing. When financing improvements, you must pay for loan points with money out of your pocket. You may not pay for them with loan proceeds obtained from the lender.

The tax law also treats refinances differently than purchases.

REFINANCING THE DREAM—TRICKY TRAPS

As a general rule, you must deduct points incurred to refinance your home evenly over the life of your loan. Since the points are not currently deductible, it does not matter whether you have the lender add them to the loan balance or you pay for them with cash.

Let's say you pay $3,000 in points on a 30-year "refi" (that's real estate lingo for refinance). You must deduct that $3,000 evenly over the life of the loan. Most loans are for 360 months, or 30 years. Three thousand dollars divided by 360 is $8.33 per month. If you refinance on July 1, you can deduct $49.98 in points on your tax return! Next year, you can deduct the full year's worth, or $99.96. It is important to keep track of the amount of points you pay, because when you pay off the loan, you can claim any points not previously deducted on that tax return.

One easy way to keep track of points is to set up a Quicken Asset Account. Use the total amount of the points as the Opening Balance. Reduce the Account balance by the amount of points you deduct on your taxes each year, as shown in Figure 8-2. You should add any points that the IRS considers capital expenses to the Asset Account you use to track your home's value.

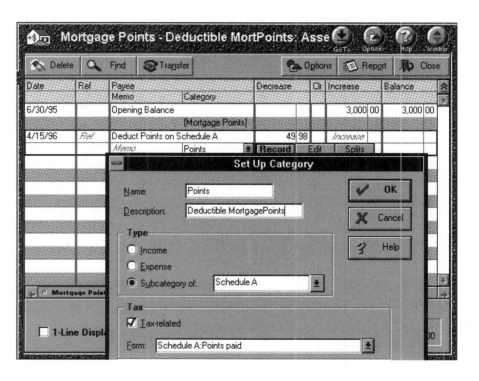

Figure 8-2. Use an Asset Account to track the number of points you deduct on your taxes each year. Don't forget to deduct any points not previously deducted when you pay a loan in full.

Now that you understand the basics, we can discuss the opportunities that lie in the exceptions. When you use a portion of the loan proceeds to improve your home, the percentage of points equal to the money used for improvements is fully deductible in the year you refinance. The IRS considers that portion of the loan new acquisition debt. Remember, you must pay the costs of those points out of your pocket to deduct them currently; the lender cannot add them to the cost of the loan.

The second opportunity lies in demographic trends. The number of people refinancing their old 30-year mortgages with new 30-year mortgages is less than it was a few years ago. Many refinances convert 30-year mortgages into 15-year mortgages. The number of balloon mortgages is also increasing. A balloon mortgage is a mortgage calculated over a longer term than the length of the loan. For example, many people get 30-year mortgages that are due in five or seven years. Whatever balance is due at the end of the term must be paid or refinanced. The tax advantage of a "due in__-years mortgage" is that the points are deductible over the shorter period. If our previous example was a "due in 5," you could deduct $49.98 each month instead of every six months!

The advantages of a balloon mortgage are that the interest rates are lower and most people move in five years or less. Why get a 30-year loan if you plan to move in five years? Other people plan to accelerate their house payments. A "30 due in 5" loan also has a lower interest rate than a 15-year mortgage. The owner simply makes the same payment that a 15-year loan requires to pay down the due-in-five loan even faster.

 Quicken has a Refinance Planner. Windows users select Plan on the main menu bar, then click the Financial Planners button and finally choose Refinance. DOS users go to the Activities menu while in any Register. Choose Financial Planning, and finally Refinance. The Refinance planner, shown in Figure 8-3, helps solve part of the puzzle of whether or not to refinance your home. Once the Refinance Planner completes its analysis, there are several more items you must consider to make a wise

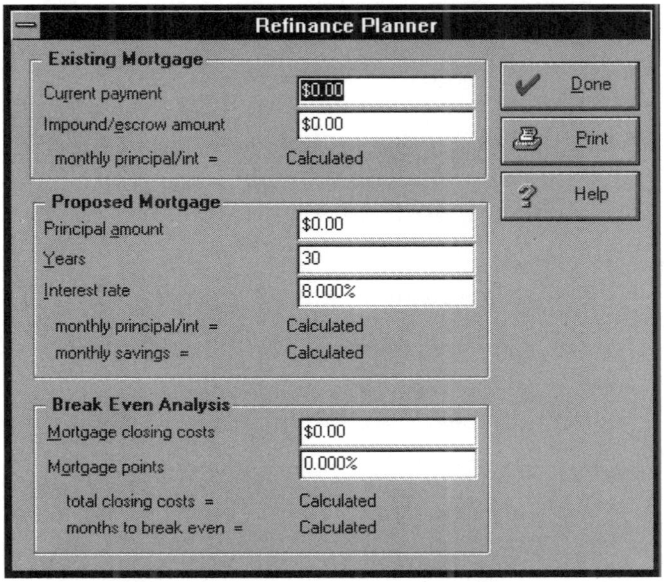

Figure 8-3. The Refinance Planner is easy to use but does not provide answers to the most important questions you need to ask when refinancing your home.

decision. We will discuss those items after we see how the Refinance Planner works.

The Refinance Planner is similar to the Savings Planner we used in Chapter 1. Simply enter in the appropriate places your current mortgage payment and the monthly amount of any impounds you pay with your current mortgage payment. The planner computes your monthly principal and interest payment.

Now enter the information on the mortgage you are considering. Enter the amount of principal you plan to finance, include any refinancing costs that you think the lender will include in the loan. Enter the number of years over which the loan is amortized—balloon payment mortgages are amortized over a longer period of time than the length of the loan, usually 30 years. Then input the interest rate that your lender quoted.

Quicken computes the new loan's monthly principal and interest payment and the amount of your monthly savings, assuming you have no closing costs.

Finally, enter the amount of closing costs that the lender gave you in the Good Faith Estimate, which tells you how much the lender expects you to pay for document preparation fees, credit checks, appraisals, and a myriad of other fees. Federal lending laws require lenders to provide this information to you when you apply for a loan. The last number you need to enter is the number of lender's points and loan discount points the lender will charge. You can include these in the closing costs, but it is better to separate them. The number of points lenders charge changes almost every day and can even change several times during a day. After you enter the closing costs and points, the Refinance Planner calculates how many months it would take to recoup the costs of refinancing based on the difference between your current and projected monthly mortgage payments.

By itself, the Refinance Planner is an extremely simplistic approach to deciding whether you should refinance. If someone convinces you to refi based on these few assumptions, that person is doing you a disservice and possibly an injustice! Consider the information in Figure8-4.

Anyone basing a refi decision simply on the information in Figure 8-4 would jump at the opportunity to refinance. You must also consider your current loan's characteristics and your financial goals. In this example, the existing 30-year fixed-rate loan has a $50,000 balance, but the beginning balance was $150,307. This loan only has 59.5 months, less than five years, left until it is paid in full. You should also know that the current interest rate is only seven percent.

Now, can you answer whether this loan is a good refinance candidate? If you said "No," you are right. However, there is more information to consider. The company the home owners work for is down-sizing. Their boss said one of them will lose their job in six months. To save their home from

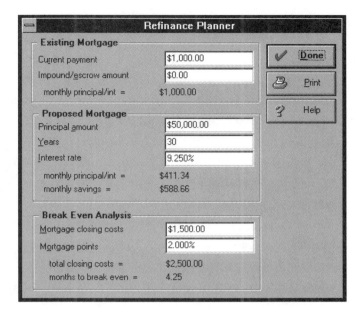

Figure 8-4. Based on the Refinance Planner in this figure, someone might be tempted to refinance without considering other important questions.

foreclosure, they must reduce the mortgage payment. This loan is good for the owners because of their circumstances, even though the loan is terrible compared with their current mortgage. It would be better for them to refinance while both are still employed, since they may not qualify for a new loan with only one income!

Before committing to a 15-year mortgage, carefully examine your economic situation. How secure is your income? Would you be better off with a 30-year mortgage with a slightly higher interest rate but a lower monthly obligation? Some former home owners have lost homes that they could have salvaged if only their payment were a little lower.

Let's consider another situation where the Refinance Planner shows inadequate information. Harry and Hillary Homestead have a 30-year mortgage. Their mortgage broker is trying to persuade them to refinance to a 15-year mortgage with the same payment their old loan has. On the surface, this sounds like a winner. The Homesteads examine their existing loan and discover that their 30-year loan only has 15 years left on it. The refi is a terrible deal. The Homesteads will pay off the loan just as fast if they do nothing. If they refinance, they will go through a tremendous amount of hassle and expense but gain nothing. If they simply use the money the mortgage broker wants to charge for closing costs and points to pay additional principal on their existing loan, they will own their home even sooner. Don't laugh. Many people find themselves with longer loan terms, higher interest rates, or higher payments simply because they didn't logically think through their situation.

Frequently, people will refinance their home and take additional money out of the house, which they use to make improvements. When you make improvements, you can deduct the same percentage of points as the percentage of money you use for the improvements.

Now we will consider a complex example that uses many of the facts explained in this chapter about refinancing. Assume you refinance your home with a $100,000 mortgage. Your old loan balance was $80,000. So, $80,000 of the refinance fees are deductible as refinance points. You use $10,000 to pay off consumer debt. Because you are under the law's home equity limits, those points are also deductible as refinance points. You use the final $10,000 to add a room onto your house, so only $10,000 of the $100,000 is used for improvements. Thus, only 10 percent of the points you pay on your refinance transaction are fully deductible as improvement—acquisition or purchase—points.

Remember, when you own a second home, you may deduct the points on all of those mortgages only over the life of each loan. You may not fully deduct those points in the year paid.

HOME OWNERSHIP

Purchasing and refinancing your home are normally of immediate significance to your income taxes in the year the event occurs. While you own your home, you will probably put a lot of money into improving its condition or appeal.

Few people keep adequate records, for tax purposes, of the improvements they make to their home. Under current law, if you never sell your home—if it is still yours when you die—there will be no income tax paid on those profits, the undocumented improvements. Your heirs will receive the home's profits free of income tax. In 1993, the Democrat controlled Congress discussed changing the law so that, when survivors inherit a piece of appreciated property, they would pay income taxes on the profits when they sell it. Your home will probably be a major source of profit. Although under current law, your taxes aren't affected if you never sell your home, the tax could be a large burden if the government ever changes the law. Therefore, it is extremely important to maintain detailed records over your entire lifetime. The market value of your home does not matter when calculating the tax value of your home. The tax value of your home is the cost, plus any non-deductible points and settlement costs added to your basis, plus any capital improvements.

Capital improvements are improvements you make to your property that add long-term value. The IRS says that a capital improvement must appreciably add to the value or substantially prolong the useful life of your home. Putting new siding on your home is a capital improvement, but painting the outside of your home is a cost of ownership. The improvement can be added to your tax basis, but the cost of ownership is not deductible or tax-related in any way, unless you own rental property. Then, costs of ownership become tax-deductible business expenses. As a home owner, you want most of your expenses to be capital improvements. If you become a landlord, you want most of your expenses to be tax-deductible business expenses. Let's review some examples of items that qualify and others that don't qualify as capital improvements.

Capital improvements include escrow costs of purchasing or refinancing a residence, including title insurance premiums, transfer taxes, and recording fees; significant roof replacement; architect's fees for completed projects; construction costs of an addition; construction costs of an in-ground swimming pool; an underground sprinkler system; electrical or plumbing installations; new flooring, including linoleum, tile, or carpeting; new installed appliances, such as dishwashers, stoves, water heaters, and furnaces; decks and patios; installed lighting that cannot be practically removed; solar heating units; wood or garden sheds; vinyl siding; fencing; concrete, brickwork, or paving that is not a minor repair or enhancement; and central heating and air conditioning.

Some items not deductible as capital improvements include above-ground swimming pools; minor plumbing or electrical repairs; financing costs on the purchase or refinance of a home; escrow costs not incurred as a result of a purchase transaction; other escrow costs, such as fire insurance, property taxes, interest, and association fees; general repairs and maintenance; painting, plastering, and wallpapering; replacing storm gutters; small-scale planting; removable air conditioning units; replacement of broken windows or new screens; and roof repairs to replace broken shingles or stop leaks.

One reason it is important to keep track of small improvements is that they add up over time. For example, if you add an electrical outlet, it is a capital improvement. It may cost you only a few dollars to buy the wire and outlet at the local hardware store, but those few dollars, multiplied by numerous improvements, can someday reduce your taxes significantly. Another advantage to keeping track of your capital improvements is that if you decide to make your house into a rental unit, those improvements are depreciable. You must depreciate the building over 27.5 years under current tax law. You can often depreciate improvements over shorter periods of time, thus increasing your tax deductions. For example, you may depreciate a dishwasher or carpeting over seven years instead of 27.5 years.

Remember, you want to maintain your records from the very first home you own until the day you die. Many of the items that are not deductible as capital expenses, if properly documented and properly done, are deductible as fixing-up expenses when you sell your home. When you are ready to sell your home, consult the most recent tax publication regarding fixing-up expenses and how to qualify such items as painting and wallpapering as tax-deductible expenses. You will report fixing-up expenses on Form 2119: Sale of Your Home.

SELLING YOUR HOME

The preceding sections discuss most of the important tax aspects of buying your home. When you sell your home, it is important to remember that items described as points for the purchaser are not deductible as points on Schedule A by the seller. When selling your home, you must use them to reduce the home's profit. Report these costs as selling expenses on Form 2119: Sale of Your Home.

The tax rules related to selling homes are very complex. We discuss only highlights of the law in this text. Please consult with your tax consultant or a good tax guide on selling your home before entering into a sales agreement.

Any time you sell your residence, you must report the sale on Form 2119. The tax law requires that one of the parties involved in a real estate transaction must report the selling price of the property to the IRS. Depending on the practice in your area, the reporting party may be your real estate agent, the title insurance company, a lawyer, the lender, or another participant in the transaction. In our area, the title insurance company usually reports the sale. When there is no title insurance company involved, the owner's real estate agent normally reports the sale.

The IRS finds out only the amount you sold the house for and the seller(s) Social Security number and name. The IRS computers then match the reported figures to the sellers' tax return. The IRS learns from Form 2119 how much profit, if any, you made and how much is taxable. There are three options: 1) you sold at a profit and chose to defer your profit, 2) you sold at a profit and will pay tax on the profit, or 3) you sold at a loss.

SELLING FOR A PROFIT

When you sell your home for a profit, you can either defer the entire profit or pay taxes on all or a portion of the profit. You can defer the taxes by purchasing another home for the same price or more than you sold your previous home. If you do not replace your home or you replace it with a lower-cost home, you must pay taxes on a portion of the profits. The only exception is for home owners who qualify for the $125,000 exclusion, which will be explained later in this section.

The whole concept of how the tax law determines profit confuses people. Most of the questions revolve around the effects of the home's mortgage on the profit. In the eyes of the IRS, the mortgage is immaterial unless you default on a loan that exceeds your basis.

The idea of profit is quite simple. All you do is compare the basis of the home to the net sales price. When the basis is less than the net sales price, you have a profit. When the basis is more than the net sales price, you lost money. The basis of your home is the net purchase price, plus improvements, less depreciation. You will have depreciation only if you claimed a home office deduction or rented out all or part of the home while you owned it. The net sales price is the total sales price less qualified fixing-up expenses, less the costs of selling the home. You calculate these figures as you work through Form 2119.

To defer the tax on your profit, you must replace your home with a home that costs as much or more than you sold your old house for. Furthermore, with extremely limited exceptions, you must physically move into your new home within 24 months of the sales date of your former home. The sale date can be 24 months in the past or future. Taxpayers have moved in 24 months and one day from the sale date and lost the tax deferral. Some taxpayers challenged the IRS in Tax Court, claiming extenuating circumstances. The Tax Court ruled in favor of the IRS, holding that the law is very clear and the limit may not be extended. This rule even applies when the new home is destroyed by a fire or a natural disaster.

When you do sell your home for a profit, the profit is taxed at the applicable capital gains tax rates which cannot exceed 28 percent under the tax laws in affect in early 1995. This can be extremely beneficial because many people make enough profit to place them in a higher tax bracket than the capital gains tax rate. For example, Randy and Roxanne Retiree had a taxable income of $30,000 in 1994. In January, 1995, they sold Randy's home. Roxanne and her late husband had used the $125,000 exclusion. Thus the $100,000 net profit after purchasing a lower-priced home is fully taxable. With $30,000 taxable income, the Retirees were in a 25 percent income tax bracket. The home profits would boost them into a 36 percent bracket if they were not eligible for the maximum 28 percent capital gains tax rate in effect at that time.

One of the goals stated in the Republican's *Contract with America* is to further reduce the maximum capital gains tax rate. The debate on this issue was still raging between the fiscally conservative Republicans and left-wing Democrats as this book went to press.

Another important consideration is the $125,000 exclusion that is available for home sellers age 55 or older. Under current law, anyone age 55 or older has the opportunity to exclude $125,000 of their profit from the sale of one home, and this is a once-in-a-lifetime exclusion. This can be tricky, because in today's society, where many people marry multiple times, the law allows you to use the deduction only one time. This exclusion is the same for married people and singles. If you and your spouse are 55 years old and you divorce, and if you sell the home after the divorce, the law entitles each of you to take a $125,000 exclusion. If you remarry and your new spouse has a home that he or she wants to sell, your new spouse may not take the exclusion after marrying someone who already took the exclusion. This is such a valuable tax benefit that the IRS has a special computer program to track everyone who participates in an exclusion until they die.

To qualify for the exclusion, at least one spouse must be 55 years old. That spouse must have owned the home and used it as a principal residence for at least three of the five years prior to the date of sale.

The government continues searching for new sources of revenue. Tax experts have suggested the $125,000 exclusion as a possible revenue enhancement item. So, if you know someone who is eligible for the exclusion, I would advise them to take it while it is available, because it may not be here much longer if the tax and spend liberals return to power.

Not everyone is fortunate enough to sell for a profit.

SELLING AT A LOSS

When you sell an *investment* at a loss, the tax law allows you to deduct those losses, with certain restrictions. When you sell your *residence* at a loss, you may not deduct any portion of the loss from your taxes.

The most confusing aspect of the law applies to home owners who owned multiple homes and deferred the gains from their prior homes into the home they now think they are selling at a loss. You can pay $100,000 for a house, sell it for $90,000, and still make a profit. There are two reasons this may happen. By deferring previous homes' profits on Form 2119, your cost basis on the home may be less than the $90,000 sales price. The second situation occurs when you use all or part of your home as a rental. When you rent all or a portion of your home, you receive depreciation deductions to help offset the rental income. Depreciation reduces the basis of your home. The end result is that you may sell your home for less than you paid for it but still make a profit for tax purposes.

If you really are selling your home at a loss, it is possible to transform that non-deductible loss into a profitable situation relative to your tax return. As one of my clients said, "If you must lose money on your house, it should at least be profitable!" This is possible by transforming your home into a business.

FINANCIAL ALERT **The recently elected Republican-controlled Congress is talking about allowing homeowners to deduct losses incurred on their residences as capital losses. If you like this idea and Congress has not yet acted, write your representative or senator and let them know you support this change in the tax law.**

RENTING YOUR HOME

Rental real estate is big business. Ibbotson Associates estimates that 54.1 percent of the wealth of the world is in the form of real estate. Much of that is rental property.

When you sell a home at a loss, it can be advantageous to rent, or prove that you tried to rent, your home at fair market value rents for at least one year and one day. You may then sell the rental house and deduct the loss as an investment loss on your tax return.

Most landlords do not get into the rental business because they want to sell their home at a loss. You may find it more financially beneficial to rent your home rather than live in it yourself. Many of the expenses that you cannot deduct as a home owner become deductible as business expenses when you are a landlord. For example, the IRS does not consider repainting the rooms inside your home a capital improvement; these costs are after-tax expenses. If you become a landlord, repainting the inside of your home is a tax-deductible business expense. All small repairs and maintenance also become tax-deductible expenses. Large repairs classify as either capital or deductible expenses, depending on the nature of the expense. For example, if you replace a broken dishwasher in your home, it is a capital improvement. If you replace the dishwasher in a rental home, it is a depreciable asset that you will deduct over the next seven years.

In fact, the entire structure of your house is a depreciable asset, so if you turn your house into a rental unit, your building will be deductible over the next 27.5 years. This also works if you rent out one room in your house to a boarder, or if you decide to have a home office. Home offices have come under attack by the IRS, and it has become much more difficult to claim them after the January 1993 Supreme Court Soliman decision. Before you claim a tax deduction for a home office, you should consult a tax advisor to find out what the latest rulings are.

As you can see, it can be financially advantageous to own a rental home and live in a rental yourself, rather than owning a home that you live in. In addition to being able to deduct many expenses that a home owner cannot, you also have the ability to participate in the appreciation of the underlying real estate. The problem with being a landlord is that it can be a hassle. Also, when you are a tenant, you do not have the freedom to renovate your accommodations to suit your needs.

PRACTICAL APPLICATIONS

When you delve into the subject, it is surprising how complex and interesting the subject of home ownership is. Hopefully, you have encountered several new ideas in this chapter that will reduce your taxes today or in the future.

There are a couple of strategies you may want to employ to maximize your home-mortgage deduction. Many people who have a lot of consumer debt refinance their homes or take out second mortgages to pay off their consumer debt. Although I do not recommend this in most situations, it can be helpful from a tax perspective. Unfortunately, it is very easy for people addicted to consumer debt to fall back into the same trap. They purchase more goods on their credit cards and end up right back where they were. From a financial planning perspective, it is preferable just to pay off your consumer debt and not roll it over into a mortgage.

It may not impact you in the near future, but if you do own a home, you need to gather all of your home improvement records. Sort through them and enter them into your home's Account. Don't forget to include any deductions for depreciation you may have claimed with a home office deduction or when you rented out all or part of your home.

If you do not own a home, consider the advantages and disadvantages of home ownership carefully before entering the rank of home owners.

The long-term benefits of owning a home are greater than the short-term benefits of lower rental payments.

CHAPTER 9

THE SECRETS OF CREATING WEALTH SYNTHESIZED

> TO ACCEPT GOOD ADVICE IS BUT TO INCREASE
> ONE'S OWN ABILITY.
> —JOHANN WOLFGANG VON GOETHE (1749–1832)

This book contains many different financial concepts and strategies. We included each of them to help you create wealth. What exactly is the secret of creating wealth? Is there a single secret, or is there a series of secrets that you must link together? Let's examine the question of success and discover the secret—or secrets—together. Before beginning, we need to consider the definition of financial success.

DETERMINE YOUR DEFINITION OF FINANCIAL SUCCESS

How do you define financial success? Is success one million dollars in net worth? Is it a mansion with a great view, or a new Ferrari? Will you consider yourself successful when you have enough money to retire comfortably at age 55?

What is your definition? When you set your definition, be careful not to use others as your benchmark. If you want to be richer than anyone in your town, or have a better car than anyone in your neighborhood, or have the biggest house on the block, you may never be financially successful. Eventually, someone will come along who is richer, has a nicer car, or owns a larger home. One of the secrets of financial success is to determine for yourself where you want to be, not how you view yourself in relationship to others. Once you have a definition of success, make it into a goal. Let's talk about keeping our eyes on the goal.

FOCUS ON YOUR FINANCIAL GOALS

It is said that financial success is not a destination; it is a journey. What path have you chosen to travel? Once you choose a path, keep your eyes on the one in front of you. Don't look to the left or the right, but focus on the road ahead. When you allow the pleasures of today to distract you from the goals of tomorrow, you will falter. You may veer off the road to success onto another path that leads nowhere. You may find, as many already have, that the secret of success is simpler than you may have thought possible.

KISS (KEEP IT SIMPLE, SILLY)

Have you ever heard of the KISS principle? Keep It Simple, Silly. Many people fail because they try to do too much or they try to make the task more difficult than it really deserves to be. When you add complexity to your goal, you are liable to obscure your view of reality.

The road to success is a series of simple steps. Each step builds on the previous step, but you must continue to master previous steps as you move on to the next step. In this book, we outlined a list of priorities that you can use as milestones on the road to riches. The financial priorities we have discussed, in my order of preference, are as follows:

1. Invest in yourself. Acquire the knowledge you need to achieve your goals. The quest for wisdom is a life-long commitment. Never stop investing in yourself.

2. Control your cash flow. This is the key to wealth creation. Even if you do not acquire great wealth, you will be rich. As Edward Gibbon said, "I am indeed rich, since my income is superior to my expense, and my expense is equal to my wishes."

3. You are now ready to begin investing your financial resources. Your goal is to invest at least 10 percent of your gross earnings. Your optimum investment strategy should include the following goals:

   a. Reduce and eliminate all consumer (non–deductible) debt.

   b. Accumulate enough cash and short-term investments to cover three to six months worth of expenses. Place this savings into a fund that you can use for contingencies, emergencies, and opportunities.

   c. Remember that one of the best investments you will ever make is to reduce and eliminate all debt from your life. Debt reduction includes accelerating your deductible debt payments, i.e. your home mortgage. Freedom from debt will allow you to live life with less stress. You can also achieve the same standard of living as your friends and neighbors with much less income and pay less of your income in taxes!

   d. Create a well-diversified portfolio of equity investments. As Jean-Jacques Rousseau advises, "Money is the seed of money."

You can achieve financial success if you determine to do so. Heed the words of Washington Irving, "Great minds have purposes, others have wishes." Throughout this process, use the power of Quicken to organize your financial records with efficiency and ease. Quicken will enable you to maximize every available tax deduction. An optimized tax strategy will allow you to increase your cash flow and enable you to create wealth even more rapidly.

As you focus on your financial goals and strategies, you will be less likely to fall into financial traps or trickery. You must quickly learn that there are no shortcuts to wealth. Don't allow yourself to be tempted by someone offering a shortcut to reach your financial goals—you may fall for a scam. The path to prosperity requires a focused, methodical approach. Like the tortoise, you will win the race to riches by continually striving to reach the reward.

One of the most popular shortcuts is using leverage to increase your earning potential. Yes, when used judiciously, leverage can enhance returns. The pitfall lies in our inability to predict the future. Ask investors who lost everything in Dallas or Denver in the mid- to late- '80s when property values plummeted instead of rising as expected. The conservative course is not to leverage your investments. When you own your property, the bank can't foreclose on you when economic calamity strikes. Few people live without experiencing economic stress at some time.

Another aspect of simplicity is to avoid becoming over-diversified. If you have too many investments, they are difficult to track mentally. Quicken will keep them organized as long as you input the pertinent data, but investors frequently find themselves overwhelmed by paperwork, even with computer assistance. You also want to use simple investments. It is easier for investment sponsors to hide self-enriching clauses in complex transactions.

Invest in what you understand. Never invest in what you do not understand. Better yet, never invest in something if you cannot explain the opportunity in terms simple enough for a child to grasp. Thoroughly examine and study opportunities that intrigue you, but don't pursue every opportunity that seems to hold promise. If you do, you will not succeed at anything. Most important of all, maintain balance in your life.

KEY CONCEPT

Don't let debt destroy your destiny.

BALANCE YOUR POCKETBOOK WITH REALITY

It is a human failing to become consumed by wealth. We call it greed. Wealth itself is not the reason you should aspire to riches. The purpose of money is to acquire and accomplish. When you have money, you may find that it isn't everything you thought it would be. Even J. Paul Getty lamented, "I find all this money a considerable burden."

As you traverse your road to success, don't forget the people around you—your companions who join you in traversing the road of life. Don't allow yourself to alienate your closest friends. Used properly, Quicken will increase the amount of time you have available to spend with your family and friends.

As you strive to maintain your humanity, become involved in worthwhile efforts. What good is financial success if you have nobody to share it with? Do you want to become a stingy old codger without family or friends with whom you can enjoy your golden years? So what is the formula for financial success? Balance, perseverance, and focus.

PRACTICAL APPLICATIONS

Review your definition of success. Is it realistic? Are you aiming too high or too low? How do your goals mesh with your definition? Are your goals realistic, or are they "pie in the sky"? Consider the complexity of your financial plans. Are they simple enough to explain in a way that a child could understand? Finally, consider your life. Is your life in balance or out of kilter?

I too need to periodically stop and review how I am doing with balancing the numerous activities, priorities, and projects in my life. As a Certified Financial Planner® and small business consultant, much of my activity is focused on creating wealth for my clients and my family. It is very easy to allow your business and financial concerns to demand more attention than they deserve, to the detriment of relationships with family and friends.

While working on the third edition of this book, I took a couple days off to attend a Promise Keepers conference. The conference allowed me a chance to regroup emotionally and spiritually. I was able to slow down long enough to reconsider my definition of success and make a few minor corrections to the course I am plotting for my life. Although the opportunity to affirm my commitment to my wonderful wife and children will pay invaluable dividends for years to come. The next time you have an opportunity to participate in an event like Promise Keepers, take it. The rewards could be eternal.

You must create balance in all areas of your life—financial, spiritual, and emotional. Then you will be truly wealthy.

QUICK KEYS

Function	DOS	Windows
Dates		
Today	T	T
First day of this Month	M	M
Last day of this Month	H	H
First day of this Year	Y	Y
Last day of this Year	R	R
Go to Date		Ctrl-G
File Operations (DOS only)		
Back up a file	Ctrl-B	Ctrl-B
Open a file	Ctrl-O	Ctrl-O
Help		
Help on current window or menu	F1	F1
Help Index	Ctrl-F1	N/A
Go to Help contents	F1+F1	Click contents
Move to selected Help topic	Enter	N/A
Print Help topic	N/A	Click Print
Return to last Help topic	Backspace	Click back

Function	DOS	Windows
Select related topic in bold or underlined	[Tab]	Click Phrase
Investments		
Action, select	[Ctrl]–[L]	N/A
Buy	[Ctrl]–[B]	N/A
Go to Portfolio View	N/A	[Ctrl]–[U]
Decrease or increase price by ⅛	[–] or [+]	[–] or [+]
Graph the price history selected security	[Ctrl]–[F]	N/A
Price History	[Ctrl]–[H]	N/A
Record Income	[Ctrl]–[C]	N/A
Register view	[Ctrl]–[R]	N/A
Reinvest Shares	[Ctrl]–[N]	N/A
Security, select or set up	[Ctrl]–[Y]	[Ctrl]–[Y]
Sell	[Ctrl]–[S]	N/A
View or Update prices	[Ctrl]–[U]	
Go to next or previous day	[Ctrl]–[<] or [>]	N/A
Go to next or previous month	[Ctrl]–[Pg Up] or [Ctrl]–[Pg Dn]	N/A
Lists		
Add new item to a list	[Ctrl]–[Ins]	N/A
Select an item a list	1st letter of the item	1st letter of the item
Main Menu Activities (DOS only)		
Account, select or set up	[Ctrl]–[A]	[Ctrl]–[A]
Back up all accounts in file	[Ctrl]–[B]	N/A
Back up all accounts in file and exit	[Ctrl]–[E]	N/A
File, select or set up	[Ctrl]–[F]	N/A
Update prices	[Ctrl]–[U]	N/A

Function	DOS	Windows
Moving Around in a Window		
Go to:		
Beginning of field	`Home`	`Home`
End of field	`End`	`End`
Next field or column	`Tab`	`Tab`
Next window or screen	`Pg Dn`	`Pg Dn`
Next or previous month	`Ctrl`–`Pg Dn` or `Ctrl`–`Pg Up`	N/A
Previous field or column	`Shift`–`Tab`	`Shift`–`Tab`
Previous window or screen	`Pg Up`	`Pg Up`
Special Keys		
Save transaction or info. in any window	`F10`	N/A
Decrease date or check number	`–`	`–`
Increase date or check number	`+`	`+`
Go to Portfolio View	N/A	`Ctrl`–`U`
Go to register	`Ctrl`–`R`	`Ctrl`–`R`
Go to View Loans	N/A	`Ctrl`–`H`
Go to Write Checks	`Ctrl`–`W`	`Ctrl`–`W`
QuickZoom on a selected report amount	`Ctrl`–`Z`	`Ctrl`–`Z`
Register & Write Checks		
Account, select or set up	`Ctrl`–`A`	`Ctrl`–`A`
Calculator Display	`Ctrl`–`O`	N/A
Calendar Display	`Ctrl`–`K`	`Ctrl`–`K`
Category, select or set up	`Ctrl`–`C`	`Ctrl`–`C`
Class, select or set up	`Ctrl`–`L`	`Ctrl`–`L`
Copy field above in splits	`'` or `"`	`'` or `"`

Function	DOS	Windows
Copy payee name to check address	`'` or `"`	`'` or `"`
Copy a field in the register	N/A	`Ctrl`-`Ins`
Copy a transaction in the register	`Ctrl`-`Ins`	N/A
Delete transaction or split line	`Ctrl`-`D`	`Ctrl`-`D`
Edit the current transaction	`Ctrl`-`E`	N/A
Electronic Payee	`Ctrl`-`Y`	N/A
Find (Go to) a transaction	`Ctrl`-`F`	`Ctrl`-`F`
Find back (search backward)	`Ctrl`-`B`	N/A
Find next (search forward)	`Ctrl`-`N`	N/A
Go to date	`Ctrl`-`G`	`Ctrl`-`G`
Go to a new transaction	N/A	`Ctrl`-`N`
Group of transactions, set up/recall	`Ctrl`-`J`	`Ctrl`-`J`
Insert a transaction or split line	`Ctrl`-`I`	`Ctrl`-`I`
Memorize a transaction	`Ctrl`-`M`	`Ctrl`-`M`
Paste a field in the register	N/A	`Shift`-`Ins`
Paste a transaction in the register	`Shift`-`Ins`	N/A
Print checks	`Ctrl`-`P`	`Ctrl`-`P`
Recall a memorized transaction	`Ctrl`-`T`	`Ctrl`-`T`
QuickFill automatic recall	Type Payee name	Type Payee name
QuickFill automatic completion	N/A	`Tab`
QuickFill list, scroll up or down	`Ctrl`-`+` or `Ctrl`-`−`	`Ctrl`-`↑` or `Ctrl`-`↓`
Record a Transaction	`Ctrl`-`Enter` or `F10`	`Enter` or `Ctrl`-`Enter`
Split transaction	`Ctrl`-`S`	`Ctrl`-`S`
Transfer, go to	`Ctrl`-`X`	`Ctrl`-`X`
Transfer, select account for	`Ctrl`-`C`	`Ctrl`-`C`
Void transaction	`Ctrl`-`V`	`Ctrl`-`V`

APPENDIX B

RESOURCES

THE CREATE WEALTH WITH QUICKEN HOME PAGE

The *Create Wealth with Quicken* home page is available from *The Computer Connection's* home page, `http://www.c3rn.com`. Visit our us for news on Quicken and finances. You will also links to other web sites of interest. We will also post information on electronic banking as the technology develops and gains acceptance.

BOOKS

The following list includes all of the books recommended in the practical applications, plus one or two others. Your local booksellers can order any of these titles that they do not stock.

Blue, Ron. *The Debt Squeeze.* Colorado Springs: Focus on the Family Publishing, 1989.
——. *Master Your Money.* Nashville: Thomas Nelson Publisher, 1991.
Burkett, Larry. *The Coming Economic Earthquake.* Chicago: Moody Press, 1991.
Case, Samuel. *The First Book of Investing.* Rocklin: Prima Publishing, 1994.
Chilton, David. *The Wealthy Barber.* Rocklin: Prima Publishing, 1991.
Clason, George S. *The Richest Man in Babylon.* New York: Signet, 1988.
Figgie, Harry E., Jr. w/ Gerald J. Swanson, Ph.D. *Bankruptcy 1995.* Boston: Little, Brown and Company, 1992.
Mrkvicka, Edward F., Jr. *The Bank Book.* New York: HarperPerennial, 1994.
Morris, Kenneth M. and Alan M. Siegal. *The Wall Street Journal Guide to Understanding Personal Finance.* New York: Lightbulb Press, Inc., 1992.

OTHER RESOURCES

The Computer Connection
The C³ Radio Network
(800) 485-5700. National toll-free talk lines open during the show
(916)727-7030. Business office open weekdays 9:30 a.m. to 5 p.m. PST
CompuServe: 72662,2547
Internet: chris@c3rn.com
World Wide Web: http://www.c3rn.com
Christopher E. Vogt, CFP, Talk Show Host
P.O. Box 625
Pleasant Grove, CA 95668-0625

Every Saturday, this nationally syndicated computer talk show "Cuts through the Chaos of Computing" from 12 to 1, Pacific Standard Time. *The Computer Connection* is America's Friendliest Computer Talk Show. Call Chris Vogt, author of *Create Wealth with Quicken*, with your computing questions. If your local talk radio station does not carry *The Computer Connection*, call the station's program director and request the program today.

Consumer Credit Counseling Services, Inc.
(800) 388-CCCS (2227) U.S. and Canada referral line
(301) 589-5600
8611 2nd Avenue, Suite 100
Silver Spring, MD 20910

This is a great resource to turn to if you are in debt and need affordable assistance in breaking debt's bonds on your life. Offices are located throughout the United States and Canada.

MetaStock Professional
Equis International
(800) 882–3040 or (801) 265–9996
World Wide Web: http://www.equis.com
3950 South 700 East, Suite 100
Salt Lake City, UT 84107

Great stock and market analysis software for DOS and Windows.

Intuit
(800) 624-8742 or (520) 295-3220
2650 East Elvira Road, Suite 100
Tucson, AZ 85706
CheckFree: electronic bill paying from Checkfree Corporation
(800) 882-5280

IntelliCharge: the Quicken credit card from Travelers Bank:
(800) 262-9323 2221
Online banking: (800) 224-1047
Technical Support: 5 a.m. 5 p.m. Pacific Standard Time
QuickFax: (800) 858-6090 order forms and documents for all versions of
Quicken and QuickBooks using document numbers 24 hours a day,
7 days a week.

DOS Support:
(505) 896-7190

Windows Support:
(505) 896-7219 Quicken standard edition
(505) 896-7220 Quicken Deluxe
(505) 896-7221 Quicken CD-ROM

Online Support:
America Online: Keyword: Intuit
BBS (8,1,0): (520) 295-3261
CompuServe: Go Intuit
Prodigy: Jump Intuit
World Wide Web: http://www.intuit.com

Morningstar Mutual Funds & Morningstar OnDisc

(800) 876–5005 or (312) 697–4404
Morningstar
53 West Jackson Blvd.
Chicago, IL, 60604

An independent rating service that includes information on over 2,000
mutual funds. Paper and software updates are available.

Social Security Administration

(800) 772–1213
Social Security Administration
P.O. Box 3600
Wilkes-Barre, PA 18767-3600

You can receive a projection of your retirement benefits by calling Social
Security. Ask for form SSA–7004, "Request for Statement of Earnings Card."
This form is also available on their Web server. Complete the card and mail it
back to Social Security, which will prepare a report of your earnings on which
you paid Social Security taxes. The report will also project your future
retirement benefits, disability benefits, and how much money your family
will receive if you die.

TurboTax (DOS, Mac, & Windows)

(800) 964-1040 or (520) 295-3110
Intuit
2650 East Elvira Road, Suite 100
Tucson, AZ 85706
   DOS, Mac, and Windows tax preparation software

United States Congress

(202) 224-3121
World Wide Web: http://www.house.gov
U.S. House of Representatives
Washington, DC 20915

U.S. Senate

(202) 224-3121
World Wide Web: http://www.senate.gov
Washington, DC 20510

Vogt Financial Concepts & Strategies, Inc.

Christopher E. Vogt, CFP, President
(916) 727–7030
CompuServe: 72662,2547
Internet: chris@c3rn.com
P.O. Box 625
Pleasant Grove, CA 95668–0625
   Financial consulting and tax preparation services for individuals, businesses, corporations, partnerships, estates, and trusts. Services available in all 50 states and for U.S. citizens living abroad.

GLOSSARY

401(k) Plan A tax–deferred salary savings plan, authorized by section 401(k) of the Internal Revenue Code. A percentage of an employee's salary is withheld and placed in a savings account or an investment fund. The salary deferral account balance grows tax–free. Income accumulates on the deferred amount until withdrawn by the employee at age 59½ or when the employee retires or leaves the company.

Account, Quicken A collection of related transactions, assets, or liabilities grouped together in Quicken. Most people establish a separate Quicken Account for each asset, cash, checking, credit card, investment, liability, money market, and savings account they have.

Accountable reimbursement plan A reimbursement arrangement with an employer that requires employees to substantiate business expenses adequately.

Acquisition debt Debt used to buy, build, or construct a principal residence or second home. This debt generally qualifies for a full mortgage interest expense deduction on Schedule A.

Adjusted basis A statutory term describing the cost used to determine your profit or loss from a sale or exchange of property. It is generally your original cost, plus capital improvements, less depreciation and other capital write–offs.

Adjusted gross income (AGI) Your total income, less adjustments, e.g., IRA contributions, one–half of self–employment taxes, self–employment insurance deductions, penalties on early withdrawals of savings, and alimony payments. This is the last number on the front of the 1040 long form. The AGI determines whether various tax benefits—such as personal exemptions, itemized deductions, and the rental loss allowance—are phased out.

After–tax return An investment's yield after paying any income taxes due.

Alternative minimum tax (AMT) When certain tax benefits reduce your regular income tax, the tax code requires alternate tax calculations on Form 6251 to compute a minimum tax due.

Amended return You may file an amended return using Form 1040X within a three–year period to correct a mistake made on an original return.

Amortizable bond premium The amount paid in excess of an obligation's face amount that is deductible.

Amortization Deducting an investment in intangible assets over their projected life.

Amortization schedule A printout showing the projected amount of principal and interest payable with each loan payment.

Amortized loan Loan in which the principal borrowed is repaid over the term of the loan (usually through monthly payments).

Annual percentage rate (APR) The rate of interest charged for a loan each year. Under the Truth–in–Lending provisions of the Consumer Credit Protection Act of 1968, all lenders must calculate the APR in a uniform manner and state the APR in advertisements so that consumers can accurately compare rates.

Annualized rate A rate for a period of less than a year computed as though for a full year.

Annuity A type of investment made with an insurance company. Under current tax law, the interest earned in an annuity is not taxable until withdrawn. When withdrawals are not made for a period of time, it is called a *deferred annuity.*

Annuity, immediate An investment with an insurance company. In exchange for the investment, the insurance company promises to make a series of periodic payments to the investor for as long as he or she lives or another specified length of time. The payment is determined by the interest rate at the time the investment is made and the length of time the payments will last.

Annuity, Tax Sheltered (TSA) People working for hospitals, schools, or other qualified nonprofit organizations may contribute a certain percentage of their income on a pre–tax basis to an account where the earnings grow tax–free. TSA plans are managed by insurance companies and mutual funds. TSAs are also known as 403(b) plans and Tax Sheltered Accounts.

Annuity, variable A deferred annuity, where the money invested is placed into accounts similar to mutual funds.

Appreciating asset An asset that increases in value with the passage of time. A house, in many cases, is a good example of an appreciating asset.

Appreciation The increase in the value of property beyond its purchase cost. Generally, the full market value is deductible as a non–cash charitable contribution when appreciated property owned more than a year is donated to a qualified non–profit organization.

Asset Anything a person or business owns, including cash, investments, receivables, real estate, and personal property.

Balloon payment A final lump–sum payment on a loan.

Bankruptcy A declaration by a court of law that a person is financially insolvent.

Basis The price paid for an asset, plus any improvements made to the asset, less any depreciation claimed on the asset. A basis is used to determine profits and losses for tax purposes.

Beneficiary One designated to receive a benefit, most commonly in connection with life insurance, IRAs, and other pension plans. When a person dies and the money from the life insurance policy or a pension plan, such as an IRA, goes directly to a named beneficiary, it does not pass through probate.

Bond A contractual agreement representing a loan for a specific amount and term. The party that purchases the bond is the lender. The party selling the bond is the borrower.

Bond, corporate An interest-paying certificate of indebtedness issued by a corporation.

Bond, municipal See *Bond, tax-free.*

Bond, tax-free An interest-paying certificate of indebtedness issued by a state or local government. The earnings are exempt from federal taxation and sometimes from state taxation.

Budget A plan or a guideline for managing cash flow.

Capital appreciation The growth in the value of an asset.

Capital asset Property you own, such as real estate, an investment, commercial property, land, or equipment, except for certain business assets or works you create. Capital assets are subject to capital gain or loss treatment on your income tax return.

Capital expenses Costs that are not currently deductible and that increase the basis of property. Capital expenses generally increase the property's value.

Capital gain dividend A payment made when a mutual fund profits from the sale of fund portfolio assets. Capital gain dividends are reported as long-term capital gains even when the mutual fund shares are held short-term.

Capital gain/loss The difference between the sales price and the basis of a capital asset. When you sell a capital asset that you have owned for at least one year, that asset's profit may qualify for favorable tax treatment. Under the Revenue Reconciliation Act of 1993, the maximum capital gains tax rate is 28 percent. Business and investment capital losses are normally deductible, with certain limitations. Short-term capital gains and losses result from the sale of an asset owned for one year or less; long-term capital gains and losses result from longer holding periods.

Cash flow The process of receiving income from various sources and spending money on various expenses. A cash flow statement looks at both income and expenses over a period of time, usually at least one month or one year.

Cashier's check See *Check, cashier's.*

Cash reserve fund See *Reserve fund.*

Cash surrender value   The amount of cash you receive if you voluntarily terminate a life insurance policy before it matures. Most policies allow you to borrow a portion of your cash value.

Cash value   *See* Cash surrender value.

Casualty loss   A tax-deductible loss from an unforeseen and sudden event. Personal losses are subject to a reduction of $100 plus ten percent of adjusted gross income.

Certificate of deposit (CD)   A bank deposit payable either on demand or at a specific date in the future, for which the customer is given a receipt. Normally, the account is for a specific deposit amount and interest rate. Generally, the longer the term, the higher the rate of interest paid. If the customer withdraws the money before the CD matures, a penalty is charged.

Certified Financial Planner® (CFP®)   A financial planner who has demonstrated competence in analyzing and developing personal and business financial plans through the completion of a series of rigorous financial planning examinations. To maintain his or her license, a planner must complete continuing education requirements each year and abide by a strict Code of Ethics. The International Board of Standards and Practices for Certified Financial Planners administers the certification requirements and disciplinary procedures for the licensees.

Charitable contributions   Donations to qualifying charities are deductible when itemized on Schedule A. For non-cash donations, the amount deductible depends on the type of property, the donee organization, your holding period, and, in some cases, how the donation is used. See also *Charitable organization, qualified.*

Charitable organization, qualified   A nonprofit philanthropic organization approved by the U.S. Treasury Department to receive tax-deductible charitable contributions.

Charitable organization, non-qualified   A nonprofit philanthropic organization not approved by the U.S. Treasury Department to receive tax-deductible charitable contributions.

Check, cashier's   A check issued by a bank on a customer's behalf. It is a direct obligation of the bank.

Check, cleared   A check that has been paid by the bank where the check's account is located.

Child and Dependent Credit   A tax credit of up to 30 percent of certain expenses incurred to allow you to work. The credit percentage is determined by the taxpayer's adjusted gross income.

Christmas club accounts   A savings account with frequent deposits. The account balance is paid to the account holder in December. In most cases, because of the interest computations on these types of accounts, the customer would be better off using a standard savings account.

Collateral   Security pledged to guarantee the repayment of a loan.

Collateral loan   A loan for which the borrower pledges an asset as security. The lender may sell the collateral if the borrower defaults on the loan.

Commodity   There are two types of commodities. Traditional commodities are raw materials such as precious metals and agricultural products. Financial commodities are financial instruments like currencies and stock indexes. Commodity futures are an agreement to buy or sell for a set price on a specific date in the future. Commodity options are the right to buy or sell a commodity futures contract for a set price for a specific period of time. Commodity purchasers hope that the value of the contract will increase enough to be profitable before the specified date arrives. Speculating in commodities usually involves a large amount of money and is extremely risky.

Common stock   Securities that represent an ownership interest in a corporation. Common stock typically has dividend and appreciation potential.

Community property   A system of property rights affecting husbands and wives. The basis of this system is that the earnings and assets of each spouse belong to both spouses. There are nine community property states; Arizona, California, Idaho, Louisiana, Nevada, New Mexico, Texas, Washington, and Wisconsin.

Compound interest   See *Interest, compound.*

Consolidation loan   A loan made for the purpose of repaying other loans. Borrowers typically use the proceeds to pay off smaller or higher-interest loans.

Consumer interest   See *Interest, consumer.*

Conveyance   Transfer of ownership of property from one owner to another.

Cosign   To jointly sign a promissory note so that a person without established credit or with a bad credit rating can obtain a loan. If the borrower fails to repay the loan, the cosigner is fully responsible.

Credit   An individual's right to borrow money, granted by a lender.

Credit limit   The prearranged maximum amount of money one is entitled to borrow.

Credit rating   One's standing in terms of borrowing capabilities. A credit rating is based on past performance in repaying loans or a borrower's ability to repay.

Data file   Quicken keeps transaction information relating to a set of Accounts in a data file. One data file actually consists of multiple related computer files that Quicken uses concurrently. *See* your Quicken manual for additional information.

Death benefit   The amount payable under a life insurance policy when an insured person dies. The death benefit is the face amount plus any additional benefits payable; e.g., some universal and variable policies pay the cash value in addition to the face amount.

Debt instrument   Money lent to an individual or organization in the form of a bond, deposit, loan, note, or other interest-bearing instrument.

Deductions   See *Itemized deductions*.

Default   When a borrower does not meet the terms of a loan, the loan is in default.

Dependency exemption   A fixed deduction allowed for every taxpayer except those who are claimed as dependents by others. An extra exemption is allowed for a spouse on a joint return. The deduction is phased out for certain high-income taxpayers.

Deposit   Money a bank owes its depositors.

Depreciable property   A business or income-producing asset with a useful life exceeding one year.

Depreciation   The decrease in the value of property over its useful life. The amount of decrease is deductible for business and investment property.

Depression   Economic inactivity usually caused by a shortage of money, high-priced credit, or both.

Devaluation   Lowering the value of a country's currency. The most memorable example of devaluation occurred in Germany between World War I and World War II. Many believe that the United States may have to opt for some form of devaluation in the foreseeable future because of its debt structure.

Disclosure statement   A statement that all lenders, under the Truth-in-Lending provisions of the Consumer Credit Protection Act of 1968, must give a borrower when a loan is made. The statement sets forth the terms of the loan, including the annual percentage rate and the finance charge.

Diversification (investment)   Spreading money among different types of investments to reduce risk.

Dividend   A payment from a corporation, distributed pro rata among outstanding shares of stock. Corporations usually pay dividends from their profits. Additional forms include interest paid on accounts by credit unions, earnings from mutual funds, and a refund of excess premiums from a life insurance policy. See also *Capital gain dividend*.

Dollar cost averaging   A method of purchasing securities on a periodic basis with a fixed amount of dollars, regardless of the prevailing price of the security. Payments buy more shares when the price is low and fewer shares as the price rises. This strategy enables investors who consistently buy in good and bad times to improve their potential for gain when they sell. It is an effective strategy for single investors to use.

Earned income   Compensation received for performing personal services.

Effective tax bracket (rate)   See *Tax bracket, effective*.

Equity   The difference between the fair market value of an asset and the balance of any outstanding loans. For example, if a home has a fair market value of $100,000 while the buyer owes $25,000 on the mortgage, the equity equals $75,000.

Estate tax   See *Tax, estate*.

Estimated tax   See *Tax, estimated*.

Executor The person or institution named in a will and approved by the probate court to act as the representative of a decedent's estate to carry out the directions in the will. A female executor is often called an *executrix*. When a person dies intestate—without a will—the proper term for the executor is administrator (*administratrix*, if female). Many states use the term *personal representative* rather than *executor* or *administrator*.

Exemption, personal See *Dependency exemption*.

Face amount *or* value The minimum amount of life insurance proceeds an insurance company promises to pay when an insured dies. This amount may be different than the actual death benefit payable. See also *Death benefit*.

Fair market value The amount of money a willing buyer will pay a willing seller when neither is under any compulsion to buy or sell.

Federal debt The total amount of money owed by the federal government to its creditors.

Federal deficit The annual shortfall between the money the government collects and the money it spends. This difference is compensated for by additional borrowing, which increases the total national debt and the interest due on the debt.

Federal Deposit Insurance Corporation (FDIC) A federal executive agency that insures deposits for member banks.

FDIC See Federal Deposit Insurance Corporation (FDIC).

Fiat Money Money declared legal by a government. The currency is not convertible to gold, silver, or any other commodity. Its value is entirely based on the faith of its users.

Fiduciary One who acts for the benefit of another in financial matters.

FIFO An acronym meaning "first in, first out."

Finance charge The total amount charged for a loan, under the Truth-in-Lending provisions of the Consumer Credit Protection Act of 1968, must be disclosed by the lender when making the loan. The longer it takes to repay a loan, the higher the finance charge collected.

Financial principle A fundamental, primary, or general financial law or truth.

Financial statement A balance sheet, or statement of condition, prepared for business or personal use.

Fiscal policy The sum of the guidelines and policies that represent the monetary policy of the country. In effect, it becomes the budgetary policy of the government.

Fixed Annuity See *Annuity*.

Fixed Investment An asset whose principal cannot grow in value; e.g., CDs, cash value life insurance, and bonds. These are debt instruments that yield interest.

Flexible spending plan A salary reduction plan that allows employees to pay for enhanced medical coverage, dependent care expenses, and other benefits with pretax earnings.

Foreclosure Legal action taken by a lender when the conditions of a mortgage are not met. The mortgage holder may institute proceedings to force the owner to pay the mortgage in full and/or sell the property.

Fringe benefit An advantage of employment employees receive in addition to their pay, such as health insurance. Some fringe benefits are taxable.

Gift tax See *Tax, gift*.

Grace period, credit card The amount of time from when your credit card statement is printed until when your payment must arrive without incurring interest charges.

Gross income The total amount of income received from all sources before exclusions and deductions.

Guaranteed account Usually, an investment option offered by an insurance company in a corporate pension plan. It is known as a fixed annuity when offered to an individual. See also *Annuity*.

Guaranteed Investment Contract See *Guaranteed account*.

Guarantor A person who promises to pay for another's debt if the other person is unable to fulfill the obligation.

Home equity debt   Debt secured by a principal residence or second home to the extent of the excess of fair market value over acquisition debt. A mortgage interest deduction is allowed for home equity debt up to $100,000 ($50,000 in the case of married taxpayers filing separately).

Home equity loan   A type of second mortgage that allows a homeowner to borrow up to 80 percent of the appraised market value of his or her home less the amount owed on the first mortgage.

Immediate annuity   See *Annuity.*

Income in respect of a decedent   Income earned by a person before he or she dies but taxable to their estate or the heir who receives it.

Individual Retirement Account (IRA)   A retirement account to which up to $2,000 in tax-deductible contributions may be made annually. Deductions for the contribution are restricted if you or your spouse are covered by a company retirement plan. Earnings on contributions accumulate tax-free until withdrawn.

Inflation   The devaluation of money caused by an increase in the volume of money and credit, relative to available goods. This process results in a substantial and continuing rise in general price levels as purchasing power declines.

Inheritance tax   See *Tax, inheritance.*

Installment loan   A loan in which the borrower pays a portion of the principal balance every month until the amount owed is completely repaid.

Insurance, automobile   A system of sharing the costs of personal injury and property damage caused by or to automobiles. The automobile owners contribute to a common fund from which claims are paid. *Collision insurance* covers losses to an insured's car if he or she has an accident and is unable to collect from other drivers or their insurance companies. *Comprehensive coverage* is for losses to the insured person's car if it is stolen or damaged by such things as fire, hail, or vandalism.

Insurance, cash value   Life insurance that accumulates cash in the contract that the owner may receive as a loan or withdrawal at a later date.

Insurance, health   A system for sharing medical expenses under which those who are insured contribute to a common fund from which claims are paid.

Insurance, homeowner's   A plan for sharing the costs of damage to houses and other residential structures, personal belongings, and injuries to people under which those who are insured contribute to a common fund from which claims are paid.

Insurance, life, modified endowment contract (MEC)   A life insurance policy that exceeds Internal Revenue Code restrictions for the amount of money that may be contributed to a life policy. MECs are subject to stricter tax guidelines than regular life insurance policies.

Insurance, property and casualty   Insurance on one's possessions and against unforeseen losses or legal claims. The most common types are automobile and homeowner's insurance.

Insurance, tenant's   Homeowner's insurance that covers the loss or theft of a renter's belongings.

Insurance, term life   Life insurance that provides low-cost protection for a specified period of time, such as one, five, or ten years. Term policies don't include a savings feature. Initial annual premiums for term insurance are less expensive than cash value plans. The cost of term insurance increases as the insured ages because the premiums are actuarially determined. As the insured's probability of death increases, the premium increases. Term insurance is suitable for temporary insurance needs.

Insurance, universal life (UL)   A hybrid life insurance product that has term and cash value insurance characteristics. Money placed in a UL policy purchases term insurance. Any excess cash earns interest. Interest earned in a UL policy is not subject to income tax unless it is withdrawn prior to the insured's death. Cash may usually be borrowed from the policy without triggering any tax consequences. After cash values accrue in a policy, the policy owner can increase, decrease, and even stop making further premium payments depending on the performance of the cash account.

Insurance, variable life (VL)   Like universal life insurance, except that the cash deposited in the policy may be invested in various investment accounts. The investment accounts are managed like mutual funds.

Insurance, whole life (WL)   Also known as traditional or cash value insurance. Whole life insurance typically offers low returns for the cash deposited in the policy.

Insurance premium   The payment an insurance policy owner makes in exchange for insurance coverage.

Interest, compound   Interest paid on the principal as well as on the accrued interest. Savings account interest may be compounded on a daily, continuous (essentially the same as daily), weekly, monthly, quarterly, semiannual, or annual basis. The more frequently the interest is compounded (calculated and paid), the greater the saver's yield is.

Interest, consumer   Interest incurred on personal debt and credit. Consumer interest is no longer deductible. Consumer interest includes all interest except business, investment, and mortgage interest.

Interest, investment   Interest on debt used to purchase investments, but not including interest expense from a passive activity. Deductions are limited to net investment income. Interest on loan proceeds used to purchase tax-free bonds is not deductible.

Intestacy   Dying without a will. State laws govern how property is distributed when a person dies intestate.

IRA   See *Individual Retirement Account.*

Itemized deductions   Items that directly reduce taxable income. Personal deductions such as for mortgage interest, state and local taxes, and charitable contributions are itemized on Schedule A. Other deductions, such as for alimony, capital losses, business losses, and IRAs and Keoghs, are deducted from gross income as adjustments to income on Form 1040.

Joint ownership   Ownership of property by more than one person. *See also: Community property, Joint tenants with rights of survivorship, Tenancy in common, and Tenancy by the entirety.*

Joint return   A tax return filed by a married couple reporting their combined income and deductions.

Joint tenants (with rights of survivorship)   Two or more people who own property with rights of survivorship, which means that when one of the joint tenants dies, the property automatically belongs to the other joint tenant(s). An owner is not able to will property at death. A deceased joint tenant's ownership rights pass by law to the surviving joint owner(s).

Keogh plan   A retirement plan, set up by a self-employed person, which allows tax-deductible contributions, tax-free income accumulations until withdrawal, and favorable averaging for qualifying lump-sum distributions.

Lease   A contract where a property owner allows a lessee or renter to use that property temporarily for a fee. Leases of personal property, e.g. a car, allow the lessee to purchase the property for a predetermined sum at the conclusion of the lease.

Legally separated   Said of a husband and wife required to live apart from each other by the terms of a decree of separate maintenance. Payments other than child support under the decree are deductible by the payer and taxable to the payee as alimony.

Leverage   The use of a small amount of money, assets, or equity to control or purchase an asset worth substantially more. This allows you to receive the appreciation on the total asset, not just the amount you have invested. Although leveraging increases your earning potential, it also increases your risk. You are obligated to repay the amount leveraged, which is a loan. Most people leverage their houses; e.g., if you put $10,000 as a down payment on a house and borrow $90,000, you have leveraged yourself into a home.

Liability   An obligation you owe. Current liabilities, such as bills, credit cards, and taxes, must technically be repaid within one year; long-term liabilities, such as home mortgages, extend for more than one year.

LIFO   An acronym meaning "last in, first out."

Line of credit   The maximum preapproved dollar amount that a person can borrow from a lender.

Liquid assets   Current assets that can immediately be turned into cash, e.g., savings accounts and other cash deposits.

Liquidity   The ability to readily convert an asset to cash at the fair market value. In other words, if you sell an asset, you will not lose value.

Load   A fee to cover the cost of the sales commission. Front-end loads are paid when one buys mutual fund shares. Back-end loads are paid when redeeming mutual fund shares.

Loan schedule See *Amortization schedule.*

Long-term capital gain or loss See *Capital gain/loss.*

Marginal Tax Bracket *or* Rate See *Tax bracket or rate, marginal.*

Maturity The due date of an obligation.

Medicare Government-sponsored health insurance for people aged 65 or over.

Memorized transaction A member of a list of frequently used transactions you can create in Quicken

Miscellaneous itemized deductions Job and investment expenses that must exceed two percent of a taxpayer's adjusted gross income before they affect the amount of income taxes due.

Modified endowment contract (MEC) See *Insurance, life, modified, endowment contract (MEC).*

Money market account A deposit account at a bank, savings and loan, or credit union that pays a fluctuating rate of interest close to market interest rates.

Money market fund A mutual fund that invests in short-term monetary instruments: Treasury Bills, U.S. Government Agency issue, commercial bank CDs, commercial paper, etc. The interest rate on a money market fund fluctuates with market interest rates. Deposits in these funds are not insured, but the investments are of high enough quality to make them safe.

Money order A negotiable instrument issued by a bank and paid for in advance by the customer.

Mortgage interest Interest on the balance of a home loan. It is fully deductible on up to two residences if acquisition debt secured by the homes is $1,000,000 or less, and if home equity debt is $100,000 or less.

Municipal bond *or* muni-bond See *Bond, tax-free.*

Mutual fund An open-ended investment trust in which people pool their money for investment in a variety of securities. Investors may put more money into the fund or take it out at the current market rate at any time. Mutual funds give people with small amounts of money to invest the opportunity to put their money into a diversified portfolio of stocks, bonds, or other vehicles at reduced brokerage fees.

Mutual fund checking account See *Money market fund.*

Net worth The total value owned minus the total value owed, i.e., all of someone's assets minus all of that person's liabilities. A negative net worth exists when obligations exceed assets.

Note See *Promissory note.*

Opportunity fund See *Reserve fund.*

Option The right to purchase or sell a security at a set price on or before a fixed date. See also *Stock option.*

Ordinary income Income other than capital gains.

Ordinary loss A loss other than a capital loss.

Original issue discount (OID) The difference between the face value of a bond and its original issue price. OID is reported to the taxpayer on an annual basis as interest income on Schedule B.

Paper loss A paper loss occurs when you own an investment that is worth less than you paid for it. There are no tax consequences to a paper loss.

Passbook savings Said of an account in which transactions are recorded for the customer in a passbook. Because of the relatively low interest, it is a good idea to use a passbook account for accumulating funds only until enough is saved to transfer into higher-yielding investments.

Passive activity loss rules Rules that limit the deduction of losses from passive activities to income from other passive activities. Passive activities include rental operations or businesses in which the taxpayer does not materially participate.

Payee The person to whom a check is made payable.

Penny stock Stock, usually common stock, whose share price is $5 or less. Penny stock is considered speculative.

Pension Payments to employees from an employer-funded retirement plan for past services.

Personal interest A tax term for non-deductible interest on personal loans and consumer credit.

Personal property tax See *Taxes, property.*

Points For tax purposes, points are many non-recurring charges incurred at the time of securing a loan. Lenders consider a point equal to one percent of the loan amount. Depending on the type of loan, points may be currently deductible or amortized over the life of the loan.

Policy loan insurance A loan against a life insurance policy. Most policy loans credit most or all of the interest paid back into the policy. When all of the interest paid is credited to the policy, it is known as a zero-net-cost loan.

Portfolio A group of investments owned by a single individual or couple.

Preferred stock Similar to common stock, preferred stock typically has less dividend and appreciation potential, but it receives a higher priority or preference over common stock in dividend payments or in the event of liquidation.

Premium See *Insurance premium.*

Present value of money The value of a future sum of money in today's dollars, taking into account interest rates, inflation, or both.

Principal (finance) A sum of capital, as opposed to interest or profit. For example, the amount of money borrowed in the form of a loan is its principal. As a loan is repaid, a portion of the payment is credited to the lender as interest, and the remainder is credited to the borrower as a reduction in the amount owed. Also, the amount of money invested.

Principle See *Financial principle.*

Probate A legal proceeding to certify the authenticity of a will by a court of law and the action taken to make sure that the terms of a will are carried out or that an estate is settled when a person dies intestate, without a will.

Promissory note A written promise to repay a debt. The note should include the amount of money borrowed; the maturity date; where, when, and to whom payments are payable; and the signature of the borrower.

Prorate To divide proportionately.

Prospectus A legal document that describes securities or investments offered for sale to the public.

Provisional income A tax term used to describe the amount of Social Security benefits taxable for income tax purposes. Provisional income is defined as adjusted gross income plus 50 percent of Social Security benefits plus any tax-free income earned. Original Issue Discount income is also included in provisional income calculations.

Purchasing power The ability of a dollar to buy products or services. Since fiat money has no intrinsic value, purchasing power is an important benchmark, as it assigns a value to the dollar.

Real Estate Property including land, buildings, and natural assets, e.g., water and minerals. Real estate also includes things attached to the land, such as trees, shrubs, and fences, as well as fixtures attached to buildings.

Recession A decline in business activity. Recessions are usually caused by monetary shortages and can sometimes lead to depressions.

Related party Under the tax law, spouses, siblings, parents, grandparents, children, grandchildren, trusts, pension plans, IRAs, and fiduciaries are related parties. In-laws are not related for tax purposes under the wash sale rule or most other purposes according to the Internal Revenue Code.

Reserve fund An amount of cash and liquid assets available for use in an emergency or when a great opportunity occurs. An individual's reserve funds should equal three to six month's expenses.

Right of Survivorship A condition of joint ownership whereby joint property automatically belongs to the surviving joint owner(s) when another joint owner dies.

Rollover A tax-free reinvestment of a distribution from a qualified retirement plan into an IRA or other qualified plan within 60 days after receipt. The date of receipt is generally considered the date the distribution check is written.

Royalty An author's, composer's, or inventor's right to a portion of the money received from the sale of a literary work, musical composition, or invention.

Savings Money set aside to spend at a later date.

Second mortgage A mortgage on a piece of real property that already has a first mortgage.

Secured loan A loan in which the borrower pledges collateral to the lender in case of default.

Security Collateral for a loan.

Securities Exchange Commission The federal government agency that regulates the investment industry.

Separate return A return filed by a married person who does not file a joint return. Filing separately may save taxes when each spouse has separate deductions, but certain tax benefits require a joint return.

Short-term loans Loans that mature within one year.

Silent partner A partner who is not involved in the management of a partnership.

Simplified Employee Pension Plan (SEP) A retirement plan for employees of companies having fewer than 25 employees.

Speculate To take risks in buying and selling securities, commodities, options, and other investments in order to make large profits. Speculation involves higher than normal risk.

Standard deduction A fixed deduction for taxpayers who do not itemize deductions on Schedule A. The amount depends on filing status, age, and presence or absence of blindness.

Stock A certificate of ownership in a corporation. Stocks may be publicly or privately traded.

Stock, common Shares in the ownership of a corporation for which one share represents the right to receive one part of the corporation's distributed earnings and the right to one vote at shareholders' meetings.

Stock, growth Common stock that is expected to grow in value but is not expected to pay relatively high, regular dividends. This type of stock is more speculative than income stock.

Stock, income Common stock that pays relatively high, regular dividends.

Stock, preferred Shares in the ownership of a corporation for which the shareholder gets certain preferential treatment, such as precedence in receiving dividends. Shareholders, however, have no voting rights unless dividends are in default. Preferred stocks often offer higher income than common stocks.

Stock, utility Shares of stock in a company that provides public services, e.g., electric, gas, and telephone companies.

Stockholder The owner of one or more shares of stock.

Stock option The contractual right to buy (*call option*) or sell (*put option*) a specified number of shares of a specific stock at a set price on or before a specified date. Each option can be bought for a fraction of the cost of the stock, giving the investor much greater potential for profit or loss. Options are very risky because the entire investment can be lost.

Surety Someone who agrees to be responsible for losses suffered because another fails to perform as agreed.

Tax A payment collected by a government. An individual's willingness to pay is irrelevant, as a fundamental premise of taxing is the government's ability to force compliance.

Tax, estate A tax imposed if the value of an individual decedent's taxable estate exceeds $600,000, after deductions. Under the Revenue Reconciliation Act of 1993, the maximum estate tax rate is 55 percent.

Tax, estimated The amount of advance payment of current tax liability based on wage withholdings or installment payments. To avoid penalties, individual taxpayers generally must pay the IRS either 90 percent of the final tax liability in a timely manner or 100 percent of the prior year's tax liability.

Tax, gift Gifts in excess of the $10,000 per donee annual exclusion are subject to a gift tax. The tax may be offset by a unified gift and estate tax credit. Under the Revenue Reconciliation Act of 1993, the maximum gift tax rate is 55 percent.

Tax, inheritance State tax on the assets of a deceased person, which is paid from the estate.

Tax, property A tax levied by a local government as a percentage of the assessed value of real or personal property.

Tax, self-employment Mandatory taxes for Social Security and Medicare coverage paid by self-employed persons with net business income over $400.

Taxable income A person's adjusted gross income minus adjustments, deductions, and exemptions.

Tax bracket *or* rate, effective   The percentage of each dollar earned that is paid in taxes. Calculate the effective tax rate by dividing the total amount of taxes paid by the gross income or total income.

Tax credit   A tax credit directly reduces tax liability, in contrast to a deduction, which reduces income subject to tax.

Tax deduction   An expense that legally may be deducted from income when computing federal income taxes.

Tax deferral   Shifting income to a later year. Contributions to qualified retirement plans provide tax deferral. Taxpayers MUST defer any gain from sale of a residence if they buy a qualifying replacement home within two years.

Tax-free bond   See *Bond, tax-free*.

Tax shelter   A legal way to avoid paying a portion of federal income taxes by taking advantage of available tax laws.

Tax Sheltered Annuity, account, *or* 403(b) plan   See *Annuity, Tax Sheltered (TSA)*.

Tenancy by the entirety   A form of joint ownership between married persons. Both the husband and the wife must agree to a transfer of an interest in the property. Generally, creditors of one spouse cannot reach property held as tenancy by the entirety.

Tenancy in common   Ownership of property by two or more persons in which each person owns a percentage of the property. Each owner is able to sell or give away his or her share or will his or her share at death.

Term insurance   See *Insurance, term life*.

Third mortgage   A mortgage on real property that already has a second mortgage.

Title   Documented proof of ownership of a specific piece of property.

Treasury Bills   Non-interest bearing, discounted notes issued by the U.S. Government. They are redeemed at face value at maturity.

Treasury Securities   U.S. Government obligations sold to the public through Federal Reserve Banks.

Trust   An arrangement under which a person transfers legal ownership of his or her assets to another person or corporation (trustee) for the benefit of one or more third persons (beneficiaries).

Universal life insurance   See *Insurance, universal life (UL)*.

Useful life   An estimate of time stipulated in the tax code that a depreciable asset is expected to last.

U.S. Government Securities   Financial obligations of the United States government.

Usury   Offering a loan at an interest rate in excess of the legal maximum.

Variable annuity   See *Annuity, variable*.

Void   Having no effect. Not binding on anyone.

Wash Sale Rule   The purpose of the Wash Sale Rule is to disallow losses on sales of stock, securities, or other investments if the investors recover their position within a short time of selling the investment. The IRS disallows tax deductions on investment losses when such a loss occurs and the investor repurchases or purchases an option to repurchase the investment within 30 days of the sale. The wash period begins 30 days prior to the sale and ends 30 days after the sale. Thus, the wash period is a total of 61 days.

Wealth   A measure of available resources.

Whole life insurance   See *Insurance, whole life (WL)*.

Will   A legal document containing a person's instructions for his or her property and other affairs after death.

Withholding   An amount taken from income as a prepayment of tax liability.

Yield   The amount of profit an investment produces, including interest, dividends, and appreciation.

Zero bracket amount   A basic amount of money, built into tax-computation formulas, that the federal government allows a taxpayer to earn tax-free.

Zero net cost policy loan   See *Policy loan*.

INDEX